REMARKABLE

PROVIDENCES

ILLUSTRATIVE OF THE EARLIER DAYS
OF AMERICAN COLONISATION.

BY

INCREASE MATHER.

WITH INTRODUCTORY PREFACE,

BY GEORGE OFFOR.

LONDON:

REEVES AND TURNER
196, STRAND.
1890.

Crescentius Matherus

INCREASE MATHER

INTRODUCTION.

——o——

THE very natural and laudable curiosity to examine and compare the past with the present, has been recently gratified to a great extent by the republication of rare and curious books. The labours of the Percy, Parker, Camden, Shakespeare, and Hansard Knollys Societies, have contributed a store of information most pleasant and profitable. The Harleian and Somers' collection of Tracts have rendered accessible a vast number of singularly interesting but rugged pamphlets, in contrast with which our popular literature sheds a benign influence over society, while it exhibits an equally superior elegance of appearance.

The volume now offered to the public is one of a series of the popular books of a bygone age, which will form a valuable library of old authors, that in their original forms are too rare and expensive to be generally accessible.

These singular narrations were collected by one of the most valuable men of a most eventful period. It exhibits a striking and interesting display of the state of public feeling of those times, as to supernatural appearances and strange or mysterious events; and the dawn of light upon an enquiring mind, imbued with godly piety, leading him to attempt to penetrate the gloom with which the human intellect has been for ages shrouded.

The subtle craft of a wily priesthood—first Pagan, and then Christian—led them to claim the exercise of dominion over the invisible world, and especially over demons. This may be traced to a pure source, which, by the craft of man, became streams most polluted. "God, who at sundry times, and in divers manners, spake in time past unto the fathers," completed his revelations by his Son, and with the death of those who were in personal communion with him, miraculous powers ceased. But as false prophets among the heathen had deceived the people, so did false apostles in the Christian church, by pretended miracles. Upon the ignorance of man they constructed a subtle system, transforming the teaching of Christianity, which by its divine Founder had been based upon the purest philanthropy, into a mine of pelf in its extent incredible as it is dishonourable. The pagan priesthood practised delusions puerile and absurd, consulting the entrails of beasts, the flight of birds, the hum of oracles; and this gave place to practises equally childish—rotten bones, relics, incantations, and holy water.

Upon the ignorance of man they built up a curious and ancient system, now fast falling to decay; and in countries where old inventions have lost their influence, as a last refuge of lies, they fly to a mystic apostolic descent, conveying some obscure undefined miraculous powers. Thus have they acquired an ascendency over their fellow-men—soul-destroying, tyrannous, and almost universal. They limit to their own order all mortal influence to appease Heaven or to overcome hell. He who dared to doubt the appearance of ghosts, witches, or goblins, and their power to torment man, and the power of the priesthood over these mysterious tormentors, was denounced as an infidel. The priest alone could cope with satanic power; and the more firmly they fixed upon the people a belief in the supernatural, the stronger became their influence over them. Terrors handed down from mother to daughter became almost indelible. How strange, how incredibly absurd is it, even at this day, to see in a doorway an article of faith, in the shape of an old horseshoe, to prevent the entrance of sprites or fairies; or to witness the "foolish sorcery," as our author calls it, of foretelling events by the white of an egg! Almost equal in absurdity, and much more mischievous, is the authority still claimed by the priesthood. Who is it that in a twinkling turns an innocent babe from being a child of the devil into being "the child of God"? Who is it that says to the sick and dying, "I absolve thee from all thy sins"? and who is it that buries the body of the vilest malefactor, "in sure and certain hope of the resurrection to eternal life"? None but a priest is supposed to possess these mysterious powers, while men, even scientific philosophers, affect to believe the potent spell.

If such things are now believed, it affords a strong plea for indulgence to Doctor Mather and our pilgrim fathers, whose minds were clouded with some of those chimeras which had overshadowed all mankind; but struggling to throw them off. To see a child totter into walking, and to hear him stammer into speech, is interesting; but how much more so to watch the progress of man when emerging with anxious care from slavery and darkness to liberty and light! He feels the solemn responsibility of private judgment—of praying for Divine guidance, instead of paying for pater-nosters to sham intercessors.

The editor of this singular collection of *Remarkable Providences* was the son of one of those seventy-seven pious clergymen who, with four thousand of their followers, found refuge among the Indians in the wilds of America from the ferocious tyranny of Archbishop Laud. Dr. Mather, who was one of the most extraordinary men of the age, was born at Dorchester, N.E., June 21, 1639, and received his name from a very extraordinary *increase* with which the colony was at that time favoured. He was educated for the ministry, and coming to England, obtained literary honours at Dublin University, being then only nineteen years of age. At that time he conversed familiarly in Latin, and had read the Old Testament in Hebrew, and the New in Greek. He was highly distinguished for his attainments in mathematics, philosophy,

history, theology, and rabbinical learning. It pleased
God, at a very early age, to baptize his spirit into divine
truth, and he became a valuable preacher in England.
Upon the accession of Charles the Second, he refused
to submit his conscience to the dictates of the state, and
chose rather to trust God's providence than to violate
the tranquillity of his mind. To escape persecution, he
returned to New-England, and was ordained pastor over
the North Church in Boston, May 27, 1664, after
having preached on probation three years. He fulfilled
his duties to that Church for sixty-two years; retaining
his full power of intellect, popularity and usefulness,
until he fell asleep in the arms of his son, and was
gathered to his fathers in the eighty-first year of his age.
He was the author of ninety-two distinct works, besides
many learned and useful prefaces.

During the long period of his ministry at Boston, he,
in a faithful proclamation of the gospel, sowed those seeds
of religious and political liberty which, when mature,
brought forth an abundant harvest. In the early part of
his ministerial career, the colony of New-England was
sorely oppressed. That tiger in human shape, Colonel
Kirk, of West-of-England notoriety, was governor. The
people determined to send their most talented man to
represent their grievances to Charles the Second, and in
their wisdom selected Dr. Mather. This alarmed the
oppressors: every effort was made to prevent his em-
barkation. A letter was forged, bearing his name, offen-

sive to Government, and was purposely intercepted in its supposed route to Holland, and sent to the English Court. His wisdom overcame all obstacles ; he escaped every snare, found access to the King, took advantage of his declaration of liberty of conscience, and obtained a re-mission of their persecutions. He had several interviews with James the Second, but all terminated with that weak monarch in good words and promises. On the accession of William, he with great difficulty obtained a new charter, and in 1692 returned in the same ship with the new governor. By these wise exertions, crowned with complete and extraordinary success, he laid the foundation upon which Washington, Franklin, and their compatriots established the vast and extending empire of the United States of America.

Such was the eminent divine, the decided patriot, the truthful historian, who to promote the best interests of man, collected, arranged, and published these *Remarkable Providences and Marvellous Escapes by Sea and Land.* They faithfully delineate the state of public opinion two hundred years ago, the most striking feature being an implicit faith in the power of the invisible world to hold visible intercourse with man ;—not the angels to bless poor erring mortals, but of demons imparting power to witches and warlocks to injure, terrify, and destroy.

These superstitions prevailed in all nations in propor-tion to ignorance and priestly domination. All professed to believe in witchcraft, excepting only those few enlightened philosophers who were branded as "impious atheists." It was at this period, when oppressed by the ruthless hand of persecution, our pilgrim fathers, threatened with torture and death, succumbed not to man, but, trusting on an Almighty arm, braved the dangers of an almost unknown ocean, and threw themselves into the arms of men called savages, who proved more beneficent than rational Christians. Their exodus was unlike that of the Israelites, fenced about with miracles, guided by an inspired leader, and in one great body. Our refugees divided into small parties, fled in frail vessels more fit for ferry-boats over an arm of the sea than to brave the billows of the Bay of Biscay, the stormy perils of the great Atlantic, and the foggy dangers of Newfoundland. Theirs was a solemn covenant, that at all hazards they would render unto God the homage of the heart in obeying his high commands, however contrary to human laws, which are void of obligation when they infringe the rights of conscience.

They sought an asylum in an unknown wilderness, and there founded a mighty nation, which when purified from slave-holding, bids fair to become the greatest nation in the world. Kingdoms governed by despots will melt away, while those where religious freedom reigns must flourish. The exiles took with them their educational prejudices, which the solitariness of the wilderness had a tendency to increase. Their faith in supernatural appearances, possessions by devils or by the souls of deceased persons, and in witchcraft, was strengthened. Their belief was supported by plausible arguments, apparently well-attested facts, and embraced by the great, the wise, and the good.   Nor did they feel the difference between faith in unseen spiritual existences and faith in their visible appearance to man.   Dreams, like that of Dr. Frith[1], are told by one narrator to another, with additions and embellishments, until they became visions. The French scholar,[1] having spent the produce of robbery in debauchery, goes on to shed blood—his conscience drives him mad—he raves of having sold his soul to the fiend, and sealed the contract with blood. The priests assemble; they pray and exorcise; the bystanders are amazed. It may have been that one of them, who had previously written and threw it up, catches a paper fluttering in the air ; it is signed and sealed with blood ; it is the accursed deed, and is torn in fragments. The maniac recovers, like the rich man in the humorous tale of the Cobbler, by Samuel Wesley. Who could doubt but that the devil had so befooled himself ? One such tale was quite enough to be told with a thousand variations—all derived from one original, and all attested by the same spectators. The most cruel and mischievous of all these delusions was that of witchcraft.   Poor defenceless old women, especially the ill-favoured and ill-tempered, were sacrificed to that horrid Moloch.   The history of their sufferings, with that of the martyrs, forms the most gloomy, the blackest, and most

[1] See Preface.

revolting pages of history. The prevailing opinion was that under the Mosaic law כָּשַׁף, answering to the Greek word φαρμακεία,[1] conveyed the same idea as the English word "witch," and that such characters were, by divine command, sentenced to death. These words convey no such meaning as a Satanic compact, but allude to an acquired human knowledge, as skill in medicine sometimes perverted to administering poison, and at others to poisoning the mind with the cruel ceremonies of idolatry. Thus it was with Manasseh,[2] who persuaded the people to murder their offspring as an act of religion. A witch is defined by the statute to be "One that shall use, practise, or exercise any invocation or conjuration of any evil or wicked spirit, or consult, covenant with, entertain, or employ, feed or reward any evil or wicked spirit," &c., "whereby any person shall be killed, destroyed, wasted, consumed, pined, or lamed in his or her body, or any part thereof."[3] So early as Edward VI, 1547, Cranmer's *Articles of Visitation* inquires of every parish officer: "Item. Whether you know any that use charms, sorcery, enchantments, witches, or any like craft invented by the devil." The Virgin Queen continues this inquiry with the addition, "and especially in the time of women's travel." The fear was lest the devil should steal away the

[1] Gal. v, 19, 20.
[2] 2 Chron. xxxiii, 6. The word אוֹב, "Obi Man," is still used in Africa for doctor, or wise man.
[3] 5 Eliz. and 1 James.

soul of the infant, and introduce an imp of his own in its place—a superstitious notion derived from the Jews. In the same reign, some Jesuits practised extraordinary delusions at the mansion of Lord Vaux, at Hackney, near London. Weston and Campian were the chief performers; their abettors were Sarah Williams and some other abandoned young women. They were taught to throw themselves into a kind of mesmeric trance, and, with strange distortions of body, uttered a pretended inspiration from the world of spirits. There were awful denunciations of wrath upon all who embraced the doctrines of the Reformation, as being possessed by Satan and doomed to eternal misery. These young women were restored from these paroxysms by the aid of holy water, purgatives, and emetics, and, when these failed, the foul fiend was driven out by the application of reliques in a most indelicate manner.[1]

The Stuart race kept all these delusions in fashion, especially witchcraft. King James asserts the compact between Satan and the witch; and, among many amusing ceremonies, states that the devil teaches his disciples how to draw *triangular circles*—a most potent spell; but unfortunately, his Majesty of England does not furnish us with a diagram to illustrate his infernal majesty's problem. At length, in the latter part of the seventeenth

---

[1] Published, with the confession of the poor woman, in a small 4to, in possession of the writer.

century, witchcraft became a dreadful epidemic, and the number of lives that were sacrificed will never be known. Drowning, hanging, and even burning the victims, only increased the horrid appetite for such slaughter. A Scotch witch-finder was tempted at Newcastle and in Northumberland to condemn poor women as witches for a reward of twenty shillings for every one that, on his evidence, was put to death. When he was hung for some villany in Scotland, he confessed that he had been the death of above two hundred and twenty women.[1]

Matthew Hopkins, another of these wretches, hanged no less than sixty reputed witches in one year in Essex alone. Dr. Zachary Grey saw a list of between three and four thousand persons who suffered death for witch-craft. These cruelties were permitted while the victims were poor, old, decrepid women, but attacks on the wealthier classes occasioned alarm. A highly respectable Quaker lady, named Morlin, was tried for witchcraft, and saved from an ignominious death by the wisdom of Judge Windham. The evidence—a lewd woman named Pryer—swore that the lady appeared at her bedside one night, about two years ago; took her from her husband's side, turned her into a bay mare, and rode her several miles up dirty lanes to a meeting; that on her return her husband did not discover it. In answer to the judge, she said her feet were a little sore, but not her hands; nor was she

---

[1] See the testimony upon oath in Gardiner's *England's Grievance.*

dirty. Upon promise of a reward she had made it known. The judge directed an acquittal, ascribing the evidence to a dream, but did not punish the perjured wretch.[1]

Many of the poor creatures were subjected to cruel tortures, until they confessed anything that was suggested them. At length Sir Robert Filmer published an advertisement to the jurymen of England touching witches. In this he shows the difference between a Hebrew and an English witch, and proves that the devil is the principal, and the witch only an accessary before the fact. Now, an accessary cannot be convicted before the principal is tried or outlawed upon summons for non-appearance; that he could not be tried by his peers, who, if he could, would never convict him; and that, by the rules of common law, the devil could neither be summoned nor outlawed, and therefore a witch could not be tried.

As the people became enlightened, these cruel outrages became less frequent. Even Luther says—" When I was a child there were many witches, which bewitched both cattle and men, especially children. But now these things be not so commonly heard of, for the gospel thrusteth the devil out of his seat."[2]

It was reserved to Lord Chief Justice Holt to put an end to witchcraft in England, which he most effectually accomplished, by ordering prosecutions against all prose-

[1] Strange and Terrible News from Cambridge proved to be a Lie. Small 4to.
[2] Com. on Gal. v, 19.

cutors who pretended to have been bewitched. One was convicted, and, as an impostor, stood in the pillory ; and Lord Campbell adds—"No female was ever after in danger of being hanged or burned for being old, wrinkled, or paralytic."[1] Soon after this, the laws against witchcraft were repealed, as a disgrace to the statutes of the realm. Thus ended witchcraft in England, after a long, brutal, sanguinary reign. Satan was despoiled of his power to carry old women through the air on broomsticks to his nocturnal assemblies, or of diverting himself with good people's butter, cheese, pigs and geese.

The Rev. Walter Scott, in his *Congregational Lecture*, has entered with great skill into this difficult question, which can now be discussed without much fear of being branded with infidelity, "The existence and agency of evil spirits." The existence of good and evil spirits is generally admitted, but their agency is disputed. It requires no argument to prove that an immaterial invisible being can neither be seen by day or night. Mr. Scott fully admits that a disordered imagination, or disease in the organs of vision, has often led mankind to a firm belief in that which never existed, and gives some very amusing instances of it, well authenticated. We know from divine revelation, that an impassable barrier, a great gulf, is fixed between this world and that of departed spirits—impenetrable to either side.[2] Which is the infidel:

[1] Lives of Justices, ii, 170.
[2] See page 150.

he who believes this solemn portion of holy writ, or he who believes it not?

A desire to pry into futurity—to be wise above what is written, has been interwoven into fallen nature. The Almighty, by the wisest of men, has told us that "man knoweth not that which shall be."[1] This is reiterated by the inspired apostle—"Ye know not what shall be on the morrow."[2] Universal experience proves that foreknowledge is limited to the Most High; yet man is so exceedingly weak and wicked as to apply to vagabond fortune-tellers or conjurors, and thus prove his faith in the promise made by the father of lies, "Ye shall be as gods." To this evil spirit we owe all that craft, deception and robbery displayed by conjurors and wizards. Man has all the foreknowledge that he needs, in Job iv, 8, and Gal. vi., 7, 8, 9.

If such learned and pious men as Dr. Preston and Judge Hale were carried away by the popular delusions, we may bear with Dr. Mather, more especially as he was one of the first divines who discovered that many very strange events, which were considered preternatural, had occurred in the course of nature or by deceitful juggling;[3] that the devil could not speak English,[4] nor prevail with Protestants;[5] the smell of herbs alarms the devil;[6] that medicine drove out Satan![7]

[1] Ecc. viii, 7.
[2] James iv, 14.
[3] Pp. 132—138.
[4] Page 142.
[5] Page 144.
[6] Page 180.
[7] Page 186.

All the narratives, many of which are deeply affecting, bear the evidence of a truthful conviction on the part of the relators ; but most of them were handed down, doubtless with some embellishments. They are arranged in methodical order, and form a very amusing volume, more especially as it conveys a faithful portrait of the state of society, when the doctrine of a peculiar providence and of personal intercourse between this world and that which is unseen was fully believed.

We are bound to admire the accuracy and beauty of this specimen of typography. Following in the path of my late friend William Pickering, our publisher rivals the Aldine and Elzevir presses, which have been so universally admired. May every success attend his efforts.

GEORGE OFFOR.

Hackney,
    Dec. 1, 1855.

THE PREFACE.

———o———

*A*BOUT six-and-twenty years ago, a *Design for the Recording of Illustrious Providences* was under serious consideration among some eminent ministers in England and in Ireland. That motion was principally set on foot by the learned Mr. Matthew Poole, whose *Synopsis Criticorum*, and other books by him emitted, have made him famous in the world. But before any thing was brought to effect, the persons to have been employed had their thoughts diverted another way ; nevertheless there was a MS. (the com poser whereof is to me unknown) then written, wherein the subjects proper for this record, and some rules for the better managing a design of this nature, are described. In that MS. I find notable stories related and attested, which elsewhere I never met with, particularly the story of Mr. Earl of Colchester, and another mentioned in our subsequent essay. And besides those, there are some

b

very memorable passages written, which have not as yet been published, so far as I understand. There are in that **MS.** several remarkables about apparitions: *e. g.* it is there said that Dr. Frith (who was one of the prebends belonging to Windsor), lying on his bed, the chamber doors were thrown open, and a corps, with attending torches, brought to his bed-side upon a bier—the corps representing one of his own family. After some pause there was such another shew, till he, the said doctor, his wife and all his family, were brought in on the bier in such order as they all soon after died. The doctor was not then sick, but quickly grew melancholly, and would, rising at midnight, repair to the graves and monuments at Eton Colledge, saying that he and his must shortly take up their habitation among the dead. The relater of this story (a person of great integrity) had it from Dr. Frith's son, who also added, " My fathers vision is already executed upon all the family but myself ; my time is next, and near at hand."

In the mentioned MS. there is also a marvelous relation concerning a young Scholar in France ; for it is there affirmed, that this prophane student, having by extravagant courses outrun his means, in his discontent walking solitarily, a man came to him, and enquired the cause of his sadness ; which he owning to be want of money, had presently a supply given him by the other. That being quickly consumed upon his lusts, as soon as his money was gone, his discontent returned ; and in his former walk he met with his former reliever, who again offered to supply him, but askt him to contract with him to be his, and to sign the contract with his blood. The woful wretch consented; but not long after, considering that this contract was made with the devil, the terrors of his conscience became insupportable, so as that he endeavoured to kill himself to get out of them. Some ministers, and other Christians, being informed how matters were circum stanced, kept dayes of prayer for him and with him; and he was carefully watched that so he might be kept from self-murder. Still he continued under terror, and said he should do so, as long as the covenant which he had signed remained in the hands of the devil. Hereupon the ministers resolve to keep a day of fasting and prayer in that very place of the field were the distressed creature had made the woful bargain, setting him in the midst of them. Thus they did; and being with special actings of faith much enlarged to pray earnestly to the Lord to make known his power over Satan, in constraining him to give up that contract; after some hours continuance in prayer, a cloud was seen to spread itself over them; and out of it the very contract signed with the poor creatures blood was dropped down amongst them; which being taken up and viewed, the party concerned took it and tore it in pieces. The relator had this from the mouth of Mr. Beaumond, a minister of note at Caen in Normandy, who assured him that he had it from one of the ministers that did assist in carrying on the day of prayer when this memorable providence hapned. Nor is the relation impossible to be true ; for Luther speaks of a providence, not unlike unto this, which hapned in his congregation.

This MS. doth also mention some most remarkable judgments of God upon sinners, as worthy to be recorded for posterity to take notice of. It is there said, that when Mr. Richard Juxon was a fellow of Kings Colledge in Cambridge, he led a most vicious life ; and whereas such of the students as were serious in matters of religion did endeavour, by solemn fasting and prayer, to prepare themselves for the communion which was then (this was about the year 1636) on Easter-Day. This Juxon spent all the time of preparation in drunken wild meetings, and was up late and drunk on the Saturday night. Nevertheless, on the Lords Day, he came with others to the communion, and sat next to the relater, who, knowing his disorder the night before, was much troubled, but had no remedy, Church-discipline not being then so practised as ought to have been. The Communion being ended, such of the scholars as had the fear of God in their hearts, repaired to their closets. But this Juxon went immediately to a drunken meeting, and there to a cockfight, where he fell to his accustomed madness, and pouring out a volley of oaths and curses ; while these were between his lips, God smote him dead in the twinkle of an eye. And though Juxon were but young, and of a comely person, his carcase was immediately so corrupted as that the stench of it was insufferable, insomuch that no house would receive it, and his friends were forced to hire some base fellows to watch the carcase till night; and then with pitch, and such-like gums, covered him in a coffin, and so made a shift to endure his interment. There stood by a scholar, whose name was George Hall, and who acted his part with Juxon in his prophaneness, but he was so astonished with this amazing providence of God, as that he fell down upon his knees, begging pardoning mercy from Heaven, and vowing a reformation; which vow the Lord enabled him to keep, so as that afterwards he became an able and famous minister of the Gospel.

One strange passage more I shall here relate out of the MS. which we have thus far made mention of. Therein I find part of a letter transcribed, which is as followeth:—

"Lismore, Octob. 2, 1658. In another part of this countrey, a poor man being suspected to have stollen a sheep was questioned for it; he forswore the thing, and wished, that if he had stollen it, God would cause the horns of the sheep to grow upon him. This man was seen within these few dayes by a minister of great repute for piety, who saith, that the man has an horn growing out of one corner of his mouth, just like that of a sheep; from which he hath cut seventeen inches, and is forced to keep it tyed by a string to his ear, to prevent its growing up to his eye. This minister not only saw but felt this horn, and reported it in this family this week, as also a gentleman formerly did, who was himself an eye-witness thereof. Surely such passages are a demonstrative evidence that there is a God who judgeth in the earth, and who, though he stay long, will not be mocked alwayes."

I shall say no more concerning the MS. only that it was sent over to Reverend Mr. Davenport by (as I suppose) Mr. Hartlib. How it came to lie dormient in his hands I know not; though I had the happiness of special intimacy with that worthy man, I do not remember that ever I heard him speak any thing of it. But since his death, looking over his MSS. I met with this, and communicated it to other ministers, who highly approved of the noble design aimed at therein. Soon after which, some proposals, in order to the reviving of this work, were drawn up, and presented at a general meeting of the ministers in this colony, May 12, 1681, which it may not be unsuitable here to recite.

"*Some Proposals concerning the Recording of Illustrious Providences.*

"I. In order to the promoving of a design of this nature, so as shall be indeed for Gods glory and the good of posterity, it is necessary that utmost care shall be taken that all and only *Remarkable Providences* be recorded and published.

"II. Such Divine judgements, tempests, floods, earthquakes, thunders as are unusual, strange apparitions, or whatever else shall happen that is prodigious, witchcrafts, diabolical possessions, remarkable judgements upon noted sinners, eminent deliverances, and answers of prayer, are to be reckoned among illustrious providences.

"III. Inasmuch as we find in Scripture, as well as in ecclesiastical history, that the ministers of God have been improved in the recording and declaring the works of the Lord, and since they are in divers respects under peculiar advantages thereunto, it is proposed, that each one in that capacity may diligently enquire into and record such illustrious providences as have hapned, or from time to time shall happen, in the places whereunto they do belong; and that the witnesses of such notable occurrents be likewise set down in writing.

"IV. Although it be true that this design cannot be brought into perfection in one or two years, yet it is much to be desired that something may be done therein out of hand, as a specimen of a more large volume, that so this work may be set on foot, and posterity may be encouraged to go on therewith.

"V. It is therefore proposed that the elders may concurre in desiring some one that hath leisure and ability for the management of such an undertaking, with all convenient speed to begin therewith.

"VI. And that, therefore, other elders do without delay make enquiry concerning the remarkable occurrents that have formerly fallen out, or may fall out hereafter, where they are concerned, and transmit them unto the aforesaid person, according to the directions above specified, in order to a speedy publication.

"VII. That notice be given of these proposals unto our brethren, the elders of the neighbour colonies, that so we may enjoy their concurrence and assistance herein.

"VIII. When any thing of this nature shall be ready for the presse, it appears on sundry grounds very expedient that it should be read and approved of at some meeting of the elders, before publication."

These things being read and considered, the author of this essay was desired to begin the work which is here done; and I am engaged to many for the materials and informations which the following collections do consist of. It is not easie to give an account of things, and yet no circumstantial mistakes attend what shall be related. Nor dare I averr that there are none such in what follows; only I have been careful to prevent them; and as to the substance of each passage, I am well assured it is according to truth. That rare accident about the lightning, which caused a wonderful change in the compasses of a vessel then at sea, was as in the book expressed, pages 91, 92; only it is uncertain whether they were then exactly in the latitude of 38, for they had not taken an observation for several dayes; but the master of the vessel affirms that to be the latitude so near as they could conjecture. Since the needle was changed by the lightning, if a lesser compass be set over it, the needle therein (or any other touched with the loadstone) will alter its polarity, and turn about to the south, as I have divers times to my great admiration experimented. There is near the north point a dark spot, like as if it were burnt with a drop of brimstone, supposed to be caused by the lightning. Whether the magnetic impressions on that part of the needle being dissipated by the heat of the lightning, and the effluvia on the south end of the needle only remaining untouched thereby, be the true natural reason of the marvelous alteration, or whether it ought to be ascribed to some other cause, the ingenious may consider.

There is another remarkable passage about lightning which hapned at Duxborough, in New England, concerning which I have lately received this following account :—

September 11, 1653 (being the Lords Day), there were small drizling showers, attended with some seldome and scarce perceivable rumbling thunders, until towards the evening; at what time, Mr. Constant Southworth of Duxbury returning home after evening exercise, in company with some neighbours, discoursing of some extraordinary thunder-claps with lightning, and the awful effects and consequents thereof, being come into his own house (there were present in one room, himself, his wife, two children, viz. Thomas, he was afterwards drowned, and Benjamin, he was long after this killed by the Indians, with Philip Delano, a servant), there broke perpendicularly over the said house and room a most awful and amazing clap of thunder, attended with a violent flash, or rather flame of lightning, which brake and shivered one of the needles of the katted or wooden chimney, carrying divers splinters seven or eight rods distance from the house. It filled the room with smoke and flame; and set fire in the thatch of a lean-to which was on the back-side of a room adjoyning to the former, in which the five persons above mentioned were. It melted some pewter, so that it ran into drops on the outside, as is often seen on tin ware; melted round holes in the top of a fire-shovel proportionable in quantity to a small goose-shot; struck Mrs. Southworths arm so that it was for a time benummed; smote the young child Benjamin in his mothers arms, deprived it of breath for a space, and to the mothers apprehension squeased it as flat as a planck; smote a dog stone dead which lay within two foot of Philip Delano; the dog never moved out of his place or posture in which he was when smitten, but giving a small yelp, and quivering with his toes, lay still, blood issuing from his nose or mouth. It smote the said Philip, made his right arm senseless for a time, together with the middle finger in special (of his right hand), which was benummed, and turned as white as chalk or lime, yet attended with little pain. After some few hours, that finger began to recover its proper colour at the knuckle, and so did gradually whiten unto its extremity; and although the said Delano felt a most violent heat upon his body, as if he had been scorched in the midst of a violent burning fire, yet his clothes were not singed, neither had the smell of fire passed thereon.

I could not insert this story in its proper place, because I received it after that chapter about thunder and lightning was printed. Some credible persons, who have been eye-witnesses of it, inform me that the lightning in that house at Duxborough, did with the vehemency of its flame, cause the bricks in the chimney to melt like molten lead : which particular was as remarkable as any of the other mentioned in the narrative, and therefore I thought good here to add it.

In this essay I design no more than a specimen ; and having (by the good hand of God upon me) set this wheel a going, I shall leave it unto others, whom God has fitted and shall incline thereto, to go on with the undertaking.

Some digressions I have made in distinct chapters, handling several considerable *Cases of Conscience*, supposing it not unprofitable or improper so to do, since the things related gave the occasion. Both leisure and exercise of judgement are required in the due performance of a service of this nature. There are some that have more leisure, and many that have greater abilities, than I have : I expect not tnat they should make my method their standard ; but they may follow a better of their own, as they shall see cause. The addition of parallel stories is both pleasing and edifying ; had my reading and remembrance of things been greater, I might have done more that way, as I hope others will in the next essay.

I could have mentioned some very memorable passages of Divine Providence, wherein the countrey in general hath been concerned : some remarkables of that kind are to be seen in my former relations of the troubles occasioned by the Indians in New-England. There are other particulars no less worthy to be recorded, but in my judgement this is not so proper a season for us to divulge them. It has been in my thoughts to publish a discourse of *Miscellaneous Observations concerning Things Rare and Wonderful, both as to the Works of Creation and Providence,* which in my small readings I have met with in many authors; but this must suffice for the present. I have often wished that the Natural History of New-England might be written and published to the world; the rules and method described by that learned and excellent person Robert Boyle, Esq., being duely observed therein. It would best become some scholar that has been born in this land to do such a service for his countrey. Nor would I myself decline to put my hand (so far as my small capacity will reach) to so noble an undertaking, did not manifold diversions and employments prevent me from attending that which I should account a profitable recreation. I have other work upon me which I would gladly finish before I leave the world, and but a very little time to do it in. Moreover, not many years ago, I *lost* (and that's an afflictive *loss* indeed!) several moneths from study by sickness. Let every God-fearing reader joyn with me in prayer, that I may be enabled to redeem the time, and (in all wayes wherein I am capable), to serve my generation.

INCREASE MATHER.

Boston in New-England,
  January 1, 168$\frac{3}{4}$.

CONTENTS.

———o———

CHAPTER I.

CONTENTS

CONTENTS.

CONTENTS.

REMARKABLE
PROVIDENCES

———o———

CHAPTER I.

OF REMARKABLE SEA DELIVERANCES.

Mr. Anthony Thacher's relation concerning his and his wife's being mar-
vellously preserved alive, when all the ship's company perished. The
wonderful preservation of Major Gibbons and his company. Several
other remarkable sea-deliverances mentioned by Mr. Janeway, wherein
New England men were concerned. Mr. Grafton's preservation. A
vessel lately coming from Bristol for New England saved out of great
distress at sea. Some providentially met with by a New England vessel
in an open boat, many leagues off from any shore, strangely preserved.
An account of a remarkable sea-deliverance which happened this present
year. Another like unto it which happened above twenty years ago.

THE royal pen of the prophet David hath most
truly affirmed, "that they who go down to the
sea in ships, that do business in great waters,
see the works of the Lord, and his wonders
in the deep." And, in special, they see wonders of Divine
goodness in respect of eminent deliverances wrought
by the hand of the Most High, who stills the noise
of the seas, the noise of their waves. It is meet that
such providences should be ever had in remembrance, as
most of all by the persons concerned in them, so by others,
that the God of Salvation, who is the confidence of them
that are afar off upon the sea, may have eternal praise.

1

Many remarkable stories of this kind are to be seen in books already published:—*e.g.* in Mandelslo's *Travels;* Hackluyt and Linschoten's *Voyages;* Wanley's *History;* Caussin's *Holy Court;* Mr. Burton's Treatises, lately printed; and in Mr. Janeway's *Sea Deliverances.* I shall in this chapter confine myself unto things which have happened either in New England, or wherein New England vessels have been concerned. We shall begin with that remarkable sea-deliverance which Mr. Anthony Thacher did experience at his first coming to New England. A full and true relation whereof I find in a letter directed to his brother, Mr. Peter Thacher, then a faithful minister of Christ in Sarum in England (he was father to my worthy dear friend, Mr. Thomas Thacher, late pastor of one of the churches in this Boston). This letter of Mr. Anthony Thacher to his brother, being written within a few days after that eminent providence happened unto him, matters were then fresh in his memory; I shall, therefore, here insert his narrative in his own words, who expresseth himself as followeth :—

"I must turn my drowned pen and shaking hand to indite the story of such sad news as never before this happened in New England. There was a league of perpetual friendship between my cousin Avery (note that this Mr. Avery was a precious holy minister, who came out of England with Mr. Anthony Thacher) and myself never to forsake each other to the death, but to be partakers of each others misery or welfare, as also of habitation in the same place. Now, upon our arrival in New England there was an offer made unto us. My Cousin Avery was invited to Marble-head, to be their pastor in due time, there being no church planted there as yet, but a town appointed to set up the trade of fishing. Because many there (the most being fishermen) were something loose and remiss in their behaviour, my Cousin Avery was unwilling to go thither, and so refusing we went to Newbery, intending there to sit down. But being solicited so often, both by the men of the place and by the magistrates, and by Mr. Cotton and most of the ministers, who alleged what a benefit we might be to the people there, and also to the country and commonwealth: at length we embraced it, and thither consented to go. They of Marble-head forthwith sent a pinnace for us and our goods. We embarked at Ipswich, August 11, 1635, with our families and substance, bound for Marble-head, we being in all twenty-three souls, viz., eleven in my cousin's family, seven in mine, and one Mr. William Eliot, sometimes of New Sarum, and four mariners. The next morning, having commended ourselves to God, with cheerful hearts we hoisted sail; but the Lord suddenly turned our cheerfulness into mourning and lamentations; for on the 14th of this August, 1635, about ten at night, having a fresh gale of wind, our sails being old and done, were split. The mariners, because that it was night, would not put to new sails, but resolved to cast anchor till the morning. But before daylight it pleased the Lord to send so mighty a storm, as the like was never known in New England since the English came, nor in the memory of any of the Indians. It was so furious that our anchor came home. Whereupon the mariners let out more cable, which at last slipped away. Then our sailors knew not what to do, but we were driven before the wind and waves. My cousin and I perceived our danger, solemnly recommended ourselves to God, the Lord both of earth and seas, expecting with every wave to be swallowed up and drenched in the deeps. And as my cousin, his wife, and my tender babes, sat comforting and cheering one the other in the Lord against ghastly death, which every moment stared us in the face, and sat triumphing upon each one's forehead, we were by the violence of the waves and fury of the winds (by the Lord's permission), lifted up upon a rock between two high rocks, yet all was one rock, but it raged with the stroke which came into the pinnace, so as we were presently up to our middles in water as we sat. The waves came furiously and violently over us, and against us; but by reason of the rock's proportion could not lift us off, but beat her all to pieces. Now look with me upon our distress, and consider of my misery, who beheld the ship broken, the water in her, and violently overwhelming us, my goods and provisions swimming in the seas, my friends almost drowned, and mine own poor children so untimely (if I may so term it without offence), before mine eyes drowned, and ready to be swallowed up, and dashed to pieces against the rocks by the merciless waves, and myself ready to accompany them.   But I must go on to an end of this woful relation. In the same room whereas he sat, the master of the pinnace not knowing what to do, our foremast was cut down, our mainmast broken in three pieces, the fore part of the pinnace beat away, our goods swimming about the seas, my children bewailing me, as not pitying themselves, and myself bemoaning them; poor souls, whom I had occasioned to such an end in their tender years, when as they could scarce be sensible of death.   And so likewise my cousin, his wife, and his children, and both of us bewailing each other, in our Lord and only Saviour Jesus Christ, in whom only we had comfort and cheerfulness, insomuch that from the greatest to the least of us, there was not one screech or outcry made, but all as silent sheep were contentedly resolved to die together lovingly, as since our acquaintance we had lived together friendly. Now as I was sitting in the cabin-room door, with my body in the room, when lo! one of the sailors, by a wave, being washed out of the pinnace was gotten in again, and coming in to the cabin-room over my back, cried out, 'We are all cast away! the Lord have mercy upon us! I have been washed overboard into the sea, and am gotten in again!' His speeches made me look forth. And looking towards the sea, and seeing how we were, I turned myself to my cousin and the rest, and spake these words: 'Oh, cousin! it hath pleased God to cast us here between two rocks, the shore not far off from us, for I saw the tops of trees when I looked forth.' Whereupon the master of the pinnace looking up at the scuttle-hole of the quarter-deck, went out at it, but I never saw him afterwards. Then he that had been in the sea went out again by me, and leaped overboard towards the rocks, whom afterwards also I could not see. Now none were left in the barque that I knew or saw, but my cousin, his wife and children, myself and mine, and his maid-servant. But my cousin thought I would have fled from him, and said unto me—'Oh, cousin, leave us not, let us die together,' and reached forth his hand unto me. Then I, letting go my son Peter's hand, took him by the hand, and said—'Cousin, I purpose it not, whither shall I go? I am willing and ready here to die with you and my poor children. God be merciful to us, and receive us to himself,' adding these words, 'the Lord is able to help and deliver us.' He replied, saying—'Truth, cousin; but what his pleasure is we know not; I fear we have been too unthankful for former deliverances, but he hath promised to deliver us from sin and condemnation, and to bring us safe to heaven through the all-sufficient satisfaction of Jesus Christ, *this therefore we may challenge of him.* To which I replying, said, 'that is all the deliverance I now desire and expect.' Which words I had no sooner spoken, but by a mighty wave I was with the piece of the barque, washed out upon part of the rock, where the wave left me almost drowned, but recovering my feet I saw above me on the rock my daughter Mary, to whom I had no sooner gotten, but my cousin Avery, and his eldest son came to us, being all four of us washed out by one and the same wave, we went all into a small hole on the top of the rock, whence we called to those in the pinnace, to come unto us, supposing we had been in more safety than they were in. My wife seeing us there, was crept into the scuttle of the quarter deck to come unto us, but presently came another wave, and dashing the pinnace all to pieces, carried my wife away in the scuttle, as she was, with the greater part of the quarter-deck unto the shore, where she was cast safely, but her legs were something bruised, and much timber of the vessel being there also cast, she was sometime before she could get away, being washed by the waves. All the rest that were in the barque were drowned in the merciless seas. We four, by that wave, were clean swept away from off the rock also, into the sea ; the Lord, in one instant of time, disposing of fifteen souls of us, according to His good pleasure and will; His pleasure and wonderful great mercy to me, was thus: standing on the rock as before you heard with my eldest daughter, my cousin and his eldest son, looking upon and talking to them in the barque, when as we were by that merciless wave washed off the rock as before you heard. God in his mercy caused me to fall by the stroke of the wave, flat on my face, for my face was toward the sea, insomuch, that as I was sliding off the rock into the sea, the Lord directed my toes into a joint in the rock's side, as also the tops of some of my fingers with my right hand, by means whereof, the wave leaving me, I remained so, having in the rock only my head above the water. When on the left hand I espied a board or plank of the pinnace ; and as I was reaching out my left hand to lay hold on it, by another coming over the top of the rock, I was washed away from the rock, and by the violence of the waves, was driven hither and thither in the seas a great while, and had many dashes against the rocks. At length, past hopes of life, and wearied in body and spirits, I even gave over to nature, and being ready to receive in the waters of death, I lifted up both my heart and hands to the God of heaven. For note, I had my senses remaining perfect with me all the time that I was under and in water, who at that instant lifted up my head above the top of the water, that so I may breathe without any hindrance by the waters. I stood bolt upright as if I had stood upon my feet, but I felt no bottom, nor had any footing for to stand upon, but the waters. While I was thus above the waters, I saw by me a piece of the mast, as I suppose about three feet long, which I laboured to catch into my arms. But suddenly I was overwhelmed with water, and driven to and fro again, and at last I felt the ground with my right foot. When immediately, whilst I was thus groveling on my face, I presently recovering my feet, was in the water up to my breast, and through God's great mercy had my face unto the shore, and not to the sea. I made haste to get out, but was thrown down on my hands with the waves, and so with safety crept to the dry shore. Where blessing God, I turned about to look for my children and friends, but saw neither, nor any part of the pinnace, where I left them as I supposed. But I saw my wife about a butt length from me, getting herself forth from amongst the timber of the broken barque; but before I could get unto her, she was gotten to the shore; I was in the water after I was washed from the rock, before I came to the shore, a quarter of an hour at least. When we were come to each other, we went and sat under the bank. But fear of the seas roaring, and our coldness, would not suffer us there to remain. But we went up into the land and sat us down under a cedar tree which the wind had thrown down, where we sat about an hour almost dead with cold. But now the storm was broken up, and the wind was calm, but the sea remained rough and fearful to us. My legs were much bruised, and so was my head, other hurt had I none, neither had I taken in much quantity of water; but my heart would not let me sit still any longer, but I would go to see if any more were gotten to the land in safety, especially hoping to have met with some of my own poor children, but I could find none, neither dead nor yet living. You condole with me my miseries, who now began to consider of my losses. Now came to my remembrance the time and manner, how and when I last saw and left my children and friends. One was severed from me sitting on the rock at my feet, the other three in the pinnace; my little babe (ah! poor Peter) sitting in his sister Edith's arms, who to the uttermost of her power sheltered him from the waters, my poor William standing close unto them, all three of them looking ruefully on me on the rock; their very countenances calling unto me to help them, whom I could not go unto, neither could they come at me, neither would the merciless waves afford me space or time to use any means at all, either to help them or myself. Oh! I yet see their cheeks, poor silent lambs, pleading pity and help at my hands. Then on the other side to consider the loss of my dear friends, with the spoiling and loss of all our goods and provisions, myself cast upon an unknown land, in a wilderness, I knew not where, nor how to get thence. Then it came to my mind how I had occasioned the death of my children, who caused them to leave their native land, who might have left them there, yea, and might have sent some of them back again, and cost me nothing: these and such like thoughts do press down my heavy heart very much. But I must let this pass, and will proceed on in the relation of God's goodness unto me in that desolate island on which I was cast. I and my wife were almost naked, both of us, and wet and cold even unto death. I found a knapsack cast on the shore, in which I had a steel and flint and powder horn. Going further I found a drowned goat, then I found a hat, and my son William's coat, both which I put on. My wife found one of her petticoats, which she put on. I found also two cheeses and some butter, driven ashore. Thus the Lord sent us some clothes to put on, and food to sustain our new lives which we had lately given unto us; and means also to make fire, for in an horn I had some gunpowder, which to my own (and since to other men's) admiration was dry; so taking a piece of my wife's neckcloth, which I dried in the sun, I struck fire, and so dried and warmed our wet bodies, and then skinned the goat; and having found a small brass pot, we boiled some of her. Our drink was brackish water; bread we had none. There we remained till the Monday following. When about three of the clock, in the afternoon, in a boat that came that **way**, we went off that desolate island, which I named after my name, Thacher's Woe ; and the rock, Avery his Fall : to the end that their fall and loss, and mine own, might be had in perpetual remembrance.   In the isle lieth buried the body of my cousin's eldest daughter, whom I found dead on the shore. On the Tuesday following, in the afternoon, we arrived at Marble-head."

Thus far is Mr. Thacher's relation of this memorable providence.   We proceed to some other :

Remarkable was that deliverance mentioned both by Mr. Janeway and Mr. Burton, wherein that gallant commander, Major Edward Gibbons, of Boston, in New England, and others were concerned.   The substance of the story is this :—A New England vessel going from Boston to some other parts of America, was, through the continuance of contrary winds, kept long at sea, so that they were in very great straits for want of provision ; and seeing they could not hope for any relief from earth or sea, they apply themselves to heaven in humble and hearty prayers ; but no calm ensuing, one of them made this sorrowful motion, that they should cast lots, which of them should die first to satisfy the ravenous hunger of the rest.   After many a sad debate, they come to a result, the lot is cast, and one of the company is taken, but where is the executioner to be found to act this office upon a poor innocent ?   It is death now to think who shall act this bloody part in the tragedy.   But before they fall upon this involuntary execution, they once more went unto their prayers ; and while they were calling upon God, he answered them, for there leaped a mighty fish into the boat, which was a double joy to them, not only in relieving their miserable hunger, which, no doubt, made them quick cooks, but because they looked upon it to be sent from God, and to be a token of their deliverance. But alas! the fish is soon eaten, and their former exigencies come upon them, which sink their spirits into despair, for they know not of another morsel. To lot they go again a second time, which falleth upon another person; but still none can be found to sacrifice him : they again send their prayers to heaven with all manner of fervency, when, behold a second answer from above! a great bird alights, and fixes itself upon the mast, which one of the company espies, and he goes, and there she stands till he took her with his hand by the wing. This was life from the dead a second time, and they feasted themselves herewith, as hoping that second providence was a forerunner of their complete deliverance. But they have still the same disappointments; they can see no land; they know not where they are. Hunger increaseth again upon them, and they have no hopes to be saved but by a third miracle. They are reduced to the former course of casting lots; when they were going to the heart-breaking work, to put him to death whom the lot fell upon, they go to God, their former friend in adversity, by humble and hearty prayers; and now they look and look again; but there is nothing. Their prayers are concluded, and nothing appears, yet still they hoped and stayed; till at last one of them espies a ship, which put new life into all their spirits. They bear up with their vessel, they man their boat, and desire and beg like perishing, humble supplicants to board them, which they are admitted. The vessel proves a French vessel—yea, a French pirate.

Major Gibbons petitions them for a little bread, and offers ship and cargo for it. But the commander knows the Major (from whom he had received some signal kindnesses formerly at Boston), and replied readily and cheerfully—"Major Gibbons, not a hair of you or your company shall perish, if it lie in my power to preserve you." And accordingly he relieveth them, and sets them safe on shore.

Memorable also is that which Mr. Janeway, in his *Remarkable Sea Deliverances*, p. 35, hath published. He there relates, that in the year 1668, a ketch, whereof Thomas Woodbery was master, sailing from New England for Barbadoes; when they came in the latitude 35 deg., because there was some appearance of foul weather, they lowered their sails, sending up one to the top of the mast, he thought he saw something like a boat floating upon the sea; and calling to the men below, they made towards it, and when they came near, it appeared to be a long-boat with eleven men in it, who had been bound for Virginia; but their ship proved leaky, and foundered in the sea, so that they were forced suddenly to betake themselves to their long-boat, in the which they had a capstan-bar, which they made use of for a mast, and a piece of canvas for a sail, so did they sail before the wind. But they having no victuals with them, were soon in miserable distress. Thus they continued five days, so that all despaired of life. Upon the sixth day they concluded to cast lots for their lives, viz., who should die, that the rest might eat him and have their lives preserved. He that the lot fell upon, begged for his life a little longer; and being in their extremity, the wonder-working providence of God was seen, for they met with this New England vessel, which took them in and saved their lives. An hour after this a terrible storm arose, continuing forty hours, so that if they had not met the vessel that saved them in the nick of opportunity, they had all perished ! and if the New England men had not taken down some of their sails, or had not chanced to send one up to tallow the mast, this boat and men had never been seen by them. Thus admirable are the workings of Divine Providence in the world

Yet further :

That worthy and now blessed minister of God, Mr. James Janeway, hath published several other *Remarkable Sea Deliverances,* of which some belonging to New England were the subjects. He relates (and I am informed that it was really so) that a small vessel—the master's name Philip Hungare—coming upon the coast of New England suddenly sprang a leak, and so foundered. In the vessel there were eighteen souls, twelve of which got into the long-boat. They threw into the boat some small matters of provision, but were wholly without fire. These twelve men sailed five hundred leagues in this small boat, being by almost miraculous providences preserved therein for five weeks together. God sent relief to them by causing some flying-fish to fall into the boat, which they eat raw, and were well pleased therewith. They also caught a shark, and opening his belly, sucked his blood for drink. At the last the Divine Providence brought them to the West Indies. Some of them were so weak that they soon died ; but most of them lived to declare the works of the Lord.

Again, he relates that Mr. Jonas Clark, of New England,

going for Virginia, the vessel was cast ashore in the night. They hoped to get their ship off again; to which end the master with some others going in the boat, when they were about sixty fathoms from the shore there arose a great sea, which broke in upon them, and at last turned the boat over. Four men were drowned. Mr. Clark was held under water till his breath was gone, yet, through the good hand of a gracious God, he was set at liberty, and was enabled to swim to the shore, where the providence of God did so overrule the hearts of barbarians, as that they did them no hurt; until at last they were brought safe unto the English plantations. These things have (as was said) been related by Mr. Janeway. I proceed therefore to mention some other sea deliverances. And that notable preservation deserves to be here inserted and recorded, wherein Mr. John Grafton and some other of his ship's company were concerned; who as they were bound in a voyage from Salem in New England, for the West Indies, in a ketch called the Providence, on September 16, 1669, their vessel suddenly struck upon a rock at the which they were amazed, it being then a dark and rainy night; the force of the wind and sea broke their vessel in a moment. Their company was ten men in number, whereof six were drowned. The master and the mate were left upon the rock. As they sat there the sea came up to their waists. There did they embrace each other, looking for death every moment; and if the tide had risen higher it would have carried them off. By the same rock was one of the seamen, being much wounded and grievously groaning. In the morning they saw an island about half a mile off from them. The rocks were so sharp and cragged that they could not tread upon them with

their bare feet, nor had they shoes or stockings. But
they found a piece of tarpauling, which they wrapped
about their feet, making it fast with rope yarns; so getting
each of them a stick, they sometimes went on their feet,
and sometimes crept, until at last they came to the island,
where they found another of their company ashore, being
carried thither by a piece of the vessel. Upon the island
they continued eight days, four of which they had no fire.
Their provision was salt-fish and rain-water, which they
found in the holes of the rocks. After four days they
found a piece of touchwood, which the mate had formerly
in his chest, and a piece of flint, with which, having a
small knife, they struck fire. A barrel of flour being cast
on shore, they made cakes thereof. Now their care was
how to get off from the island, there being no inhabitants
there. Finding a piece of the mainsail, and some hoops
of cask, they framed a boat therewith. Yet had they no
tools to build it with. But Providence so ordered, that
they found a board twelve feet long, and some nails; also
a box was cast ashore, wherein was a bolt-rope needle;
they likewise found a tar-barrel, wherewith they tarred
their canvas. Thus did they patch up a boat, in fashion
like a birchen canoe; and meeting with some thin boards
of ceiling, which came out of the cabin, they made paddles
therewith; so did they venture in this dangerous vessel
ten leagues, until they came to Anguilla and St. Martin's,
where they were courteously entertained, the people ad-
miring how they could come so many leagues in such a
strange kind of boat. Besides all these particulars, which
have been declared, information is brought to me concerning some sea preservations which have happened more
lately.

There was a small vessel set sail from Bristol to New England, September 22, 1681 ; the master's name William Dutten. There were seven men in the vessel, having on board provisions for three months, but by reason of contrary winds, they were twenty weeks before they could make any land ; and some unhappy accidents fell out, which occasioned their being put to miserable straits for victuals, but most of all for drink. The winds were fair and prosperous until October 28, when they supposed themselves to be gotten 600 leagues westward. But after that, the north-west winds blew so fiercely that they were driven off from the coast of New England, so that, December 12, they concluded to bear away for Barbadoes. But before this, one of their barrels of beer had the head broken out, and the liquor in it lost. They had but seven barrels of water, three of which proved leaky, so that the water in them was lost. When their victuals failed, the providence of God sent them a supply, by causing dolphins to come near to the vessel ; and that still as their wants were greatest, nor could they catch more than would serve their present turn. But still their misery upon them was great, through their want of water. Sometimes they would expose their vessels to take the rain-water ; but oft, when it rained, the winds were so furious that they could save little or no rain ; yet so it fell out, that when they came near to the latitude of Bermudas they saved two barrels of rain-water, which caused no little joy amongst them. But the rats did unexpectedly eat holes through the barrels, so that their water was lost again. Once when a shower of rain fell they could save but a pint, which, though it was made bitter by the tar, it seemed very sweet to them. They divided this pint of rain-water amongst seven, drinking a thimbleful at a time, which went five times about, and was a great refreshing to them. On January 27, a good shower of rain fell; that so they might be sure to save some water, and not be again deprived thereof by the rats, they laid their shirts open to the rain, and wringing them dry, they obtained seven gallons of water, which they put into bottles, and were, for a time, much refreshed thereby. But new straits come upon them. They endeavoured to catch the rats in the vessel, and could take but three or four, which they did eat, and it seemed delicate meat to their hungry souls. But the torment of their drought was insufferable. Sometimes, for a week together, they had not one drop of fresh water. When they killed a dolphin they would open his belly and suck his blood, a little to relieve their thirst; yea, their thirst was so great that they fell to drinking of salt water. Some drank several gallons, but they found that it did not allay their thirst. They greedily drank their own urine when they could make any. They would go overboard, with a rope fastened to their bodies, and put themselves into the water hoping to find some refreshment thereby. When any of them stood to steer the vessel, he would think a little to refresh himself by having his feet in a pail of sea-water. In this misery, some of the seamen confessed that it was just with God thus to afflict them, in that they had been guilty of wasting good drink, and of abusing themselves therewith before they came to sea. The divine Providence so ordered, that on February 7, they met with a vessel at sea, which happened to be a Guiny-man; (Samuel Richard, master). Their boat was become leaky, that they could not go aboard, if it had been to save their lives; but the master of the other

2

vessel understanding how it was with them, very courteously sent his own boat to them, with ten pieces of Guiny-beef, two ankors of fresh water, and four bushels of Guiny-corn, whereby they were sustained until they arrived at Barbadoes; being weak and spent with their hardships, but within a fortnight they were all recovered, and came the next summer to New England. This account I received from the mate of the vessel, whose name is Joseph Butcher.

Remarkable, also, is the preservation of which some belonging to Dublin, in Ireland, had experienced, whom a New England vessel providentially met, in an open boat, in the wide sea, and saved them from perishing. Concerning which memorable providence, I have received the following narrative :—A ship of Dublin, burdened about seventy tons, Andrew Bennet, master, being bound from Dublin to Virginia: this vessel having been some weeks at sea, onward of their voyage, and being in the latitude of 39, about 150 leagues distant from Cape Cod, in New England, on April 18, 1681, a day of very stormy weather, and a great sea, suddenly there sprang a plank in the fore part of the ship, about six o'clock in the morning; whereupon the water increased so fast in the ship, that all their endeavours could not keep her from sinking above half an hour; so when the ship was just sinking, some of the company resolved to launch out the boat, which was a small one: they did accordingly, and the master, the mate, the boatswain, the cook, two foremast men, and a boy, kept such hold of it, when a cast of the sea suddenly helped them off with it, that they got into it. The heaving of the sea now suddenly thrust them from the ship, in which there were left nineteen souls, viz., sixteen men and three women, who all perished in the mighty waters, while they were trying to make rafters by cutting down the masts, for the preservation of their lives, as long as might be. The seven in the boat apprehended themselves to be in a condition little better than that of them in the ship, having neither sails nor oars, neither bread nor water, and no instrument of any sort, except a knife and a piece of deal board, with which they made sticks, and set them up in the sides of the boat, and covered them with some Irish cloth of their own garments, to keep off the spray of the sea, as much as could be by so poor a matter. In this condition they drave with a hard wind and high sea all that day and the night following. But in the next morning, about six o'clock, they saw a ketch (the master whereof was Mr. Edmund Henfield, of Salem, in New England) under sail, which ketch coming right with them, took them up and brought them safe to New England. And it is yet further remarkable, that when the ship foundered, the ketch which saved these persons was many leagues to the westward of her, but was, by a contrary wind, caused to stand back again to the eastward, where these distressed persons were, as hath been said, met with and relieved.

Another remarkable sea-deliverance, like unto this last mentioned, happened this present year; the relation whereof take as followeth :—A ship called the Swallow, Thomas Welden, of London, master, on their voyage from St. Christopher's towards London, did, on March 23 last, being then about the latitude of 42, meet with a violent storm. That storm somewhat allayed, the ship lying in

2a

the trough of the sea, her rudder broke away; whereupon the mariners veered out a cable, and part of a mast to steer by; but that not answering their expectation, they took a hogshead of water, and fastened it to the cable to steer the ship; that also failing, they laid the ship by, as the seamen's phrase is. And on March 25 an exceeding great storm arose, which made the vessel lie down with her hatches under water, in which condition she continued about two hours; and having much water in the hold, they found no other way to make her rise again but by cutting down her masts; and accordingly her mainmast and her mizenmast being cut down, the ship righted again. The storm continuing, on March 28 the ship made very bad steerage, by reason of the loss of her rudder and masts. The sea had continual passage over her, and one sea did then carry away the larboard quarter of the ship, and brake the side from the deck, so that there was an open passage for the sea to come in at that breach; and, notwithstanding their endeavours to stop it with their bedding, clothes, &c., so much water ran in by the sides of the ship, that it was ready to sink. Now, all hopes of saving their lives being gone, the Divine Providence so ordered, that there appeared a vessel within sight, which happened to be a French ship, bound from St. John de Luce to Grand Placentia, in Newfoundland; this vessel took in the distressed Englishmen, and carried them away to Grand Placentia; from whence the master and sundry of the mariners procured a passage in a ketch bound for Boston in New England. There did they arrive, June 21, 1683, declaring how they had seen the wonders of God in the deep, as hath been expressed.

There was another memorable sea-deliverance like unto these two last. The persons concerned in it being now gone out of the world, I have not met with any who perfectly remember the particular year wherein that remarkable providence happened; only that it was about twenty-two years ago, when a ship (William Laiton, master), bound from Pascataqua, in New England, to Barbadoes, being 250 leagues off from the coast, sprang a leak. They endeavoured what they could to clear her with their pump for fourteen hours. But the vessel fillin᷄ with water, they were forced (being eight persons) to betake themselves to their boat, taking with them a good supply of bread and a pot of butter; the master declaring that he was persuaded they should meet with a ship at sea that would relieve them: but they had little water, so that their allowance was at last a spoonful in a day to each man. In this boat did they continue thus distressed for nineteen days together. After they had been twelve days from the vessel, they met with a storm which did very much endanger their lives, yet God preserved them. At the end of eighteen days a flying-fish fell into their boat, and having with them a hook and line, they made use of that fish for bait, whereby they caught two dolphins. A ship then at sea, whereof Mr. Samuel Scarlet was commander, apprehending a storm to be near, that so they might fit their rigging, in order to entertain the approaching storm, suffered their vessel to drive right before the wind, and by that means they happened to meet with this boat, full of distressed seamen. Captain Scarlet's vessel was then destitute of provision; only they had on board water enough and to spare. When the mariners first saw the boat, they desired the master not to take the men in, because they had no bread nor other victuals for them ; so that by receiving eight more into their company, they should all die with famine.   Captain Scarlet who as after he left using the sea, he gave many demonstrations, both living and dying, of his designing the good of others, and not his own particular advantage only, did at this time manifest the same spirit to be in him ; and therefore, would by no means hearken to the selfish suggestions of his men, but replied to them (as yet not knowing who they were)— "It may be these distressed creatures are our own countrymen, or if not, they are men in misery, and therefore, whatever come of it, I am resolved to take them in, and to trust in God, who is able to deliver us all."   Nor did God suffer him to lose anything by this noble resolution. For as in Captain Scarlet's ship there was water which the men in the boat wanted, so they in the boat had bread and the two dolphins lately caught, whereby all the ship's company were refreshed.   And within few days they all arrived safe in New England.

CHAPTER II.

A FURTHER ACCOUNT OF SOME OTHER REMARKABLE PRESERVATIONS.

Of a child that had part of her brains struck out, and yet lived and did well. Remarkable deliverances of some in Windsor. Of several in the late Indian War. The relation of a captive. Skipper How's memorable preservation. Several examples somewhat parallel wherein others in other parts of the world were concerned.

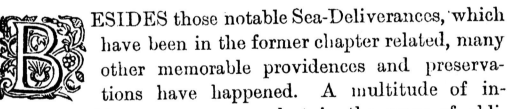

ESIDES those notable Sea-Deliverances, which have been in the former chapter related, many other memorable providences and preservations have happened. A multitude of instances to this purpose are now lost in the grave of oblivion, because they were not recorded in the season of them. But such observables as I have been by good hands acquainted with, I shall here further relate.

Remarkable was the preservation and restoration which the gracious providence of God vouchsafed to Abigail Eliot, the daughter of elder Eliot, of Boston, in New England; concerning whom, a near and precious relation of hers informs me, that when she was a child about five years old, playing with other children under a cart, an iron hinge, being sharp at the lower end, happened to strike her head, between the right ear and the crown of her head, and pierced into the skull and brain. The child making an outcry, the mother came, and immediately drew out the iron, and thereupon some of the brains of her child, which stuck to the iron, and other bits, were scattered on her forehead. Able chyrurgeons were sent for—in special Mr. Oliver and Mr. Prat. The head being uncovered, there appeared just upon the place where the iron pierced the skull, a bunch as big as a small egg. A question arose, whether the skin should not be cut and dilated from the orifice of the wound to the swelling, and so take it away This Mr. Prat inclined unto, but Mr. Oliver opposed, pleading that then the air would get to the brain, and the child would presently die. Mr. Oliver was desired to undertake the cure; and thus was his operation :—He gently drove the soft matter of the bunch into the wound, and pressed so much out as well he could ; there came forth about a spoonful ; the matter which came forth was brains and blood (some curdles of brain were white and not stained with blood): so did he apply a plaister. The skull wasted where it was pierced to the bigness of a half-crown piece of silver or more. The skin was exceeding tender, so that a silver plate, like the skull, was always kept in the place to defend it from any touch or injury. The brains of the child did swell and swage according to the tides :—when it was spring-tide her brain would heave up the tender skin, and fill the place sometimes : when it was neap-tide, they would be sunk and fallen within the skull. This child lived to be the mother of two children; and (which is marvellous) she was not by this wound made defective in her memory or understanding.

In the next place we shall take notice of some remarkable preservations which sundry in Windsor in New England have experienced ; the persons concerned therein being desirous that the Lord's goodness towards them may be ever had in remembrance : wherefore a faithful hand has given me the following account :—

Jan. 13, 1670.—Three women, viz., the wives of Lieut Filer, and of John Drake, and of Nathaniel Lomas, having crossed Connecticut river upon a necessary and neighbourly account, and having done the work they went for, were desirous to return to their own families, the river being at that time partly shut up with ice, old and new, and partly open. There being some pains taken aforehand to cut a way through the ice, the three women above said got into a canoe, with whom also there was Nathaniel Bissel and an Indian. There was likewise another canoe with two men in it, that went before them to help them in case they should meet with any distress, which indeed quickly came upon them ; for just as they were getting out of the narrow passage between the ice, being near the middle of the river, a greater part of the upper ice came down upon them, and struck the end of their canoe, and broke it to pieces, so that it quickly sunk under them. The Indian speedily got upon the ice, but Nathaniel Bissel, and the above said women, were left floating in the middle of the river, being cut off from all manner of human help besides what did arise from themselves and the two men in the little canoe, which was so small that three persons durst seldom, if ever, venture in it. They were indeed discerned from one shore, but the dangerous ice would not admit from either shore one to come near them. All things thus circumstanced, the suddenness of the stroke and distress (which is apt to amaze men, especially when no less than life is concerned), the extreme coldness of the weather, it being a sharp season, that persons out of the water were in danger of freezing, the unaptness of the persons to help themselves, being mostly women, one big with child, and near the time of her travail (who was also carried away under the ice), the other as unskilled and inactive to do anything for self-preservation as almost any could be, the waters deep, that there was no hope of footing, no passage to either shore, in any eye of reason, neither with their little canoe, by reason of the ice, nor without it, the ice being thin and rotten, and full of holes. Now, that all should be brought off safely without the loss of life, or wrong to health, was counted in the day of it a *Remarkable Providence.* To say how it was done is difficult, yet something of the manner of the deliverance may be mentioned. The above said Nathaniel Bissel, perceiving their danger, and being active in swimming, endeavoured, what might be, the preservation of himself and some others ; he strove to have swum to the upper ice, but the stream being too hard, he was forced downwards to the lower ice, where, by reason of the slipperiness of the ice, and disadvantage of the stream, he found it difficult getting up ; at length, by the good hand of Providence, being gotten upon the ice, he saw one of the women swimming down under the ice, and perceiving a hole, or open place, some few rods below, there he waited, and took her up as she swam along. The other two women were in the river, till the two men in the little canoe came for their relief ; at length all of them got their heads above the water, and had a little time to pause, though a long and difficult, and dangerous way to any shore ; but by getting their little canoe upon the ice, and carrying one at a time over hazardous places, they did (though in a long while) get all safe to the shore from whence they came.

Remarkable also was the deliverance which John and Thomas Bissel, of Windsor aforesaid, did at another time receive. John Bissel, on a morning, about break of day, taking nails out of a great barrel, wherein was a considerable quantity of gunpowder and bullets, having a candle in his hand, the powder took fire. Thomas Bissel was then putting on his clothes, standing by a window, which though well fastened, was by the force of the powder carried away at least four rods ; the partition-wall from another room was broken in pieces ; the roof of the house opened and slipt off the plates about five feet down ; also the great girt of the house at one end broke out so far, that it drew from the summer to the end most of its tenant. The woman of the house was lying sick, and another woman under it in bed, yet did the divine Providence so order things as that no one received any hurt, excepting John Bissel, who fell through two floors into a cellar, his shoes being taken from his feet, and found at twenty feet distance, his hands and his face very much scorched, without any other wound in his body.

It would fill a volume to give an account of all the memorable preservations in the time of the late war with the Indians.

Remarkable was that which happened to Jabez Mus grove, of Newbery ; who, being shot by an Indian, the bullet entered in at his ear, and went out at his eye, on the other side of his head, yet the man was preserved from death, yea, and is still in the land of the living.

Likewise several of those that were taken captive by the Indians are able to relate affecting stories concerning the gracious Providence of God, in carrying them through many dangers and deaths, and at last setting their feet in a large place again. A worthy person hath sent me the account which one lately belonging to Deerfield (his name is Quintin Stockwell), hath drawn up respecting his own captivity and redemption, with the more notable occurrences of Divine Providence attending him in his distress, which I shall, therefore, here insert in the words by himself expressed. He relateth as follows :—

"In the year 1677, September 19, between sunset and dark, the Indians came upon us, I and another man being together, we ran away at the outcry the Indians made, shouting and shooting at some other of the English that were hard by. We took a swamp that was at hand for our refuge. The enemy espying us so near them, ran after us, and shot many guns at us; three guns were discharged upon me, the enemy being within three rods of me, besides many other, before that. Being in this swamp that was miry, I slumpt in, and fell down, whereupon one of the enemy stepped to me, with his hatchet lifted up to knock me on the head, supposing that I had been wounded, and so unfit for any other travel. I, as it happened, had a pistol by me, which, though uncharged, I presented to the Indian, who presently stepped back, and told me, if I would yield I should have no hurt; he said (which was not true) that they had destroyed all Hatfield, and that the woods were full of Indians, whereupon I yielded myself, and so fell into the enemy's hands, and by three of them was led away unto the place whence first I began to make my flight, where two other Indians came running to us; and the one lifting up the butt end of his gun to knock me on the head, the other with his hand put by the blow, and said I was his friend. I was now by my own house, which the Indians burned the last year, and I was about to build up again, and there I had some hopes to escape from them; they had a horse just by, which they bid me take, I did so, but made no attempt to escape thereby, because the enemy was near, and the beast was slow and dull; then was I in hopes they would send me to take my own horses, which they did, but they were so frightened that I could not come near to them, and so fell still into the enemy's hands, who now took me and bound me, and led me away, and soon was I brought into the company of captives, that were that day brought away from Hatfield, which was about a mile off; and here methoughts was matter of joy and sorrow both, to see the company; some company in this condition being some refreshing, though little help any ways. Then were we pinioned and led away in the night over the mountains, in dark and hideous ways, about four miles further, before we took up our place for rest, which was in a dismal place of wood, on the east side of that mountain. We were kept bound all that night; the Indians kept waking, and we had little mind to sleep in this night's travel; the Indians dispersed, and as they went, made strange noises, as of wolves and owls, and other wild beasts, to the end that they might not lose one another; and if followed they might not be discovered by the English.

"About the break of day, we marched again and got over the great river at Pecomptuck river mouth, and there rested about two hours. There the Indians marked out upon trays the number of their captives and slain as their manner is. Here was I again in great danger; a quarrel arose about me, whose captive I was, for three took me. I thought I must be killed to end the controversy; so when they put it to me, whose I was, I said three Indians took me, so they agreed to have all a share in me : and I had now three masters, and he was my chief master who laid hands on me first, and thus was I fallen into the hands of the very worst of all the company, as Ashpelon the Indian captain told me ; which captain was all along very kind to me, and a great comfort to the English. In this place they gave us some victuals, which they had brought from the English. This morning also they sent ten men forth to town to bring away what they could find, some provision, some corn out of the meadow they brought to us upon horses which they had there taken. From hence we went up about the falls, where we crossed that river again ; and whilst I was going, I fell right down lame of my old wounds that I had in the war, and whilst I was thinking I should therefore be killed by the Indians, and what death I should die, my pain was suddenly gone, and I was much encouraged again. We had about eleven horses in that company, which the Indians made to carry burthens, and to carry women. It was afternoon when we now crossed that river ; we travelled up that river till night, and then took up our lodging in a dismal place, and were staked down and spread out on our backs ; and so we lay all night, yea so we lay many nights. They told me their law was, that we should lie so nine nights, and by that time, it was thought we should be out of our knowledge. The manner of staking down was thus : our arms and legs stretched out were staked fast down, and a cord about our necks, so that we could stir no ways. The first night of staking down, being much tired, I slept as comfortably as ever ; the next day we went up the river, and crossed it, and at night lay in Squakheag meadows; our provision was soon spent; and while we lay in those meadows the Indians went a hunting, and the English army came out after us : then the Indians moved again, dividing themselves and the captives into many companies, that the English might not follow their tract. At night having crossed the river, we met again at the place appointed. The next day we crossed the river again on Squakheag side, and there we took up our quarters for a long time ; I suppose this might be about thirty miles above Squakheag, and here were the Indians quite out of all fear of the English ; but in great fear of the Mohawks ; here they built a long wigwam. Here they had a great dance (as they call it) and concluded to burn three of us, and had got bark to do it with, and as I understood afterwards, I was one that was to be burnt, Sergeant Plimpton another, and Benjamin Wait his wife the third : though I knew not which was to be burnt, yet I perceived some were designed thereunto, so much I understood of their language : that night I could not sleep for fear of next day's work, the Indians being weary with that dance, lay down to sleep and slept soundly. The English were all loose, then I went out and brought in wood and mended the fire, and made a noise on purpose, but none awaked, I thought if any of the English would wake, we might kill them all sleeping ; I removed out of the way all the guns and hatchets ; but my heart failing me, I put all things where they were again. The next day when we were to be burnt, our master and some others spake for us, and the evil was prevented in this place : and hereabouts we lay three weeks together. Here I had a shirt brought to me to make, and one Indian said it should be made this way, a second another way, a third his way; I told them

I would make it that way that my chief master said ;
whereupon one Indian struck me on the face with his fist ;
I suddenly rose up in anger ready to strike again, upon
this happened a great hubbub, and the Indians and
English came about me ; I was fain to humble myself to
my master, so that matter was put up.   Before I came to
this place, my three masters were gone a hunting ; I was
left with another Indian.   All the company being upon a
march, I was left with this Indian, who fell sick, so that I
was fain to carry his gun and hatchet, and had opportunity
and had thought to have despatched him, and run away ;
but did not, for that the English captives had promised
the contrary to one another, because if one should run
away, that would provoke the Indians, and endanger the
rest that could not run away.   Whilst we were here, Benjamin Stebbins going with some Indians to Wachuset hills,
made his escape from them, and when the news of his
escape came we were all presently called in and bound ;
one of the Indians, a captain among them, and always our
great friend, met me coming in, and told me Stebbins was
run away, and the Indians spake of burning us, some of
only burning and biting off our fingers bye and bye.   He
said there would be a court, and all would speak their
minds, but he would speak last, and would say, that the
Indian that let Stebbins run away was only in fault, and
so no hurt should be done us, fear not : so it proved
accordingly.   Whilst we lingered hereabout, provision
grew scarce, one bear's foot must serve five of us a whole
day ; we began to eat horse-flesh, and eat up seven in all
three were left alive and were not killed.   Whilst we had
been here, some of the Indians had been down and fallen
upon Hadley, and were taken by the English, agreed with

and let go again, and were to meet the English upon such a plain, there to make further terms. Ashpalon was much for it, but the Wachuset Sachims, when they came, were much against it, and were for this: that we should meet the English indeed, but there fall upon them and fight them, and take them. Then Ashpalon spake to us English, not to speak a word more to further that matter, for mischief would come of it. When those Indians came from Wachuset, there came with them Squaws, and Children about four-score, who reported that the English had taken Uncas, and all his men, and sent them beyond seas; they were much enraged at this, and asked us if it were true; we said no; then was Ashpalon angry, and said, he would no more believe Englishmen. For they examined us every one apart; then they dealt worse by us for a season than before: still provision was scarce. We came at length to a place called Squaw-Maug river; there we hoped for Sammon, but we came too late. This place I account to be above two hundred miles above Deerfield: then we parted into two companies; some went one way and some went another way; and we went over a mighty mountain; we were eight dayes a going over it, and travelled very hard, and every day we had either snow or rain: we noted that on this mountain all the water run northward. Here also we wanted provision; but at length met again on the other side of the mountain, viz. on the north side of this mountain, at a river that run into the lake, and we were then half a dayes journey off the lake; we stayed here a great while to make canoos to go over the lake; here I was frozen, and here again we were like to starve: all the Indians went a hunting, but could get nothing: divers days they powow'd, but got nothing;

3

then they desired the English to pray, and confessed they could do nothing; they would have us pray, and see what the Englishman's God could do. I prayed, so did Serjeant Plimpton, in another place. The Indians reverently attended, morning and night; next day they got bears; then they would needs have us desire a blessing, return thanks at meals : after a while they grew weary of it, and the Sachim did forbid us. When I was frozen they were very cruel towards me, because I could not do as at other times. When we came to the lake we were again sadly put to it for provision; we were fain to eat touchwood fryed in bears greace; at last we found a company of racoons, and then we made a feast; and the manner was, that we must eat all. I perceived there would be too much for one time, so one Indian that sat next to me bid me slip away some to him under his coat, and he would hide it for me till another time. This Indian, as soon as he had got my meat, stood up and made a speech to the rest, and discovered me, so that the Indians were very angry, and cut me another piece, and gave me racoon grease to drink, which made me sick and vomit. I told them I had enough, so that ever after that they would give me none, but still tell me I had racoon enough; so I suffered much, and being frozen was full of pain, and could sleep but a little, yet must do my work. When they went upon the lake, and as they came to the lake, they light of a moose and killed it, and staid there till they had eaten it all up And entering upon the lake, there arose a great storm; w thought we should all be cast away; but at last we got t an island, and there they went to Powawing. The Powa said that Benjamin Wait and another man was comin; and that storm was raised to cast them away. This afte ward appeared to be true, though then I believed them not. Upon this island we lay still several dayes, and then set out again, but a storm took us, so that we lay to and fro upon certain islands about three weeks; we had no provision but racoons, so that the Indians themselves thought they should be starved. They gave me nothing, so that I was sundry days without any provision. We went on upon the lake upon that isle, about a dayes journey : we had a little sled upon which we drew our load. Before noon I tired, and just then the Indians met with some Frenchmen : then one of the Indians that took me came to me and called me all manner of bad names, and threw me down upon my back. I told him I could not do any more ; then he said he must kill me. I thought he was about it, for he pulled out his knife and cut out my pockets, and wrapped them about my face, helped me up, and took my sled and went away, and gave me a bit of biscake, as big as a walnut, which he had of the Frenchman, and told me he would give me a pipe of tobacco. When my sled was gone I could run after him, but at last I could not run, but went a foot-pace; then the Indians were soon out of sight; I followed as well as I could ; I had many falls upon the ice ; at last I was so spent I had not strength enough to rise again, but I crept to a tree that lay along, and got upon it, and there I lay. It was now night, and very sharp weather ; I counted no other but that I must die there. Whilest I was thinking of death an Indian hallowed, and I answered him ; he came to me and called me bad names, and told me if I could not go he must knock me on the head ; I told him he must then so do. He saw how I had wallowed in that snow, but could not rise : then he took his coat and wrapt me in it, and went back, and sent two Indians with a sled. One said he must knock me on the head; the other said no, they would carry me away and burn me: then they bid me stir my instep, to see if that were frozen; I did so; when they saw that they said that was 'wurregen.' There was a chirurgeon at the French that could cure me. Then they took me upon the sled and carried me to the fire, and they then made much of me, pulled off my wet, and wrapped me in dry clothes, made me a good bed. They had killed an otter, and gave me some of the broth, and a bit of the flesh. Here I slept till towards day, and then was able to get up and put on my clothes. One of the Indians awaked, and seeing me go, shouted as rejoycing at it. As soon as it was light, I and Samuel Russel went before on the ice upon a river; they said I must go where I could on foot, else I should frieze. Samuel Russel slipt into the river with one foot; the Indians called him back and dried his stockins, and then sent us away, and an Indian with us to pilot us, and we went four or five miles before they overtook us. I was then pretty well spent; Samuel Russel was (he said) faint, and wondred how I could live, for he had (he said) ten meals to my one. Then I was laid on the sled, and they ran away with me on the ice; the rest and Samuel Russel came softly after. Samuel Russel I never saw more, nor know what became of him: they got but half way, and we got through to Shamblee about midnight. Six miles of Shamblee (a French town) the river was open; and when I came to travail in that part of the ice I soon tired; and two Indians run away to town, and only one was left: he would carry me a few rods, and then I would go as many, and that trade we drave, and so were long a going six miles. This Indian now was kind, and told me that if he did not carry me I would die, and so I should have done. sure enough; and he said I must tell the English how he helped me. When we came to the first house there was no inhabitant: the Indian spent, both discouraged; he said we must now both die; at last he left me alone, and got to another house, and thence came some French and Indians and brought me in: the French were kind, and put my hands and feet in cold water, and gave me a dram of brandey, and a little hasty pudding and milk; when I tasted victuals I was hungry, and could not have forborn it, but that I could not get it; now and then they would give me a little as they thought best for me; I lay by the fire with the Indians that night, but could not sleep for pain: next morning the Indians and French fell out about me, because the French, as the Indian said, loved the English better than the Indians. The French presently turned the Indians out of doors and kept me; they were very kind and careful, and gave me a little something now and then; while I was here all the men in that town came to see me: at this house I was three or four dayes, and then invited to another, and after that to another; at this place I was about thirteen dayes, and received much civility from a young man, a batchelour, who invited me to his house, with whom I was for the most part; he was so kind as to lodge me in the bed with himself; he gave me a shirt, and would have bought me, but could not, for the Indians asked a hundred pounds for me. We were then to go to a place called Surril, and that young man would go with me, because the Indians should not hurt me: this man carried me on the ice one dayes journey, for I could not now go at all; then there was so much water on the ice, we could go no

further : so the Frenchman left me, and provision for me ;
here we stayed two nights, and then travailed again, for
then the ice was strong ; and in two dayes more I came
to Surril ; the first house we came to was late in the night ;
here again the people were kind.   Next day being in
much pain, I asked the Indians to carry me to the Chirur-
geons, as they had promised, at which they were wroth,
and one of them took up his gun to knock me, but the
Frenchmen would not suffer it, but set upon him, and
kicked him out of doors : then we went away from thence
to a place two or three miles off, where the Indians had
wigwams ; when I came to these wigwams, some of the
Indians knew me and seemed to pity me.   While I was
here, which was three or four dayes, the French came to
see me, and it being Christmas time, they brought cakes
and other provisions with them, and gave to me, so that
I had no want : the Indians tried to cure me, but could
not ; then I asked for the chirurgeon, at which one of the
Indians, in anger struck me on the face with his fist ; a
Frenchman being by, the Frenchman spake to him—I
knew not what he said—and went his way.   By and by
came the captain of the place into the wigwam with about
twelve armed men, and asked where the Indian was that
struck the Englishman, and took him and told him he
should go to the bilboes, and then be hanged : the Indians
were much terrified at this, as appeared by their countenances and trembling.   I would have gone too, but the
Frenchman bid me not fear, the Indians durst not hurt
me.   When that Indian was gone, I had two masters still ;
I asked them to carry me to that captain, that I might
speak for the Indian ; they answered, I was a fool, did I
think the Frenchmen were like to the English, to say one

thing and do another? they were men of their words. But I prevailed with them to help me thither, and I spake to the captain by an interpreter. and told him I desired him to set the Indian free, and told him what he had done for me; he told me he was a rogue and should bo hanged; then I spake more privately, alleging this reason, because all the English captives were not come in, if he were hanged it might fare the worse with them; then the captain said that was to be considered: then he set him at liberty, upon this condition, that he should never strike me more, and every day bring me to his house to eat victuals. I perceived that the common people did not like what the Indians had done and did to the English. When the Indian was set free. he came to me, and took me about the middle, and said I was his brother, I had saved his life once, and he had saved mine (he said) thrice. Then he called for brandy, and made me drink, and had me away to the wigwams again; when I came there, the Indians came to me one by one, to shake hands with me, saying 'Wurregen Netop,' and were very kind, thinking no other but that I had saved the Indians life. The next day he carried me to that captains house, and set me down; they gave me my victuals and wine, and being left there a while by the Indians, i shewed the captain my fingers, which when he and his wife saw, he and his wife run away from the sight, and bid me lap it up again, and sent for the chirurgeon, who, when he came, said he could cure me, and took it in hand, and dressed it. The Indians towards night came for me; I told them I could not go with them; they were displeased, called me rogue. and went away. That night I was full of pain; the French did fear that I would die; five men did watch with me, and strove to keep me chearly, for I was sometimes ready to faint; often times they gave me a little brandy. The next day the chirurgeon came again, and dressed me, and so he did all the while I was among the French. I came in at Christmass, and went thence May 2d. Being thus in the captain's house, I was kept there till Ben Waite came, and my Indian master being in want of money, pawned me to the captain for 14 beavers, or the worth of them, at such a day; if he did not pay, he must lose his pawn, or else sell me for twenty-one beavers; but he could not get beaver, and so I was sold." But by being thus sold, he was in Gods good time set at liberty, and returned to his friends in New England again.

Thus far is this poor captive's relation concerning the changes of Providence which passed over him.

There is one remarkable passage more affirmed by him : for he saith, in their travails they came to a place where was a great wigwam (*i.e.* Indian house) ; at both ends was an image; here the Indians in the war time were wont to powaw (*i.e.* invocate the devil), and so did they come down to Hatfield, one of the images told them they should destroy a town ; the other said no, half a town, This god (said that Indian) speaks true ; the other was not good, he told them lies. No doubt but others are capable of declaring many passages of Divine Providence no less worthy to be recorded than these last recited; but inasmuch as they have not been brought to my hands, I proceed to another relation.

Very memorable was the Providence of God towards Mr. Ephraim How, of New-Haven, in New England, who was for a whole twelvemoneth given up by his friends as a dead man ; but God preserved him alive in a desolate island where he had suffered shipwrack, and at last returned him home to his family.

The history of this providence might have been mentioned amongst "Sea Deliverances," yet considering it was not only so, I shall here record what himself (being a godly man) did relate of the Lords marvelous dispensations towards him, that so others might be encouraged to put their trust in God, in the times of their greatest straits and difficulties.

On the 25th of August, in the year 1676, the said Skipper How, with his two eldest sons, set sail from New-Haven for Boston, in a small ketch, burden 17 tun, or thereabout. After the dispatch of their business there, they set sail from thence for New-Haven again, on the 10th of September following; but contrary winds forced them back to Boston, where the said How was taken ill with a violent flux, which distemper continued near a moneth, many being at that time sick of the same disease, which proved mortal to some. The merciful providence of God having spared his life, and restored him to some measure of health, he again set sail from Boston, October 10. By a fair wind they went forward so as to make Cape Cod ; but suddenly the weather became very tempestuous, so as that they could not seize the Cape, but were forced off to sea, where they were endangered in a small vessel by very fearful storms and outrageous winds and seas. Also, his eldest son fell sick and died in about eleven days after they set out to sea. He was no sooner dead but his other son fell sick and died too. This was a bitter cup to the good father. It is noted in 1 Chron. vii, 22, "that when the sons of Ephraim were dead, Ephraim their father mourned many days, and his brethren came to comfort him." This Ephraim when his sons were dead his friends on shore knew it not, nor could they come to comfort him; but when his friends and relations could not, the Lord himself did, for they died after so sweet, gracious, and comfortable a manner, as that their father professed he had joy in parting with them. Yet now their outward distress and danger was become greater, since the skipper's two sons were the only help he had in working the vessel. Not long after, another of the company, viz. Caleb Jones (son to Mr. William Jones, one of the worthy magistrates in New-Haven), fell sick and died also, leaving the world with comfortable manifestations of true repentance towards God, and faith in Jesus Christ. Thus the one-half of their company was taken away, none remaining but the skipper himself, one Mr. Augur, and a boy. He himself was still sickly, and in a very weak estate, yet was fain to stand at the helm thirty-six hours and twenty-four hours at a time: in the meantime the boisterous sea overwhelming the vessel, so as that if he had not been lasht fast he had certainly been washed overboard. In this extremity he was at a loss in his own thoughts, whether they should persist in striving for the New England shore, or bear away for the southern islands. He proposed that question to Mr. Augur; they resolved that they would first seek to God by prayer about it, and then put this difficult case to an issue, by casting a lot. So they did, and the lot fell on New England. By that time a moneth was expired, they lost the rudder of their vessel, so that now they had nothing but God alone to rely upon. In this deplorable state were they for a fortnight. The skipper (though infirm, as has been expressed), yet for six weeks together was hardly ever dry ; nor had they the benefit of warm food for more than thrice or thereabouts. At the end of six weeks, in the morning betimes, the vessel was driven on the tailings of a ledge of rocks, where the sea broke violently ; looking out they espied a dismal rocky island to the leeward, upon which, if the Providence of God had not by the breakers given them timely warning, they had been dashed in pieces. And this extremity was the Lords opportunity to appear for their deliverance ; they immediately let go an anchor, and get out the boat ; and God made the sea calm. The boat proved leaky ; and being in the midst of fears and amazements they took little out of the vessel. After they came ashore, they found themselves in a rocky desolate island (near Cape Sables), where was neither man nor beast to be seen, so that now they were in extream danger of being starved to death. But a storm arose which beat violently upon the vessel at anchor, so as that it was staved in pieces, and a cask of powder was brought ashore (receiving no damage by its being washed in the water), also a barrel of wine, and half a barrel of molosses, together with many things useful for a tent to preserve them from cold. This notwithstanding, new and great distresses attended them ; for though they had powder and shot, there were seldom any fowls to be seen in that dismal and desolate place, excepting a few crows, ravens, and gulls ; these were so few as that for the most part the skipper shot at one at a time. Many times half of one of these fowls, with the liquor, made a meal for three. Once they lived five dayes without any sustenance, at which time they did not feel themselves pincht with hunger as at other times, the Lord in mercy taking away their appetites when their food did utterly fail them. After

they had been about twelve weeks in this miserable island,
Mr. How's dear friend and consort, Mr. Augur, died, so
that he had no living creature but the lad before mentioned to converse with ; and on April 2, 1677, that lad
died also, so that the master was now left alone upon the
island, and continued so to be above a quarter of a year,
not having any living soul to converse with.   In this time
he saw several fishing vessels sailing by, and some came
nearer the island than that which at last took him in ; but
though he used what means he could that they might be
acquainted with his distress, none came to him, being
afraid ; for they supposed him to be one of those Indians
who were then in hostility against the English. The good
man, whilest he was in his desolate estate, kept many dayes
of fasting and prayer, wherein he did confess and bewail
his sins, the least of which deserved greater evils than any
in this world ever were or can be subject unto ; and begged
of God that he would find out a way for his deliverance.
At last it came into his mind that he ought very solemnly
to praise God (as well as pray unto him) for the great
mercies and signal preservations which he had thus far
experienced.   Accordingly he set apart a day for that end,
spending the time in giving thanks to God for all the
mercies of his life, so far as he could call them to mind,
and in special, for those Divine favours which had been
mingled with his afflictions ; humbly blessing God for his
wonderful goodness in preserving him alive by a miracle
of mercy.   Immediately after this, a vessel, belonging to
Salem in New England, providentially passing by that
island, sent their boat on shore, and took in Skipper How,
who arrived at Salem, July 18, 1677, and was at last
returned to his family in New-Haven.

Upon this occasion it may not be amiss to commemorate a providence not altogether unlike unto the but now related preservation of Skipper How. The story which I intend is mentioned by Mandelslo in his *Travails,* page 280, and more fully by Mr. Clark in his *Examples,* vol. ii, page 618, Mr. Burton in his *Prodigies of Mercies,* page 209. Yet inasmuch as but few in this countrey have the authors mentioned, I shall here insert what has been by them already published. The story is in brief as followeth : —

"In the year 1616, a Fleming, whose name was Pickman, coming from Norway in a vessel loaden with boards, was overtaken by a calm, during which the current carried him upon a rock or little island towards the extremities of Scotland. To avoid a wreck he commanded some of his men to go into the shallop, and to tow the ship ; they having done so, would needs go up into a certain rock to look for birds eggs ; but as soon as they were got up into it, they at some distance perceived a man, whence they imagined that there were others lurking thereabouts, and that this man had made his escape thither from some pyrates, who, if not prevented, might surprise their ship : and therefore they made all the haste they could to their shallop, and so returned to their ship ; but the calm continuing, and the current of the sea still driving them upon the island, they were forced to get into the long-boat, and to tow her off again. The man whom they had seen before was in the meantime come to the brink of the island, and made signs with his hands lifted up, and sometimes falling on his knees, and joyning his hands together, begging and crying to them for relief. At first they made some difficulty to get to him, but at last, being overcome by his lamentable signs, they went nearer the island, where they saw something that was more like a ghost than a living person; a body stark naked, black and hairy, a meagre and deformed countenance, with hollow and distorted eyes, which raised such compassion in them, that they essayed to take him into the boat; but the rock was so steepy thereabouts, that it was impossible for them to land; whereupon they went about the island, and came at last to a flat shore, where they took the man aboard. They found nothing at all in the island, neither grass nor tree, nor ought else from which a man could procure any subsistence, nor any shelter, but the ruins of a boat, wherewith he had made a kind of a hutt, under which he might lie down and shelter himself against the injuries of wind and weather. No sooner were they gotten to the ship, but there arose a wind that drave them off from the island; observing this providence they were the more inquisitive to know of this man, what he was, and by what means he came unto that uninhabitable place? Hereunto the man answered :—

" I am an Englishman, that about a year ago, was to pass in the ordinary passage-boat from England to Dublin in Ireland; but by the way we were taken by a French pirate, who being immediately forced by a tempest, which presently arose, to let our boat go; we were three of us in it, left to the mercy of the wind and waves, which carried us between Ireland and Scotland into the main sea : in the meantime we had neither food nor drink, but only some sugar in the boat; upon this we lived, and drank our own urine, till our bodies were so dried up, that we could make no more; whereupon one of our company, being quite spent, died, whom we heaved overboard; and awhile after a second was grown so feeble, that he had laid himself along in the boat, ready to give up the ghost : but in this extremity it pleased God that I kenned this island afar off, and thereupon encouraged the dying man to rouse up himself with hopes of life ; and accordingly, upon this good news, he raised himself up. and by and by our boat was cast upon this island, and split against a rock. Now we were in a more wretched condition than if we had been swallowed up by the sea, for then we had been delivered out of the extremities we were now in for want of meat and drink ; yet the Lord was pleased to make some provision for us : for on the island we took some sea-mews, which we did eat raw : we found also in the holes of the rocks, upon the sea-side, some eggs ; and thus had we through God's good Providence wherewithal to subsist, as much as would keep us from starving : but what we thought most unsupportable, was thirst, in regard that the place afforded no fresh water but what fell from the clouds, and was left in certain pits, which time had made in the rock. Neither could we have this at all seasons by reason that the rock being small, and lying low, in stormy weather the waves dashed over it, and filled the pits with salt-water. When they came first upon the island, about the midst of it they found two long stones pitched in the ground, and the third laid upon them, like a table, which they judged to have been so placed by some fishermen to dry their fish upon, and under this they lay in the nights, till with some boards of their boat, they made a kind of an hutt to be a shelter for them. In this condition they lived together for the space of about six weeks, comforting one another, and finding some ease in their common calamity, till at last, one of them being left alone, the burden became almost insupportable : for one day, awaking in the morning, he missed his fellow, and getting up, he went calling and seeking all the island about for him ; but when he could by no means find him, he fell into such despair that he often resolved to have cast himself down into the sea, and so to put a final period to that affliction, whereof he had endured but the one-half whilst he had a friend that divided it with him.   What became of his comrade he could not guess, whether despair forced him to that extremity, or whether getting up in the night, not fully awake, he fell from the rock, as he was looking for birds eggs ; for he had discovered no distraction in him, neither could imagine that he could on a sudden fall into that despair, against which he had so fortified himself by frequent and fervent prayer.   And his loss did so affect the survivor, that he often took his leer, with a purpose to have leaped from the rocks into the sea ; yet still his conscience stopped him, suggesting to him, that if he did it, he would be utterly damned for his self-murther.

"Another affliction also befel him, which was this : his only knife, wherewith he cut up the sea-dogs and sea-mews, having a bloody cloth about it, was carried away (as he thought) by some fowl of prey ; so that not being able to kill any more, he was reduced to this extremity, with much difficulty to get out of the boards of his hutt a great nail, which he made shift so to sharpen upon the stones, that it served him instead of a knife.   When winter came on, he endured the greatest misery imaginable ; for many times the rock and his hutt were so covered with snow, that it was not possible for him to go abroad to provide his food, which extremity put him upon this invention :— He put out a little stick at the crevice of his hutt, and baiting it with a little sea-dogs fat, by that means he got some sea-mews, which he took with his hand from under the snow, and so kept himself from starving. In this sad and solitary condition he lived for about eleven months, expecting therein to end his dayes, when Gods gracious providence sent this ship thither which delivered him out of the greatest misery that ever man was in. The master of the ship, commiserating his deplorable condition, treated him so well, that within a few dayes he was quite another creature; and afterwards he set him a shore at Derry, in Ireland; and sometimes after he saw him at Dublin, where such as heard what had happened unto him, gave him money wherewithal to return into his native countrey of England."

Thus far is that relation.

I have seen a manuscript, wherein many memorable passages of Divine Providence are recorded, and this, which I shall now mention, amongst others.

About the year 1638, a ship fell foul upon the rocks and sands called the Rancadories, sixty leagues distant from the Isle of Providence. Ten of the floating passengers got to a spot of land, where having breathed awhile, and expecting to perish by famine, eight of them chose rather to commit themselves to the mercy of the waters; two only stood upon the spot of land, one whereof soon died, and was in the sands buried by his now desolate companion. This solitary person in the midst of the roaring waters was encompassed with the goodness of Divine Providence. Within three dayes God was pleased to send this single person (who now alone was lord and subject in this his little commonwealth) good store of fowl, and to render them so tame, that the forlorn man could pick and chuse where he list. Fish also were now and then cast up within his reach, and somewhat that served for fuel, enkindled by flint, to dress them. Thus lived that insulary anchorite for about two years, till at last, having espied a Dutch vessel, he held a rag of his shirt upon the top of a stick towards them, which being come within view of, they used means to fetch him off the said spot of sand, and brought him to the Isle of Providence. The man having in so long a time conversed only with Heaven, lookt at first very strangely, and was not able at first conference promptly to speak and answer.

CHAPTER III.

CONCERNING REMARKABLES ABOUT THUNDER AND LIGHTNING.

One at Salisbury in New England struck dead thereby. Several at Marsh-field. One at North-Hampton. The captain of the castle in Boston. Some remarkables about lightning in Rocksborough, Wenham, Marble-head, Cambridge; and in several vessels at sea. Some late parallel instances. Of several in the last century. Scripture examples of men slain by lightning.

THERE are who affirm, that although terrible lightnings with thunders have ever been frequent in this land, yet none were hurt thereby (neither man nor beast) for many years after the English did first settle in these American desarts, but that of later years fatal and fearful slaughters have in that way been made amongst us, is most certain; and there are many who have in this respect been as brands plucked out of the burning, when the Lord hath over-thrown others as God overthrew Sodom and Gomorrah. Such solemn works of Providence ought not to be for-gotten. I shall now, therefore, proceed in giving an account of remarkables respecting thunder and lightning, so far as I have received credible information concerning them; the particulars whereof are these which follow :—

In July, 1654, a man whose name was Partridge, es-teemed a very godly person, at Salisbury in New England, was killed with thunder and lightning, his house being set on fire thereby, and himself with others endeavouring the quenching of it, by a second crack of thunder with lightning (he being at the door of his house), was struck dead, and never spake more. There were ten other persons also that were struck and lay for dead at the present, but they all revived, excepting Partridge. Some that viewed him report that there were holes (like such as were made with shot) found in his clothes and skin One side of his shirt and body was scorched, and not the other. His house, though (as was said) set on fire by the lightning in divers places, was not burnt down, but preserved by an abundance of rain falling upon it.

July 31, 1658, there hapned a storm of thunder and lightning with rain, in the town of Marshfield, in Plymouth colony in New England. Mr. Nathanael Thomas, John Philips, and another belonging to that town, being in the field, as they perceived the storm a coming, betook themselves to the next house for shelter. John Philips sat down near the chimney, his face towards the inner door. A black cloud flying very low, out of it there came a great ball of fire, with a terrible crack of thunder; the fire-ball fell down just before the said Philips; he seemed to give a start on his seat, and so fell backward, being struck dead, not the least motion of life appearing in him afterwards. Captain Thomas, who sat directly opposite to John Philips, about six feet distance from him, and a young child that was then within three feet of him, through the providence of God, received no hurt; yet many of the bricks in the chimney were beaten down, the principal rafters split, the battens next the chimney in the chamber were broken, one of the main posts of the house into which the summer was framed rent into shivers, and a great part of it was carried several rod from the house ; the door before Philips, where the fire came down was broken.

On the 28th of April, A.D. 1664, a company of the neighbours being met together at the house of Henry Condliff, in North-Hampton in New England, to spend a few hours in Christian conferences and in prayer, there hapned a storm of thunder and rain ; and as the good man of the house was at prayer, there came a ball of lightning in at the roof of the house, which set the thatch on fire, grated on the timber, pierced through the chamber-floor, no breach being made on the boards, only one of the jouyces somewhat rased. Matthew Cole, who was son-in-law to the said Condliff, was struck stone dead as he was leaning over a table, and joyning with the rest in prayer. He did not stir nor groan after he was smitten, but continued standing as before, bearing upon the table. There was no visible impression on his body or clothes, only the sole of one of his shoes was rent from the upper leather. There were about twelve persons in the room ; none else received any harm, only one woman (who is still living) was struck upon the head, which occasioned some deafness ever since. The fire on the house was quenched by the seasonable help of neighbours.

July 15, 1665, there were terrible cracks of thunder : an house in Boston was struck by it, and the dishes therein melted as they stood on the shelves ; but no other hurt done in the town, only Captain Davenport, a worthy man, and one that had in the Pequot war ventured his life, and did great service for the countrey, then residing in the castle, where he commanded, having that day wrought himself weary, and thinking to refresh himself with sleep, was killed with lightning as he lay upon his bed asleep. Several of the soldiers in the castle were struck at the same time, but God spared their lives. It has been an old opinion, mentioned by Plutarch (*Sympos.* lib. 4, q. 2), that men asleep are never smitten with lightning ; to confirm which it has been alledged, that one lying asleep, the lightning melted the money in his purse, without doing him any further harm ; and that a cradle, wherein a child lay sleeping, was broken with the lightning, and the child not hurt; and that the arrows of King Mithridates, being near his bed, were burnt with lightning, and yet himself being asleep received no hurt. But as much of all this may be affirmed of persons awake ; and this sad example (*triste jaces lucis evitandumque bidental*) of Captain Davenport, whom the lightning found and left asleep, does confute the vulgar error mentioned. And no doubt but that many the like instances to this have been known in the world, the records whereof we have not. But I proceed.

June 23, 1666. In Marshfield, another dismal storm of rain with thunder and lightning hapned. There were then in the house of John Philips (he was father of that John Philips who was slain by lightning in the year 1658) fourteen persons; the woman of the house calling earnestly to shut the door, that was no sooner done, but an astonishing thunder-clap fell upon the house, rent the chimney, and split the door. All in the house were struck. One of them (who is still living) saith, that when he came to himself, he saw the house full of smoke, and perceived a grievous smell of brimstone, and saw the fire lie scattered, though whether that fire came from heaven or was violently hurled out of the hearth, he can give no account. At first he thought all the people present, except himself, had been killed; but it pleased God to revive most of them. Only three of them were mortally wounded with Heaven's arrows, viz., the wife of John Philips, and another of his sons, a young man about twenty years old, and William Shertly, who had a child in his arms, that received no hurt by the lightning when himself was slain. This Shertly was at that time a sojourner in John Philips his house. The wife of this Shertly was with child and near her full time, and struck down for dead at present, but God recovered her, so that she received no hurt, neither by fright nor stroke. Two little children sitting upon the edge of a table, had their lives preserved, though a dog, which lay behind them under the table, was killed.

In the same year, in the latter end of May, Samuel Ruggles, of Rocksborough in New England, going with a loaden cart, was struck with lightning. He did not hear the thunder-clap, but was by the force of the lightning, e're he was aware, carried over his cattle about ten foot distance from them. Attempting to rise up, he found that he was not able to stand upon his right leg, for his right foot was become limber, and would bend any way, feeling as if it had no bone in it; nevertheless, he made a shift with the use of one leg to get to his cattle (being an horse and two oxen), which were all killed by the lightning. He endeavoured to take off the yoak from the neck of one of the oxen, but then he perceived that his thumb and two fingers in one hand were stupified that he could not stir them; they looked like cold clay, the blood clear gone out of that part of his hand; but by rubbing his wounded leg and hand, blood and life came into them again. As he came home, pulling off his stocking, he found that on the inside of his right leg (which smarted much) the hair was quite burnt off, and it looked red; just over his ankle his stocking was singed on the inside, but not on the outside, and there were near upon twenty marks, about as big as pins heads, which the lightning had left thereon; likewise the shoe on his left foot was by the lightning struck off his foot, and carried above two rods from him. On the upper leather, at the heel of the shoe, there were five holes burnt through it, bigger than those which are made with duck shot. As for the beasts that were slain, the hair upon their skins was singed, so that one might perceive that the lightning had run winding and turning strangely upon their bodies, leaving little marks no bigger than corns of gun-powder behind it. There was in the cart a chest, which the lightning pierced through, as also through a quire of paper and twelve napkins, melting some pewter dishes that were under them.

At another time in Rocksborough, a thunder storm happning, broke into the house of Thomas Bishop, striking off some clapboards, splitting two studs of the end spar, and running down by each side of the window, where stood a bed with three children in it. Over the head of the bed were three guns and a sword, which were so melted with the lightning that they began to run. It made a hole through the floor, and coming into a lower room, it beat down the shutter of the window, and running on a shelf of pewter, it melted several dishes there; and descending lower, it melted a brass morter, and a brass kettle. The children in the bed were won- derfully preserved; for a lath at the corner of it was burnt, and splinters flew about their clothes and faces, and there was not an hands breadth between them and the fire, yet received they no hurt.

On the 18th of May (being the Lords day) A.D. 1673, the people at Wenham (their worthy pastor, Mr. Antipas Newman, being lately dead) prevailed with the Reverend Mr. Higginson of Salem to spend that Sabbath amongst them. The afternoon sermon being ended, he, with several of the town, went to Mr. Newman his house. Whilst they were in discourse there about the word and works of God, a thunder-storm arose. After a while, a smart clap of thunder broke upon the house, and especially into the room where they were sitting and discoursing together; it did for the present deafen them all, filling the room with smoke, and a strong smell as of brimstone. With the thunder-clap came in a ball of fire as big as the bullet of a great gun, which suddenly went up the chimney, as also the smoke did. This ball of fire was seen at the feet of Richard Goldsmith, who sat on a leather chair next the chimney, at which instant he fell off the chair on the ground. As soon as the smoke was gone, some in the room endeavoured to hold him up, but found him dead; also the dog that lay under the chair was found stone dead, but not the least hurt done to the chair. All that could be perceived by the man, was, that the hair of his head, near one of his ears, was a little singed. There were seven or eight in that room, and more in the next; yet (through the merciful providence of God) none else had the least harm. This Richard Goldsmith, who was thus slain, was a shoemaker by trade, being reputed a good man for the main; but had blemished his Christian profession by frequent breaking of his promise; it being too common with him (as with too many professors amongst us), to be free and forward in engaging, but backward in performing; yet this must further be added, that half a year before his death, God gave him a deep sense of his evils, that he made it his business, not only that his peace might be made with God, but with men also, unto whom he had given just offence. He went up and down bewailing his great sin in promise-breaking; and was become a very conscientious and lively Christian, promoting holy and edifying discourses, as he had occasion. At that very time when he was struck dead, he was speaking of some passages in the sermon he had newly heard, and his last words were, *Blessed be the Lord.*

In the same year, on the 21st of June, being Saturday, in the afternoon, another thunder-storm arose, during which storm Josiah Walton, the youngest son of Mr. William Walton, late minister of Marble-head, was in a ketch coming in from sea, and being before the harbours mouth, the wind suddenly shifted to the northward; a violent gust of wind coming down on the vessel, the seamen concluded to hand their sails; Josiah Walton got upon the main yard to expedite the matter, and foot down the sail, when there hapned a terrible flash of lightning, which breaking forth out of the cloud, struck down three men who were on the deck, without doing them any hurt. But Josiah Walton being (as was said) on the main-yard, the lightning shattered his thigh-bone all in pieces, and did split and shiver the main-mast of the vessel, and scorcht the rigging. Josiah Walton falling down upon the deck, his leg was broken short off. His brother being on the deck, did (with others) take him up, and found him alive, but sorely scorched and wounded. They brought him on shore to his mothers house. At first he was very sensible of his case, and took leave of his friends, giving himself to serious preparation for another world. His relations used all means possible for his recovery, though he himself told them he was a dead man, and the use of means would but put him to more misery. His bones were so shattered, that it was not possible for the art of man to reduce them; also, the violent heat of the weather occasioned a gangrene. In this misery he continued until the next Wednesday morning, and then departed this life. He was an hopeful young man.

In the year 1678, on the 29th of June, at Cambridge in New-England, a thunder-clap with lightning broke into the next house to the colledge. It tore away and shattered into pieces a considerable quantity of the tyle on the roof. In one room there then hapned to be the wife of John Benjamin, daughter to Thomas Swetman, the owner of the house, who then had an infant about two moneths old in her arms; also another woman. They were all of them struck; the child being by the force of the lightning carried out of the mothers arms, and thrown upon the floor some distance from her. The mother was at first thought to be dead, but God restored her, though she lost the use of her limbs for some considerable time. Her feet were singed with the lightning, and yet no sign thereof appearing on her shoes. Also the child and the other woman recovered. In the next room were seven or eight persons who received no hurt. It was above a quarter of an hour before they could help the persons thus smitten, for the room was so full of smoke (smelling like brimstone) that they could not see them. Some swine being near the door as the lightning fell, were thrown into the house, and seemed dead awhile, but afterwards came to life again. A cat was killed therewith. A pewter candlestick standing upon a joynt-stool, some part of it was melted and carried away before the lightning, and stuck in the chamber-floor over head, like swan shot, and yet the candlestick itself was not so much as shaken off from the stool whereon it stood.

June 12, 1680. There was an amazing thunder-storm at Hampton in New England. The lightning fell upon the house of Mr. Joseph Smith, strangely shattering it in divers places. His wife (the grand-daughter of that eminent man of God, Mr. Cotton, who was the famous teacher of the church of Christ, first in Old and then in New Boston) lay as dead for the present, being struck down with the lightning near the chimney; yet God mercifully spared and restored her; but the said Smith his mother (a gracious woman) was struck dead, and never recovered again.

Besides all these which have been mentioned, one or two in Connecticut colony, and four persons dwelling in the northern parts of this countrey, were smitten with the fire of God, about sixteen years ago; the circumstances of which providences (though very remarkable) I have not as yet received from those that were acquainted therewith and therefore cannot here publish them. Also, some remarkables about thunder hapned the last year.

A reverend friend in a neighbour colony, in a letter bearing August 3, 1682, writeth thus :—

"We have had of late great storms of rain and wind, and some of thunder and lightning, whereby execution has been done, though with sparing mercy to men. Mr. Jones his house in New-Haven was broken into by the lightning, and strange work made in one room especially, in which one of his children had been but a little before. This was done June 8th, 1682. A little after which, at Norwalk, there were nine working oxen smitten dead at once, within a small compass of ground. The next moneth, at Greenwich, there were seven swine and a dog killed with the lightning, very near a dwelling-house, where a family of children (their parents not at home when lightning hapned) were much frighted, but received no other hurt. What are these but warning pieces, shewing that mens lives may go next?" Thus he.

I proceed now to give an account of some late remarkables about thunder and lightning, wherein several vessels at sea were concerned.

July 17, 1677. A vessel, whereof Mr. Thomas Berry was master, set sail from Boston in New England, bound for the island of Madeira. About 3 h. P.M., being halfway between Cape Cod and Brewsters Islands, they were becalmed; and they perceived a thunder-shower arising in the north-north-west. The master ordered all their sails (except their two courses) to be furled. When the shower drew near to them, they had only the foresail abroad; all the men were busie in lashing fast the long-boat; the master was walking upon the deck, and as he came near the main-mast, he beheld something very black fly before him, about the bigness of a small mast, at the larboard side; and immediately he heard a dreadful and amazing noise, not like a single canon, but as if great armies of men had been firing one against another; presently upon which the master was struck clear round, and fell down for dead upon the deck, continuing so for about seven minutes; but then he revived, having his hands much burnt with the lightning. The ship seemed to be on fire; and a very great smoke, having a sulphurous smell, came from between the decks, so that no man was able to stay there for more than half an hour after this surprising accident hapned. The main-mast was split from the top-gallant-mast head to the lower deck. The partners of the pump were struck up at the star-board side; and one end of two cabbins staved down betwixt decks. Two holes were made in one of the pumps, about the bigness of two musquet bullets. They were forced to return to Boston again, in order to the fitting of the vessel with a new mast. Through the mercy of the Most High, no person in the vessel received any hurt, besides what hath been expressed. Yet it is remarkable, that the same day, about the same time, two men in or near Wenham were killed with lightning, as they sat under a tree in the woods.

On June the 6th, A.D. 1682, a ship called the Jamaica Merchant, Captain Joseph Wild commander, being then in the Gulph of Florida, lat. 27 gr., about 1 h. P.M. was surprized with an amazing thunder-shower. The lightning split the main-mast, and knocked down one of the seamen, and set the ship on fire between decks in several places. They used utmost endeavour to extinguish the fire, but could not do it. Seeing they were unable to overcome those flames, they betook themselves to their boat. The fire was so furious between the cabbin and the deck in the steeridge, that they could not go to the relief of each other, insomuch that a man and his wife were parted. The man leaped overboard into the sea, and so swam to the boat ; his wife and a child were taken out of a gallery window into the boat. Three men more were saved by leaping out of the cabbin window. There were aboard this vessel which Heaven thus set on fire, thirty-four persons ; yet all escaped with their lives : for the gracious providence of God so ordered, as that Captain John Bennet was then in company, who received these distressed and astonished creatures into his ship : so did they behold the vessel burning, until about 8 h. P.M., when that which remained sunk to the bottom of the sea. The master with several of the seamen were, by Captain Bennet, brought safe to New England, where they declared how wonderfully they had been delivered from death, which God both by fire and water had threatned them with.

March 16, 1682-3. A ship, whereof Robert Luist is master, being then at sea (bound for New England), in lat. 27 gr., about 2 h. A.M., it began to thunder and lighten. They beheld three corpusants (as mariners call them) on the yards. The thunder grew fiercer and thicker than before. Suddenly their vessel was filled with smoke and the smell of brimstone, that the poor men were terrified with the apprehension of their ships being on fire.

There came down from the clouds a stream or flame of fire, as big as the ships mast, which fell on the middle of the deck, where the mate was standing, but then was thrown flat upon his back, with three men more that were but a little distance from him. They that were yet untouched, thought not only that their fellow mariners had been struck dead, but their deck broken in pieces by that blow, whose sound seemed to them to exceed the report of many great guns fired off at once. Some that were less dangerously hurt, made an out-cry that their legs were scalded, but the mate lay speechless and senseless. When he began to come to himself, he made sad complaints of a burden lying upon his back. When day came, they perceived their main-top-mast was split, and the top-sail burnt. The lightning seemed like small coals of fire blown overboard.

There is one remarkable more about thunder and lightning, which I am lately informed of by persons concerned therein : some circumstances in the relation being as wonderful as any of the preceding particulars. Thus it was :—On July 24, in the year 1681, the ship called Albemarl (whereof Mr. Edward Ladd was then master), being an hundred leagues from Cape Cod, in lat. 38, about 3h. P.M., met with a thunder-storm. The lightning burnt the main-top-sail, split the main-cap in pieces, rent the mast all along. There was in special one dreadful clap of thunder, the report bigger than of a great gun, at which all the ships company were amazed ; then did there fall something from the clouds upon the stern of the boat, which broke into many small parts, split one of the pumps, the other pump much hurt also. It was a bituminous matter, smelling much like fired gunpowder. It continued burning in the stern of the boat; they did with sticks dissipate it, and poured much water on it, and yet they were not able by all that they could do to extinguish it, until such time as all the matter was consumed. But the strangest thing of all is yet to be mentioned. When night came, observing the stars, they perceived that their compasses were changed. As for the compass in the biddikil, the north point was turned clear south. There were two other compasses unhung in the locker in the cabin : in one of which the north point stood south, like that in the biddikil; as for the other, the north point stood west, so that they sailed by a needle whose polarity was quite changed. The seamen were at first puzzled how to work their vessel right, considering that the south point of their compass was now become north; but, after a little use, it was easy to them. Thus did they sail a thousand leagues. As for the compass, wherein the lightning had made the needle to point westward, since it was brought to New-England, the glass being broke, it has, by means of the air coming to it, wholly lost its vertue. One of those compasses, which had quite changed the polarity from north to south, is still extant in Boston, and at present in my custody. The north point of the needle doth remain fixed to this day as it did immediately after the lightning caused an alteration ; the natural reason of which may be enquired into in the next chapter. But before I pass to that, it may be, it will be grateful to the reader for me here to commemorate some parellel instances, which have lately hapned in other parts of the world, unto which I proceed, contenting myself with one or two examples, reserving others for the subsequent chapter, where we shall have further occasion to take notice of them.

The Authors of *Ephemeridum Medico-Physicarum Germanicarum* have informed the world, that on August 14, 1669, it thundred and lightned as if heaven and earth would come together. And at the house of a gentleman, who lived near Bergen, the fiery lightning flashed through four inner rooms at once; entering into a beer cellar, with its force it threw down the earthen vessels, with the windows and doors where it came; but the tin and iron vessels were partly melted, and partly burnt, with black spots remaining on them. Where it entred the cellar, the barrels were removed out of their right places; where it went out, it left the taps shaking. In one room, the binding was taken off from the back of a Bible, and the margin was accurately cut by the lightning without hurting the letters, as if it had been done by the hands of some artist, beginning at the Revelation, and (which is wonderful) ending with the twelfth chapter of 1 Epistle to the Corinthians, which chapter fell in course to be expounded in public the next Lords day. Six women sitting in the same chimney, filled with a sulphurous and choaking mist, that one could scarce breathe, not far from the bed of a woman that was then lying-in, were struck down, the hangings of the room burnt, and the mother of the woman in child-bed lay for dead at present; but, after a while, the other recovering their sences, examined what hurt was done to the woman thought to be dead: her kerchief was burnt, as if it had been done with gunpowder; she had about her a silver chain, which was melted and broke into five parts; her under-garments were not so much as singed; but just under her paps she was very much burnt. After she came to herself she was very sensible of pain in the place where the lightning had caused that wound. To lenifie which, womens milk was made use of; but blisters arising, the dolour was increased, until a skilful physician prescribed this unguent:—*R. Mucil, sem. cydoniorum c. aq. malv.* half an ounce. *Succ. Plantag. rec.* an ounce and half. *Lytharg. aur. subt. pert.* half a drachm, *m. ad. fict.* Whereby the inflamation was allayed.

By the same authors, it is also related, that in June, A.D. 1671, an house was struck with lightning in four places; in some places the timber was split, and in other places had holes made in it, as if bored through with an awger, but no impression of fire were any where to be seen. A girl, fifteen years old, sitting in the chimney, was struck down, and lay for dead the space of half an hour; and it is probable, that she had never recovered, had not an able physician been sent for, who viewing her, perceived that the clothes about her breast were made to look blewish by the lightning: it had also caused her paps to look fiery and blackish, as if they had been scorched with gunpowder. Under her breast the lightning had left creases across her body, of a brownish colour: also, some creases made by the lightning, as broad as ones finger, run along her left leg reaching to her foot. The physician caused two spoonfuls of apoplectick water to be poured down her throat, upon which she instantly revived, complaining of a great heat in her jaws, and much pain in the places hurt by the lightning. Half a drachm of *Pulvis*

Bezoarticus Anglicus, in the water of sweet chervil was given to her, which caused a plentiful sweat, whereby the pain in her jaws was diminished. Being still feaverish, an emulsion, made with poppy seed, millet, carduus benedictus, &c. was made use of, upon which the patient had ease and recovered. It appears by this, as well as other instances, that great care should be had of those that are thunder-struck, that they be not given up for quite dead, before all means be used in order to their being revived. Paulus Zacchias, in *Questionibus Medicis,* giveth rules whereby it may be known whether persons smitten with lightning be dead past all recovery or no. And the history put forth by Jacobus Javellus, in an epistle emitted with his *Medicinæ Compendium,* describes the cure of persons struck with lightning. I have not myself seen those books, but whoso shall see cause to obtain and consult them, will I suppose find therein things worth their reading and consideration. Something to this purpose I find in the *Scholion,* on the *Germ. Ephem.* for the year 1671, obs. 37, p. 69. The reader that is desirous to see more remarkable instances about thunder and lightning, wherein persons living in former age were concerned, if he please to look into Zuinger his *Theatrum vit. Human.* vol. ii, lib. 2, p. 322, and lib. 7, p. 475, 545, and vol. iii. lib. 1, p. 621, and vol. v, lib. 4, p. 1371, he will find many notable and memorable passages which that industrious author hath collected. Though none more awful (to my remembrance) than that which hapned A.D. 1546, when Meckelen (a principal city in Brabant) was set on fire, and suffered a fearful conflagration by lightning; so it was, that at the very time when this thunder-storm hapned, an inn-keeper (whose name was Croes) had in his house, some guests, who were playing at cards. The inn-keeper going into his wine-cellar to fetch drink for his merry guests, at that moment the furious tempest plucked up the house and carried it a good way off. Every one of the men that were playing at cards were found dead with their cards in their hands, only the inn-keeper himself, being in the wine-cellar (which was arched) escaped with his life.

This brings to mind a strange passage related by Cardan (*De Variet*, lib. 8, c. 43), who saith, that eight men, sitting down together under an oak, as they were at supper, a flash of lightning smote and slew them all; and they were found in the very posture that the lightning surprized them in: one with the meat in his mouth, another seemed to be drinking, another with a cup in his hand, which he intended to bring to his mouth, &c. They looked like images made black with the lightning.

As for Scripture examples of men slain by lightning, it is the judgement of the judicious and learned Zuinger, that the Sodomites, and those 250 that being with Corah in his conspiracy, presumed to offer incense (Numb. xvi, 35), and Nadab and Abihu, and the two semicenturions, with their souldiers, who came to apprehend the prophet Elijah, were all killed by lightning from heaven.

CHAPTER IV.

SOME PHILOSOPHICAL MEDITATIONS.

Concerning Antipathies and Sympathies. Of the loadstone. Of the nature and wonderful effects of lightning. That thunder-storms are often caused by Satan, and sometimes by good angels. Thunder is the voice of God and, therefore, to be dreaded. All places in the habitable world are subject to it, more or less. No amulets can preserve men from being hurt thereby. The miserable estate of wicked men upon this account, and the happiness of the righteous, who may be above all disquieting fears with respect unto such terrible accidents.

HAVING thus far related many Remarkable Providences which have hapned in these goings down of the sun, and some of the particulars (especially in the last chapter) being tragical stories, the reader must give me leave upon this occasion, a little to divert and recreate my mind with some philosophical meditations, and to conclude with a theological improvement thereof. There are wonders in the works of Creation as well as Providence, the reason whereof the most knowing amongst mortals are not able to comprehend. "Dost thou know the ballancings of the clouds, the wondrous works of Him who is perfect in knowledge?"

I have not yet seen any who give a satisfactory reason of those strange fountains in New Spain, which ebb and flow with the sea, though far from it, and which fall in rainy weather, and rise in dry; or concerning that pit near St. Bartholmew's, into which if one cast a stone, though never so small, it makes a noise as great and terrible as a clap of thunder. It is no difficult thing to produce a world of instances, concerning which, the usual answer is, an occult quality is the cause of this strange operation, which is only a fig-leaf whereby our common philosophers seek to hide their own ignorance. Nor may we (with Erastus) deny that there are marvelous sympathies and antipathies in the natures of things. We know that the horse does abominate the camel; the mighty elephant is afraid of a mouse; and they say that the lion, who scorneth to turn his back upon the stoutest animal, will tremble at the crowing of a cock. Some men also have strange antipathies in their natures against that sort of food which others love and live upon. I have read of one that could not endure to eat either bread or flesh; of another that fell into a swoonding fit at the smell of a rose; others would do the like at the smell of vineger, or at the sight of an eel or a frog. There was a man that if he did hear the sound of a bell, he would immediately die away; another if he did happen to hear any one sweeping a room, an inexpressible horror would seize upon him; another if he heard one whetting a knife, his gumms would fall a bleeding; another was not able to behold a knife that had a sharp point without being in a strange agony. Quercetus speaketh of one that died as he was sitting at the table, only because an apple was brought into his sight. There are some who, if a cat accidentally come into the room, though they neither see it, nor are told of it, will presently be in a sweat, and ready to die away. There was lately one living in Stow-Market, that when ever it thundred, would fall into a violent vomiting, and so continue until the thunder-storm was over. A woman had such an antipathy against cheese that if she did but eat a piece of bread, cut with a knife, which a little before had cut cheese, it would cause a deliquium; yet the same woman when she was with child delighted in no meat so much as in cheese. There was lately (I know not but that he may be living still) a man, that if pork, or any thing made of swines flesh, were brought into the room, he would fall into a convulsive Sardonian laughter; nor can he for his heart leave as long as that object is before him, so that, if it should not be removed, he would certainly laugh himself to death. It is evident that the peculiar antipathies of some persons are caused by the imaginations of their parents. There was one that would fall into a syncope if either a calves head or a cabbage were brought near him. There were *nævi materni* upon the *hypocondria* of this person; on his right side there was the form of a calves head, on his left side a cabbage imprinted there by the imagination of his longing mother. Most wonderful is that which Libavius and others report, concerning a man that would be surprised with a lipothymy at the sight of his own son—nay, upon his approaching near unto him, though he saw him not; for which some assigned this reason, that the mother when she was with child, used to feed upon such meats as were abominable to the father (concerning the rationality of this conjecture see Sir Kenelm Digby's *Discourse of Bodies*, p. 409, 410); but others said that the midwife who brought him into the world was a witch.

Nor are the sympathies in nature less wonderful than the antipathies. There is a mutual friendship between the ilive-tree and the myrtle. There is a certain stone called pantarbe, which draws gold unto it; so does the adamas hairs and twigs. The sympathy between the load-stone and iron, which do mutually attract each other, is admirable : there is no philosopher but speaketh of this; some have published whole treatises (both profitable and pleasant) upon this argument—in special, Gilbert, Ward, Cabeus, Kepler, and of late Kircherus.

I know many fabulous things have been related concerning the load-stone by inexperienced philosophers, and so believed by many others, *e.g.* that onions, or garlick, or ointments, will cause it to lose its vertue. Johnston (and from him Dr. Browne in his *Vulgar Errors*) hath truly asserted the contrary. Every one knoweth that the head of a needle touched therewith will continue pointing towards the north pole; so that the magnet leaveth an impression of its own nature and vertue upon the needle, causing it to stand pointed as the magnet itself doth. The loadstone it self is the hardest iron ; and it is a thing known, that such mines are naturally so (notwithstanding the report of one who saith, that lately in Devonshire, loadstones were found otherwise) posited in the earth. Just under the Line the needle lieth parallel with the horizon ; but sailing north or south it begins to incline and increase according as it approacheth to either pole, and would at last endeavour to erect itself ; whence some ascribe these strange effects to the north star, which they suppose to be very magnetical. There is reason to believe that the earth is the great magnet. Hence (as Mr. Seller observes), when a bar of iron has stood long in a window, that end of it which is next to the earth will have the same vertue which the loadstone it self has.

Some place the first meridian at the Azores, because there the needle varies not ; but the like is to be said of some other parts of the world ; yea, under the very same meridian, in divers latitudes, there is a great variation as to the pointing of the needle. It is affirmed that between the shore of Ireland, France, Spain, Guiny, and the Azores, the north point varies towards the east, as some part of the Azores it deflecteth not. On the other side of the Azores, and this side of the æquator, the north point of the needle wheeleth to the west ; so that in the lat. 36, near the shore, the variation is about 11 gr., but on the other side of the æquator, it is quite otherwise, for in Brasilia the south point varies 12 gr, unto the west, but elongating from the coast of Brasilia toward the shore of Africa it varies eastward, and arriving at the Cape De las Aguillas, it rests in the meridian and looketh neither way. Dr. Browne, in his *Pseudodoxia Epidemica*, p. 63, does rationally suppose that the cause of this variation may be the inequality of the earth, variously disposed and indifferently mixed with the sea. The needle driveth that way where the greater and most powerful part of the earth is placed ; for whereas on this side the isles of Azores the needle varies eastward, it may be occasioned by that vast tract, viz. Europe, Asia, and Africa, seated towards the east, and disposing the needle that way ; sailing further it veers its lilly to the west, and regards that quarter wherein the land is nearer or greater ; and in the same latitude, as it approacheth the shore, augmenteth its variation ; hence, at Rome, there is a less variation (viz. but five degrees) than at London, for on the west side of Rome are seated the great continents of France, Spain, Germany ; but unto England there is almost no earth west, but the whole extent of Europe and Asia lies eastward, and therefore at London the variation is 11 degrees. Thus also, by reason of the great continent of Brasilia, the needle deflects towards the land 12 degrees: but at the straits of Magellan, where the land is narrowed, and the sea on the other side, it varies but 5 or 6 ; so because the Cape of De las Aguillas hath sea on both sides near it, and other land remote, and as it were æquidistant from it, the needle conforms to the meridian. In certain creeks and vallies it proveth irregular, the reason whereof may be some vigorous part of the earth not far distant. Thus Dr. Browne, whose arguings seem rational. Some have truly observed of *crocus martis* or steel corroded with vineger, sulphur, or otherwise, and after reverberated by fire, that the loadstone will not at all attract it, nor will it adhere, but lye therein like sand. It is likewise certain, that the fire will cause the loadstone to lose its vertue, inasmuch as its bituminous spirits are thereby evaporated. Porta (lib. 7, cap. 7) saith that he did, to his great admiration, see a sulphurous flame break out of the loadstone, which being dissipated, the stone lost its attractive vertue. Moreover, the loadstone, by being put into the fire, may be caused quite to change its polarity. The truly noble and honourable Robert Boyle, Esq., many of whose excellent observations and experiments have been advantagious, not only to the English nation but to the learned world, in his book of the *Usefulness of Natural Philosophy*, p. 15, hath these words : —" Taking an oblong loadstone, and heating it red hot, I found the attractive faculty, in not many minutes, either altogether abolisht, or, at least, so impaired and weakened, that I was scarce, if at all, able to discern it. But this hath been observed, though not so faithfully related, by more than one; wherefore I shall add,—That by refrigerating this red hot loadstone, either north or south, I found that I could give its extreams a polarity (if I may so speak), which they would readily display upon an excited needle freely placed in æquilibrium; and not only so, but I could by refrigerating the same end, sometimes north and sometimes south, in a very short time change the poles of the loadstone at pleasure, making that which was a quarter of an hour before the north pole become the south; and, on the contrary, the formerly southern pole become the northern. And this change was wrought on the loadstone, not only by cooling it directly north and south, but by cooling it perpendicularly; that end of it which was contiguous to the ground growing the northern pole, and so (according to the laws magnetical) drawing to it the south end, and that which was remotest from the contrary one; as if, indeed, the terrestrial globe were, as some magnetic philosophers have supposed it, but a great magnet, since its effluviums are able, in some cases, to impart a magnetic faculty to the loadstone it self." Thus far Mr. Boyle.

Also Dr. Browne shews, that if we erect a red-hot wire until it cool, then hang it up with wax and untwisted silk where the lower end and that which cooled next the earth does rest, that is the northern point. And if a wire be heated only at one end, according as the end is cooled upwards or downwards, it respectively acquires a verticity. He also observes, if a load-stone be made red hot in the fire, it amits the magnetical vigor it had before, and acquireth another from the earth, in its refrigeration, for that part which cooleth next the earth will acquire the respect of the north; the experiment whereof he made in a loadstone of parallelogram, or long square figure, wherein only inverting the extreames as it came out of the fire, he altered the poles or faces thereof at pleasure. Unto some such reason as this, must the wonderful change occasioned by the lightning in the compasses of Mr. Lad's vessel be ascribed; probably the heat of the lightning caused the needle to lose its vertue, and the compass in the bidikle might stand pointed to the south, and that unhung in the locker to the west, when they grew cold again, and accordingly continue pointing for ever after.

There is also that which is very mysterious and beyond humane capacity to comprehend, in thunder and lightning. The thunder of his power, who can understand? Also, can any understand the spreadings of the clouds, or the noise of His Tabernacle? Hence Elihu said (some interpreters think there was a thunder-storm at the very instant when those words were spoken) in Job, xxxvii, 5, ירעם נפלאות He thundreth marveils. It is indeed manifest that these wonderful meteors are generated out of a nitrous and sulphurous matter. Hence it is commonly out of dark and thick clouds that hail and coals of fire break forth, Psal. xviii, 11, 12. The scent which the lightning useth to leave behind it, in places where it falls, is a sufficient evidence of its being of a sulphurous nature Nay, the persons (as well as places) smitten therewith have sometimes smelt strong of brimstone. Two years ago there was a ship riding at anchor in a place in France and a furious tempest suddenly arising, the main-mast was split in pieces with a clap of thunder; the pendant on the top of the main-top-mast was burnt to ashes, twelve men were beat upon the deck, five of which lay for dead a considerable time, no pulse or breath being perceived, their eyes and teeth immovable, yet had they no visible wound, only an intolerable smell of brimstone; about half an hour after, by rubbing and forcing open their mouths, and pouring down some cordials, they recovered. At the same time six others were miserably burnt, their flesh being scorched, yet their garments not so much as singed; their skin much discoloured. See Mr. Burton's *Miracles of Nature,* p. 181.

Likewise, August 23, 1682. A man walking in the field near Darking in England was struck with a clap of thunder. One who was near him, ran to take him up, but found him dead, and his body exceeding hot, and withal smelling so strong of sulphur that he was forced to let him ly a considerable time ere he could be removed. It is reported, that sometimes thunder and lightning has been generated out of the sulphurous and bituminous matter which the fiery mountain Ætna hath cast forth. We know that when there is a mixture of nitre, sulphur, and unslaked lime, water will cause fire to break out. And when unto nitre brimstone is added, a report is caused thereby. And unquestionably, nitre is a special ingredient in the matter of thunder and lightning; this we may gather from the descension of the flame, which descends not only obliquely but perpendicularly, and that argues it does so not from any external force, but naturally. Mr. William Clark, in his *Natural History of Nitre,* observes that if the quantity of an ounce be put in a fire-shovel, and a live coal put upon it, the fire-shovel in the bottom will be red hot, and burn through whatever is under it; which demonstrates that this sort of fire does naturally burn downwards, when as all other fires do naturally ascend. For this cause *Stella cadens* is rationally concluded to be a nitrous substance; the like is to be affirmed of the lightning. Hence also is its terrible and irresistable force. The nitre in gunpowder is, as the aforesaid author expresseth it, *Anima Pyrii Pulveris*, sulphur without saltpeter has no powerful expulsion with it. The discharging great pieces of ordnance is fitly called *Artificial Thundring and Lightning*, since thereby men do in a moment blow up houses, beat down castles, batter mountains in pieces. So that there is nothing in nature does so admirably and artificially resemble the thunder and lightning, both in respect of the report, and the terrible and sudden and amazing execution done thereby *Flammas Jovis & sonitus imitatur Olympi:* Hence as those that are shot with a bullet do not hear the gun, being struck before the report cometh to their ears, so is it usually with them that are thunder-struck, the lightning is upon them before the noise is heard. Men commonly tremble at the dreadful crack, when, as if they hear any thing, the danger useth to be past as to that particular thunder-clap; though another may come and kill them before they hear it. The nitre in the lightning may likewise be esteemed the natural cause of its being of so penetrating and burning a nature. For there is not the like fiery substance in the world again as nitre is. Many have been of the opinion that there is a bolt of stone descending with the thunder; but that is a vulgar error, the fulmeen or thunder-bolt is the same with the lightning, being a nitro-sulphurious spirit. It must needs be a more subtile and spiritual body than any stone is of, that shall penetrate so as these meteors do. It is true that our translation reads the words in Psal. lxxviii, 41.   He gave their flocks to hot thunder-bolts : but the original word רשפים translated thunder-bolts, signifieth burning coals ; so that lightning is thereby intended.   Avicenna doth indeed say, that he saw a thunder-bolt which fell at Corduba in Spain, and that it had a sulphurous smell, and was like ammoniac.   It is possible that not only sulphurous and bituminous but stony substances may be generated in the clouds with the lightning.   George Agricola writeth that near Lurgea, a mass of iron being fifty pound in weight, fell from the clouds, which some attempted to make swords of, but the fire could not melt it, nor hammers bring it into form.

In the year 1492.   At Ensishemium, a stone of three hundred pound weight fell from the clouds, which is kept as a monument in the Temple there.   And in 1581, a stone came out of the clouds in Thuringia, which was so hot that it could not be touched, with which one might strike fire as with a flint.   There is now to be seen at Dresden a stone which descended out of a cloud, and is reserved amongst the *Admiranda* belonging to the Elector of Saxony : some lately living were present at the fall of that stone.   Again, An. 1618, in Bohemia, a considerable quantity of brass mettal fell from the clouds.   No longer since than May 28, 1677, at a village near Hana in Germany, there was a tempest of lightning, and a great multitude of stones of a green and partly cærulean colour fell therewith, and a considerable mass of mineral matter, in taste like vitriol, being pondrous and friable, having also metallick sparks like gold intermixed.   That which is by some called the rain-stone or thunder-bolt, was by the antients termed *Ceraunia,* because of the smell like that of an horn when put into the fire, which doth attend it. Learned Gesner (who, in respect of his vast knowledge in the works of God, may be called the Solomon of the former age) saith, that a gentleman gave him one of those stones, supposing it to be a thunder-bolt, and that it was five digits in length, and three in breath. This sort of stone is usually in form like unto an iron wedge, and has an hole quite through it. Joh. de Laet, in his treatise *de Gemmis,* lib. 2, cap. 24, relates that he saw another of those stones. Bootius (*de Gemmis,* lib. 2, cap. 261) reports that many persons worthy of credit, affirmed that when houses or trees had been broken with the thunder, they did by digging find such stones in the places where the stroke was given. Nevertheless, that fulminous stones or thunderbolts do always descend out of the clouds, when such breache are made by the lightning, is (as I said) a vulgar error.

The effects produced by the lightning are exceeding marvelous: sometimes gold, silver, brass, iron, has been melted thereby when the things wherein they have been kept, received no hurt; yea, when the wax on the bags which contained them has not been so much as melted. Liquors have been thereby exhausted out of vessels, when the vessels themselves remained untouched; and (which is more wonderful) when the cask has been broken by the lightning, the wine has remained as it were included in a skin, without being spilt; the reason whereof Sennertus supposeth to be, in that the heat of the lightning did condense the exterior parts of the wine. It is also a very strange thing, which histories report concerning Marcia (a Roman Princess), that the child in her body was smitten

6

and killed with lightning, and yet the mother received no hurt in her own body. It is hard to give a clear and satisfactory reason why if a piece of iron be laid upon the cask it prevents the thunder from marring the wine contained therein, and also keeps milk from turning. The Virtuosi of France, in their *Philosophical Conferences* (vol. ii, p. 427), suppose a sympathy between iron and the gross vapors of thunder and lightning. They say that which is commonly called the thunder-bolt does sometimes resemble steel, as it were to shew the correspondence that there is between iron and thunder: so that the air being impregnate by those noisome vapours which are of the same nature with iron, meeting with some piece of it laid on a vessel, is joyned to the iron by sympathy, the iron by its attractive vertue receives them, and by its retentive, retains them, and by that means prevents the effects. This conjecture is ingenious. Nor is it easie to give a solid reason why the lightning should hurt one creature rather than another. Naturalists observe that it is so. *Feles canes et capras magis illorum obnoxious ictibus observatio sedula dedit*, saith Johnston. Bartholinus conjectures the reason to be the halitus in the bodies of those creatures which are a fit nutriment for the fulminious spirits to prey upon. When fire is set to a train of gunpowder, it will run accordingly strait or crooked, upwards or downwards, as the matter it feeds upon is disposed : so proportionably here : but this is a subject for ingenious minds to enquire into. It is, moreover, difficult to determine how men are killed therewith, when no visible impression is made upon their bodies. Some think it is by a meer instantaneous suffocation of their animal spirits. That poysonful vapours do sometimes attend the lightning is manifest. Seneca saith, that wine which has been congealed with the lightning, after it is dissolved, and in appearance returned to its pristine state, it causeth the persons that shall drink of it, either to die or become mad. Naturalists observe that venomous creatures being struck with lightning lose their poyson; the reason of which may be, not only the heat but the venome of those vapours attracting the poyson to themselves. And that vapors will kill in a moment is past doubt. In the *Philosophical Transactions* for the year 1665 (p. 44), it is related that seven or eight persons going down stairs into a coal-pit, they fell down dead as if they had been shot: there being one of them whose wife was informed that her husband was stifled, she went near to him without any inconvenience; but when she went a little further, the vapors caused her instantly to fall down dead. And it is famously known, concerning the Lake Avernus, in Campania, that if birds attempt to fly over it, the deadly vapors thereof kill them in a moment. But the lightning doth more than meerly suffocate with mortiferous vapors. It sometimes penetrates the brain, and shrivels the heart and liver, when nothing does appear outwardly. And it does, as Dr. Goodwin, in his lately published judicious discourse about the punishment of sinners in the other world (p. 44) aptly expresseth, lick up the vital and animal spirits that run in the body, when yet the body itself remains unburnt. Those spirits are the vinculum, the tye of union between the soul and body, which the lightning may consume without so much as singing the body or cloaths there. Nevertheless, upon some it leaveth direful marks, and breaketh their very bones in pieces, and sometimes tears away the flesh from the bones. There are some remarkable instances confirming this, published in the *Philosophical Transactions*. Dr. Wallis, in a letter written at Oxford, May 12, 1666, giving an account of a very sad accident which had then newly hapned there, he saith, " That two scholars of Wadham Colledge, being alone in a boat (without a waterman) having newly thrust off from shore at Medley, to come homewards, standing near the head of the boat, were presently, with a stroke of thunder or lightning, both struck off out of the boat into the water : the one of them stark dead, in whom though presently taken out of the water (having been by relation scarce a minute in it), there was not discerned any appearance of life, sense, or motion; the other was stuck fast in the mud (with his feet downwards, and his upper parts above water) like a post, not able to help himself out ; but besides a present astonying or numness, had no other hurt ; but was for the present so disturbed in his senses that he knew not how he came out of the boat, nor could remember either thunder or lightning that did effect it : and was very feeble and faint upon it, which, though presently put into a warm bed, he had not thoroughly recovered by the next night; and whither since he have or no I know not. Others in another boat, about ten or twenty yards from these (as by their description I estimate), felt a disturbance and shaking in their boat, and one of them had his chair struck from under him, and thrown upon him, but had no hurt. These immediately made up to the others, and (some leaping into the water to them) presently drew them into the boat or on shore ; yet none of them saw these two fall into the water (not looking that way) but heard one of them cry for help presently upon the stroke, and smelt a very strong stinking smell in the air; which, when I asked him that told it me, what kind of stink, he said, like such a smell as is perceived upon the striking of flints together. He that was dead (when by putting into a warm bed, and rubbing, and putting strong waters into his mouth, &c., no life could be brought into him) was the next morning brought to town; where, among multitudes of others who came to see, Dr. Willis, Dr. Mallington, Dr. Lower, and myself, with some others, went to view the corps, where we found no wound at all in the skin; the face and neck swart and black, but not more than might be ordinary, by the setling of the blood; on the right side of the neck was a little blackish spott about an inch long, and about a quarter of an inch broad at the broadest, and was as if it had been seared with a hot iron; and as I remember, one somewhat bigger on the left side of the neck below the ear. Streight down the breast, but towards the left side of it, was a large place, about three quarters of a foot in length, and about two inches in breadth—in some places more, in some less, which was burnt and hard, like leather burnt with the fire, of a deep blackish red colour, not much unlike the scorched skin of a rosted pig; and on the forepart of the left shoulder such another spot about as big as a shilling; but that in the neck was blacker and seemed more seared. From the top of the right shoulder, sloping downwards towards that place in his breast, was a narrow line of the like scorched skin, as if somewhat had come in there at the neck, and had run down to the breast, and there spread broader.

" The buttons of his doublet were most of them off, which

some thought might have been torn off with the blast getting in at the neck, and then bursting its way out; for which the greatest presumption was (to me), that besides four or five buttons wanting towards the bottom of the breast, there was about half a dozen together clear off from the bottom of the collar downwards, and I do not remember that the rest of the buttons did seem to be near worn out, but almost new.   The collar of his doublet just over the fore-part of the right shoulder was quite broken asunder, but with a blunt tool; only the inward linen or fustian lining of it was whole, by which, and by the view of the ragg'd edges, it seemed manifest to me that it was from a stroke inward (from without), not outwards from within.

" His hat was strangely torn, not just on the crown, but on the side of the hat, and on the brim.   On the side of it was a great hole, more than to put in ones fist through it : some part of it being quite struck away, and from thence divers gashes every way, as if torn or cut with a dull tool; and some of them of a good length, almost quite to the edges of the brim.   And besides these one or two gashes more, which did not communicate with that hole in the side.   This also was judged to be by a stroke inwards; not so much from the view of the edges of those gashes (from which there was scarce any judgment to be made either way), but because the lining was not torn, only ript from the edge of the hat (where it was sown on) on that side where the hole was made. But his hat not being found upon his head, but at some distance from him, it did not appear against what part of his head that hole was made.

" Another sad disaster hapned Jan. 24th, 1665-6, when

one Mr. Brooks of Hampshire, going from Winchester towards his house near Andover, in very bad weather, was himself slain by lightning, and the horse he rode on under him ; for about a mile from Winchester he was found with his face beaten into the ground, one leg in the stirrup, the other in the horses main ; his cloathes all burnt off his back, not a piece as big as an handkerchief left intire, and his hair and all his body singed. With the force that struck him down, his nose was beaten into his face, and his chin into his breast, where was a wound cut almost as low as to his navil ; and his clothes being as aforesaid torn, the pieces were so scattered and consumed, that not enough to fill the crown of a hat could be found. His gloves were whole, but his hands in them singed to the bone. The hip-bone and shoulder of his horse burnt and bruised, and his saddle torn in little pieces."

Very remarkable also was that which hapned forty-five years ago at another place in England, viz., Withycomb in Devonshire, where, on October 21, A.D. 1638, being Sabbath day, whilest the people were attending the publick worship of God, a black cloud coming over the church, there was suddenly an amazing clap of thunder, and with it a ball of fire came in at the window, whereby the house was very much damnified, and the people many of them struck down. Some of the seats in the body of the church were turned upside down, yet they that sat in them received no hurt. A gentleman of note there (one Mr. Hill), sitting in his seat by the chancil, had his head suddenly smitten against the wall, by which blow he died that night. Another had his head cloven, his skull rent in three pieces, and his brains thrown upon the ground whole.   The hair of his head, through the violence of the blow, stuck fast to the pillar that was near him.   A woman, attempting to run out of the church, had her clothes set on fire, and her flesh on her back torn almost to the very bone.   See Mr. Clarks *Examples*, vol. i, chap. 104, p. 501.

It is not heresie to believe that Satan has sometimes a great operation in causing thunder-storms.   I know this is vehemently denied by some : the late witch-advocates call it blasphemy ; and an old council did anathematize the men that are thus perswaded ; but, by their favour, an orthodox and rational man may be of the opinion, that when the devil has before him the vapors and materials out of which the thunder and lightning are generated, his art is such as that he can bring them into form.   If chymists can make their *Aurum fulminans*, what strange things may this infernal chymist effect ?   The Holy Scriptures intimate as much as this cometh to.   In the sacred story concerning Job, we find that Satan did raise a great wind, which blew down the house where Job's children were feasting.   And it is said, chap. i, ver. 16, that the fire of God fell from heaven, and burnt up the sheep and the servants.   This אש אלהים, fire of God, was no doubt thunder and lightning, and such as was extraordinary, and is therefore expressed with the name of God, as is usual amongst the Hebrews.   Satan had a deep policy in going that way to work, thereby hoping to make Job believe God was his enemy.   Mr. Caryl (according to his wonted manner) does both wittily and judiciously paraphrase upon the place.   " The fire of God (saith he) here, is conceived to have been some terrible flash of lightning ; and it is the more probable, because it is said to fall down from

Heaven, that is, out of the air. There Satan can do mighty things, command much of the magazine of Heaven, where that dreadful artillery which makes men tremble, those fiery meteors, thunder and lightning, are stored and lodged. Satan, let loose by God, can do wonders in the air: he can raise storms, he can discharge the great ordnance of Heaven, thunder and lightning; and, by his art, can make them more terrible and dreadful than they are in their own nature." Satan is said to be "the Prince of the Power of the Air," Eph. ii, 2. And we read of the working of Satan with all power and signs, and lying words, 2 Thess. ii, 9. It is, moreover, predicted in the Revelation, that Antichrist should cause fire to come down from heaven, Rev. xiii, 13. Accordingly, we read in history, that some of the Popes have, by their skill in the black art, caused balls of fire to be seen in the air. So then it is not beyond Satans power to effect such things, if the great God give him leave, without whose leave he cannot blow a feather, much less raise a thunder-storm. And, as the Scriptures intimate Satan's power in the air to be great, so histories do abundantly confirm it by remarkable instances. One of the scholars of Empedocles has testified that he saw his master raising winds and laying them again; and there were once many witnesses of it, whence they called Empedocles κωλυσάνεμαν. Clemens Alexandrinus mentions this as unquestionably true. Our great Rainold (*de libris Apocryphis*, lect. 202) saith, that we may from Job conclude it was not impossible for Empedocles, by the devils aid, to do as has been reported of him. Dio relates, that when the Roman army, in the dayes of the Emperour Claudius, pursuing the Africans, was in extream danger of perishing by drought, a magician undertook to procure water for them; and presently, upon his incantations, an astonishing shower fell. Jovianus Pontanus reports, that when King Ferdinand besieged the city Suessa, all the waters in the cisterns being dried up, the citizens had like to have lost their lives by the prevailing drought. The Popish priests undertook, by conjuration, to obtain water. The magical ceremonies by them observed were most horrid and ridiculous: for they took an asse, and put the sacrament of the eucharist into his mouth, sang funeral verses over him, and then buried him alive before the church doors. As soon as these rites, so pleasing to the devil, were finished, the heavens began to look black, and the sea to be agitated with winds, and anon it rained and lightned after a most horrendous manner. Smetius, in his *Miscellanies*, lib. 5, relates, that a girl, foolishly imitating the ceremonies of her nurse, whom she had sometimes seen raising tempests, immediately a prodigious storm of thunder and lightning hapned, so as that a village near Lipsia was thereby set on fire. This relation is mentioned by Sennertus as a thing really true. At some places in Denmark, it is a common and a wicked practice to buy winds, when they are going to sea. If Satan has so far the power of the air as to cause winds, he may cause storms also. Livy reports, concerning Romulus, that he was by a tempest of thunder and lightning transported no man knew whither, being after that never heard of. Meurerus (in *Comment. Meteorolog.*) speaketh of a man, that going between Lipsia, and Torga, was suddenly carried out of sight by a thunder-storm, and never seen more. And the truth of our assertion seems to be confirmed by one of those sad effects of lightning mentioned in the preceding chapter; for I am informed, that when Matthew Cole was killed with the lightning at North-Hampton, the dæmons which disturbed his sister, Ann Cole (forty miles distant), in Hartford, spoke of it, intimating their concurrence in that terrible accident.

The Jewish rabbins affirm, that all great and suddain destructions are from Satan, the angel of death. That he has frequently an hand therein is past doubt : and if the fallen angels are able (when God shall grant them a commission) to cause fearful and fatal thunders, it is much more true concerning the good and holy angels. 2 Kings i, 14, 15. When the law was given at Mount Sinai, there were amazing thundrings and lightnings, wherein the great God saw meet to make use of the ministry of holy angels (Acts vii, 53 ; Gal. iii, 19; Heb. ii, 2). Some think that Sodom was destroyed by extraordinary lightning. Its certain that holy angels had an hand in effecting that desolation, Gen. xix, 13. We know that one night the angel of the Lord smote in the camp of the Assyrians 185,000. It is not improbable but that those Assyrians were killed with lightning; for it was with respect to that tremendous providence that those words were uttered — "Who amongst us shall dwell with the devouring fire?" Isa. xxxiii, 14. Ecclesiastical history informs us, that the Jews, being encouraged by the apostate Julian, were resolved to re-build their temple, but lightning from heaven consumed not only their work, but all their tools and instruments wherewith that cursed enterprize was to have been carried on, so was their design utterly frustrate. Why might not holy angels have an hand in that lightning? There occurs to my mind a remarkable passage, mentioned by Dr. Beard, in his chapter about the protection of holy angels over them that fear God (p. 443). He saith, that a certain man, travelling between two woods in a great tempest of thunder and lightning, rode under an oak to shelter himself; but his horse would by no means stay under that oak, but, whither his master would or no, went from that tree, and stayed very quietly under another tree not far off. He had not been there many minutes before the first oak was torn all to fitters with a fearful clap of thunder and lightning. Surely there was the invisible guardianship of an holy angel in that providence.

But though it be true, that both natural causes and angels do many times concurre when thunder and lightning, with the awful effects thereof, happen, nevertheless, the supream cause must not be disacknowledged: the Eternal Himself has a mighty hand of providence in such works. He thundreth with the voice of His excellency. Among the Greeks thunder was stiled φωνη Διος, and the Scripture calls it "The Voice of the Lord." "The God of glory thundreth." "The voice of the Lord is very powerful; the voice of the Lord is full of majesty; the voice of the Lord breaketh the cedars; the voice of the Lord divideth the flames of fires." Lightnings are also said to be "the arrows of God," Psalm xviii, 14; upon which account the children of men ought to dread the hand of the Highest therein. And the more, for that all places in the habitable world are exposed unto dangers and destruction by the artillery of Heaven: though some parts of the earth are naturally subject thereunto more than others. Acosta saith, that it seldom thunders about Brazil; but such lightnings are frequent there as make the night appear brighter than the noon-day. Travellers report, that there are some snowy mountains in Africa, on which the cracks of thunder are so loud and vehement as that they are heard fifty miles off at sea. In some parts of Tartaria it will both snow and thunder at the same time. In the northern climates there use to be vehement thunders, and men are often struck dead thereby. In the province of Terravara in Spain grows the wood for the cross, to which superstitious Papists attribute a power to preserve men from thunder. So did the Gentiles of old vainly think to secure themselves from Heavens gun-shot, by carrying those things about them which they suppose would be as amulets to defend them from all harm. The tents of the old emperors were made of seal-leather, because they imagined that the sea-calf could not be thunder-struck. Tyberius wore a crown of laurel upon his head, for that the philosophers told him the lightning could not hurt the bay-tree. Rodiginus confirms the like concerning the fig-tree. But others declare they have seen the laurel smitten and withered with lightning; therefore, the Conim-bricensian philosophers acknowledge this immunity to be fictitious. The like vanity is in their opinion who suppose that the stone by philosophers called *brontias, i.e.,* the thunder-bolt, will secure them from harm by lightning. To conclude, most miserable is the state of all Christless sinners, who know not but that every thunder-storm which comes may send them to hell in a moment.

Hi sunt qui trepidant et ad omnia fulgura pallent,
Cum tonat, exanimes primo quoque murmure cœli.

The Psalmist alludes to a thunder storm, when he saith, "The Lord will rain upon the wicked snares" (the lightning cometh suddenly, and taketh men as birds, in a snare before they think of it), "fire and brimstone, and a tempest of horrors." Psalm xi, 6. The atheism of

Epicurus of old (and of some in these dayes), who taught, that inasmuch as thunder proceeds from natural causes, it is a childish thing for men to have an awe upon their hearts when they hear that voice. I say such atheism is folly and wickedness; for the great God "maketh the way for the lightning of thunder;" nor does it ever miss or mistake its way, but always lights where God has appointed it. Job xxviii, 26. He directs the lightning under the whole heaven, and unto the ends of the earth : after it a voice roareth, that they may do whatsoever he commanded them upon the face of the world in the earth. Job xxxvii, 3, 12. Yea, and good men should from this consideration be incited to endeavour that their garments be kept from defilement, and that they be alwayes walking with God, since they know not but that death may come upon them by such a way and by such means as this. As to outward evils, there is one event to the righteous and to the wicked ; to him that sacrificeth and to him that sacrificeth not ; as is the good so is the sinner. The examples mentioned in the preceding chapter do confirm it, since divers of those whom the thunder killed were good men. And they that are in Christ, and who make it their design to live unto God, need not be dismayed at the most terrifying thunder-claps, no more than a child should be afraid when he hears the voice of his loving father. Notable is that passage, related by Mr. Ambrose, in his *Treatise of Angels* (p. 265, and by Mr. Clark, vol. i, p. 512). A prophane man, who was also a persecutor of Mr. Bolton, riding abroad, it thundred very dreadfully,' at the which the man greatly trembled ; his wife, who was eminent for godliness, being with him, asked why he was so much afraid ? To whom he replied : Are not you afraid to hear these dreadful thunder claps? No (saith she), not at all, for I know it is the voice of my Heavenly Father: and should a child be afraid to hear his fathers voice? At the which the man was amazed, concluding with himself, these Puritans have a divine principle in them, which the world seeth not, that they should have peace and serenity in their souls when others are filled with dismal fears and horrors. He thereupon went to Mr. Bolton, bewailing the wrong he had done him, begging his pardon and prayers, and that he would tell him what he must do that so his soul might be saved : and he became a very godly man ever after. This was an happy thunder-storm.

CHAPTER V.

CONCERNING THINGS PRETERNATURAL WHICH HAVE HAPNED IN NEW ENGLAND.

A remarkable relation about Ann Cole, of Hartford. Concerning several witches in that colony. Of the possessed maid at Groton. An account of the house in Newberry lately troubled with a dæmon. A parallel story of an house at Tedworth, in England. Concerning another in Hartford. And of one in Portsmouth, in New-England, lately disquieted by evil spirits. The relation of a woman at Barwick, in New-England, molested with apparitions, and sometimes tormented by invisible agents.

INASMUCH as things which are preternatural, and not accomplished without diabolical operation, do more rarely happen, it is pity but that they should be observed. Several accidents of that kind have hapned in New-England, which I shall here faithfully relate, so far as I have been able to come unto the knowledge of them.

Very remarkable was that Providence wherein Ann Cole of Hartford in New-England was concerned. She was, and is accounted, a person of real piety and integrity; nevertheless, in the year 1662, then living in her fathers house (who has likewise been esteemed a godly man), she was taken with very strange fits, wherein her tongue was improved by a dæmon to express things which she herself knew nothing of; sometimes the discourse would hold for a considerable time ; the general purpose of which was, that such and such persons (who were named in the discourse which passed from her) were consulting how they might carry on mischievous designs against her and several others, mentioning sundry wayes they should take for that end, particularly that they would afflict her body, spoil her name, &c. The general answer made amongst the dæmons was, " She runs to the rock." This having continued some hours, the dæmons said, " Let us confound her language, that she may tell no more tales." She uttered matters unintelligible. And then the discourse passed into a Dutch tone (a Dutch family then lived in the town), and therein an account was given of some afflictions that had befallen divers ; amongst others, what had befallen a woman that lived next neighbour to the Dutch family, whose arms had been strangely pinched in the night, declaring by whom and for what cause that course had been taken with her. The Reverend Mr. Stone (then teacher of the church in Hartford) being by, when the discourse hapned, declared that he thought it impossible for one not familiarly acquainted with the Dutch (which Ann Cole had not in the least been) should so exactly imitate the Dutch tone in the pronunciation of English. Several worthy persons (viz., Mr. John Whiting Mr. Samuel Hooker, and Mr. Joseph Haines) wrote the intelligible sayings expressed by Ann Cole, whilest she was thus amazingly handled. The event was, that one of the persons (whose name was Greensmith, being a lewd and ignorant woman, and then in prison on suspicion for witchcraft) mentioned in the discourse as active in the mischief done and designed, was by the magistrate sent for ; Mr. Whiting and Mr. Haines read what they had

7

written, and the woman being astonished thereat, confessed those things to be true, and that she and other persons named in this preternatural discourse, had had familiarity with the devil. Being asked whether she had made an express covenant with him, she answered, she had not, only as she promised to go with him when he called, which accordingly she had sundry times done, and that the devil told her that at Christmass they would have a merry meeting, and then the covenant between them should be subscribed. The next day she was more particularly enquired of concerning her guilt respecting the crime she was accused with. She then acknowledged, that though when Mr. Haines began to read what he had taken down in writing, her rage was such that she could have torn him in pieces, and was as resolved as might be to deny her guilt (as she had done before), yet after he had read awhile, she was (to use her own expression) as if her flesh had been pulled from her bones, and so could not deny any longer : she likewise declared, that the devil first appeared to her in the form of a deer or fawn, skipping about her, wherewith she was not much affrighted, and that by degrees he became very familiar, and at last would talk with her; moreover she said that the devil had frequently the carnal knowledge of her body; and that the witches had meetings at a place not far from her house; and that some appeared in one shape, and others in another; and one came flying amongst them in the shape of a crow. Upon this confession, with other concurrent evidence, the woman was executed; so likewise was her husband, though he did not acknowledge himself guilty. Other person accused in the discourse made their escape. Thus doth the devil use to serve his clients. After the suspected witches were either executed or fled, Ann Cole was restored to health, and has continued well for many years, approving herself a serious Christian.

There were some that had a mind to try whether the stories of witches not being able to sink under water were true ; and accordingly a man and woman, mentioned in Ann Cole's Dutch-toned discourse, had their hands and feet tyed, and so were cast into the water, and they both apparently swam after the manner of a buoy, part under, part above the water. A by-stander, imagining that any person bound in that posture would be so borne up, offered himself for trial ; but being in the like matter gently laid on the water, he immediately sunk right down. This was no legal evidence against the suspected persons, nor were they proceeded against on any such account ; however, doubting that an halter would choak them, though the waters would not, they very fairly took their flight, not having been seen in that part of the world since. Whether this experiment were lawful, or rather superstitious and magical, we shall ($\sigma\nu\nu$ $\theta\epsilon\omega$) enquire afterwards.

Another thing which caused a noise in the countrey, and wherein Satan had undoubtedly a great influence, was that which hapned at Groton. There was a maid in that town (one Elizabeth Knap) who in the moneth of October, anno 1671, was taken after a very strange manner, sometimes weeping, sometimes laughing, sometimes roaring hideously, with violent motions and agitations of her body, crying out "Money, money," etc. In November following, her tongue for many hours together was draw like a semicircle up to the roof of her mouth, not to be removed, though some tried with their fingers

7*a*

to do it. Six men were scarce able to hold her in some of her fits, but she would skip about the house yelling and looking with a most frightful aspect. December 17 : Her tongue was drawn out of her mouth to an extraordinary length ; and now a dæmon began manifestly to speak in her. Many words were uttered wherein are labial letters, without any motion of her lips, which was a clear demonstration that the voice was not her own. Sometimes words were spoken seeming to proceed out of her throat, when her mouth was shut : sometimes with her mouth wide open, without the use of any of the organs of speech. The things then uttered by the devil were chiefly railings and revilings of Mr. Willard (who was at that time a worthy and faithful pastor to the church in Groton). Also the dæmon belched forth most horrid and nefandous blasphemies, exalting himself above the Most High. After this she was taken speechless for some time. One thing more is worthy of remark concerning this miserable creature. She cried out in some of her fits, that a woman (one of her neighbours) appeared to her, and was the cause of her affliction. The person thus accused was a very sincere, holy woman, who did hereupon, with the advice of friends, visit the poor wretch ; and though she was in one of her fits, having her eyes shut, when the innocent person impeached by her came in, yet could she (so powerful were Satans operations upon her) declare who was there, and could tell the touch of that woman from any ones else. But the gracious party, thus accused and abused by a malicious devil, prayed earnestly with and for the possessed creature ; after which she confessed that Satan had deluded her, making her believe evil of her good neighbour without any cause.

Nor did she after that complain of any apparition or disturbance from such an one. Yea, she said, that the devil had himself, in the likeness and shape of divers, tormented her, and then told her it was not he but they that did it.

As there have been several persons vexed with evil spirits, so divers houses have been wofully haunted by them. In the year 1679, the house of William Morse, in Newberry in New-England, was strangely disquieted by a dæmon. After those troubles began, he did, by the advice of friends, write down the particulars of those unusual accidents. And the account which he giveth thereof is as followeth :—

On December 3, in the night time, he and his wife heard a noise upon the roof of their house, as if sticks and stones had been thrown against it with great violence; whereupon he rose out of his bed, but could see nothing. Locking the doors fast, he returned to bed again. About midnight they heard an hog making a great noise in the house, so that the man rose again, and found a great hog in the house; the door being shut, but upon the opening of the door it ran out.

On December 8, in the morning, there were five great stones and bricks by an invisible hand thrown in at the west end of the house while the mans wife was making the bed; the bedstead was lifted up from the floor, and the bedstaff flung out of the window, and a cat was hurled at her; a long staff danced up and down the chimney; a burnt brick, and a piece of a weather-board, were thrown in at the window. The man at his going to bed, put out his lamp, but in the morning found that the saveall of it was taken away, and yet it was unaccountably brought into its former place. On the same day the long staff, but now spoken of, was hang'd up by a line, and swung to and fro; the man's wife laid it in the fire, but she could not hold it there, inasmuch as it would forcibly fly out; yet after much ado, with joynt strength they made it to burn. A shingle flew from the window, though no body near it; many sticks came in at the same place, only one of these was so scragged that it could enter the hole but a little way, whereupon the man pusht it out; a great rail likewise was thrust in at the window, so as to break the glass.

At another time an iron crook that was hanged on a nail, violently flew up and down; also a chair flew about, and at last lighted on the table where victuals stood ready for them to eat, and was likely to spoil all, only by a nimble catching they saved some of their meal with the loss of the rest and the overturning of their table.

People were sometimes barricado'd out of doors, when as yet there was nobody to do it; and a chest was removed from place to place, no hand touching it. Their keys being tied together, one was taken from the rest, and the remaining two would fly about making a loud noise by knocking against each other. But the greatest part of this devils feats were his mischievous ones, wherein indeed he was sometimes antick enough too, and therein the chief sufferers were, the man and his wife, and his grand-son. The man especially had his share in these diabolical molestations. For one while they could not eat their suppers quietly, but had the ashes on the hearth before their eyes thrown into their victuals, yea, and upon their heads and clothes, insomuch that they were forced up into their chamber, and yet they had no rest there; for one of the man's shoes being left below, it was filled with ashes and coals, and thrown up after them. Their light was beaten out, and, they being laid in their bed with their little boy between them, a great stone (from the floor of the loft) weighing above three pounds was thrown upon the man's stomach, and he turning it down upon the floor, it was once more thrown upon him. A box and a board were likewise thrown upon them all; and a bag of hops was taken out of their chest, therewith they were beaten, till some of the hops were scattered on the floor, where the bag was then laid and left.

In another evening, when they sat by the fire, the ashes were so whirled at them, that they could neither eat their meat nor endure the house. A peel struck the man in the face. An apron hanging by the fire was flung upon it, and singed before they could snatch it off. The man being at prayer with his family, a beesom gave him a blow on his head behind, and fell down before his face.

On another day, when they were winnowing of barley, some hard dirt was thrown in, hitting the man on the head, and both the man and his wife on the back; and when they had made themselves clean, they essayed to fill their half-bushel; but the foul corn was in spite of them often cast in amongst the clean, and the man, being divers times thus abused, was forced to give over what he was about.

On January 23 (in particular), the man had an iron pin twice thrown at him, and his inkhorn was taken away from him while he was writing; and when by all his seeking it he could not find it, at last he saw it drop out of the air, down by the fire. A piece of leather was twice thrown at him; and a shoe was laid upon his shoulder, which he catching at, was suddenly rapt from him. An handful of ashes was thrown at his face, and upon his clothes; and the shoe was then clapt upon his head, and upon it he clapt his hand, holding it so fast, that somewhat unseen pulled him with it backward on the floor.

On the next day at night, as they were going to bed, a lost ladder was thrown against the door, and their light put out; and when the man was a bed, he was beaten with an heavy pair of leather breeches, and pull'd by the hair of his head and beard, pinched and scratched, and his bed-board was taken away from him. Yet more: in the next night, when the man was likewise a bed, his bed-board did rise out of its place, notwithstanding his putting forth all his strength to keep it in; one of his awls was brought out of the next room into his bed, and did prick him; the clothes wherewith he hoped to save his head from blows, were violently pluckt from thence. Within a night or two after, the man and his wife received both of them a blow upon their heads, but it was so dark that they could not see the stone which gave it. The man had his cap pulled off from his head while he sat by the fire.

The night following they went to bed undressed, because of their late disturbances, and the man, wife, boy, presently felt themselves pricked, and upon search, found in the bed a bodkin, a knitting-needle, and two sticks picked at both ends; he received also a great blow, as on his thigh, so on his face, which fetched blood; and while he was writing, a candlestick was twice thrown at him; and a great piece of bark fiercely smote him; and a pail of water turned up without hands.

On the 28th of the mentioned moneth, frozen clods of

cow-dung were divers times thrown at the man out of the house in which they were. His wife went to milk the cow, and received a blow on her head; and sitting down at her milking work, had cow-dung divers times thrown into her pail. The man tried to save the milk, by holding a piggin side-wayes under the cowes belly; but the dung would in for all, and the milk was only made fit for hogs. On that night, ashes were thrown into the porridge which they had made ready for their supper, so as that they could not eat it; ashes were likewise often thrown into the man's eyes as he sat by the fire; and an iron hammer flying at him, gave him a great blow on his back. The man's wife going into the cellar for beer, a great iron peel flew and fell after her through the trap-door of the cellar; and going afterwards on the same errand to the same place, the door shut down upon her, and the table came and lay upon the door, and the man was forced to remove it e'er his wife could be released from where she was. On the following day, while he was writing, a dish went out of its place, leapt into the pale, and cast water upon the man, his paper, his table, and disappointed his procedure in what he was about; his cap jumpt off from his head, and on again, and the pot-lid leapt off from the pot into the kettle on the fire.

February 2. While he and his boy were eating of cheese, the pieces which he cut were wrested from them, but they were afterwards found upon the table, under an apron and a pair of breeches; and also from the fire arose little sticks and ashes, which flying upon the man and his boy, brought them into an uncomfortable pickle. But as for the boy, which the last passage spoke of, there remains much to be said concerning him and a principal sufferer in these afflictions: for on the 18th of December, he sitting by his grandfather, was hurried into great motions, and the man thereupon took him, and made him stand between his legs; but the chair danced up and down, and had like to have cast both man and boy into the fire; and the child was afterwards flung about in such a manner, as that they feared that his brains would have been beaten out; and in the evening he was tossed as afore, and the man tried the project of holding him, but ineffectually. The lad was soon put to bed, and they presently heard an huge noise, and demanded what was the matter? and he answered, that his bedstead leaped up and down; and they (*i.e.* the man and his wife) went up, and at first found all quiet, but before they had been there long, they saw the board by his bed trembling by him, and the bed-clothes flying off him; the latter they laid on immediately, but they were no sooner on than off; so they took him out of his bed for quietness.

December 29. The boy was violently thrown to and fro, only they carried him to the house of a doctor in the town, and there he was free from disturbances; but returning home at night, his former trouble began, and the man taking him by the hand, they were both of them almost tript into the fire. They put him to bed and he was attended with the same iterated loss of his clothes, shaking off his bed-board, and noises that he had in his last conflict; they took him up, designing to sit by the fire, but the doors clattered, and the chair was thrown at him; wherefore they carried him to the doctors house, and so for that night all was well. The next morning he came home quiet; but as they were doing somewhat, he cried out that he was prickt on the back; they looked, and found a three-tin'd fork sticking strangely there; which being carried to the doctors house, not only the doctor himself said that it was his, but also the doctors servant affirmed it was seen at home after the boy was gone. The boys vexations continuing, they left him at the doctors, where he remained well till awhile after, and then he complained he was pricked; they looked and found an iron spindle sticking below his back: he complained he was pricked still; they looked, and found there a long iron, a bowl of a spoon, and a piece of a pansheard. They lay down by him on the bed, with the light burning, but he was twice thrown from them, and the second time thrown quite under the bed. In the morning the bed was tossed about, with such a creaking noise as was heard to the neighbours. In the afternoon their knives were, one after another, brought, and put into his back, but pulled out by the spectators; only one knife, which was missing, seemed to the standers by to come out of his mouth. He was bidden to read; his book was taken and thrown about several times, at last hitting the boys grandmother on the head. Another time he was thrust out of his chair, and rolled up and down, with outcries that all things were on fire; yea, he was three times very dangerously thrown into the fire, and preserved by his friends with much ado. The boy also made, for a long time together, a noise like a dog, and like an hen with her chickens, and could not speak rationally.

Particularly, on December 26, he barked like a dog, and clock't like an hen; and after long distraining to speak, said, "There's Powel, I am pinched." His tongue likewise hung out of his mouth, so that it could by no means be forced in till his fit was over, and then he said 'twas forced out by Powel. He and the house also after this had rest till the 9th of January; at which time the child, because of his intolerable ravings, lying between the man and his wife, was pulled out of bed, and knockt vehemently against the bedstead boards, in a manner very perillous and amazing. In the day-time he was carried away beyond all possibility of their finding him. His grandmother at last saw him creeping on one side, and drag'd him in, where he lay miserable lame; but recovering his speech, he said, that he was carried above the doctors house, and that Powel carried him: and that the said Powel had him into the barn, throwing him against the cart-wheel there, and then thrusting him out at an hole; and accordingly they found some of the remainders of the threshed barley, which was on the barn-floor, hanging to his clothes.

At another time he fell into a swoon; they forced somewhat refreshing into his mouth, and it was turned out as fast as they put it in; e'er long he came to himself, and expressed some willingness to eat, but the meat would forcibly fly out of his mouth; and when he was able to speak, he said Powel would not let him eat. Having found the boy to be best at a neighbours house, the man carried him to his daughters, three miles from his own. The boy was growing antick as he was on the journey, but before the end of it he made a grievous hollowing; and when he lighted, he threw a great stone at a maid in the house, and fell on eating of ashes. Being at home afterwards, they had rest awhile: but on the 19th of January, in the morning he swooned, and coming to himself, he roared terribly, and did eat ashes, sticks, rug-yarn. The morning following, there was such a racket with the boy that the man and his wife took him to bed to them : a bed-staff was thereupon thrown at them, and a chamber-pot with its contents was thrown upon them, and they were severely pinched. The man being about to rise, his clothes were divers times pulled from them, himself thrust out of his bed, and his pillow thrown after him. The lad also would have his clothes plucked off from him in these winter nights, and was wofully dogg'd with such fruits of devilish spite, till it pleased God to shorten the chain of the wicked dæmon.

All this while the devil did not use to appear in any visible shape, only they would think they had hold of the hand that sometimes scratched them ; but it would give them the slip. And once the man was discernably beaten by a fist, and an hand got hold of his wrist, which he saw but could not catch ; and the likeness of a blackmore child did appear from under the rugg and blanket, where the man lay, and it would rise up, fall down, nod, and slip under the clothes, when they endeavoured to clasp it, never speaking anything.

Neither were there many words spoken by Satan all this time ; only once, having put out their light, they heard a scraping on the boards, and then a piping and drumming on them, which was followed with a voice, singing, "Revenge ! Revenge ! Sweet is revenge !" And they being well terrified with it, called upon God : the issue of which was, that suddenly, with a mournful note, there were six times over uttered such expressions as, " Alas ! me knock no more ! me knock no more !" and now all ceased.

The man does, moreover, affirm that a seaman (being a mate of a ship) coming often to visit him told him, that they wronged his wife who suspected her to be guilty of witchcraft; and that the boy (his grandchild) was the cause of this trouble; and that if he would let him have the boy one day, he would warrant him his house should be no more troubled as it had been. To which motion he consented. The mate came the next day betimes, and the boy was with him until night; since which time his house, he saith, has not been molested with evil spirits.

Thus far is the relation concerning the dæmon at William Morse his house in Newberry. The true reason of these strange disturbances is as yet not certainly known: some (as has been hinted) did suspect Morse's wife to be guilty of witchcraft.

One of the neighbours took apples, which were brought out of that house, and put them into the fire; upon which, they say, their houses were much disturbed. Another of the neighbours caused an horse-shoe to be nailed before the doors; and as long as it remained so, they could not perswade the suspected person to go into the house; but when the horse-shoe was gone, she presently visited them. I shall not here inlarge upon the vanity and superstition of those experiments, reserving that for another place; all that I shall say at present is, that the dæmons, whom the blind Gentiles of old worshipped, told their servants, that such things as these would very much affect them; yea, and that certain characters, signs, and charms, would render their power ineffectual; and accordingly they would become subject, when their own directions were obeyed. It is sport to the devils when they see silly men thus deluded and made fools of by them. Others were apt to think that a seaman, by some suspected to be a conjuror, set the devil on work thus to disquiet Morse' family ; or, it may be, some other thing, as yet kept hid in the secrets of Providence, might be the true original of all this trouble.

A disturbance not much unlike to this hapned above twenty years ago, at an house in Tedworth, in the county of Wilts, in England, which was by wise men judged to proceed from conjuration.

" Mr. Mompesson of Tedworth being in March, 1661, at Ludgershall, and hearing a drum beat there, he demanded of the bailiff of the town what it meant ; who told him, they had for some dayes been troubled with an idle drummer, pretending authority and a pass under the hands of some gentlemen. Mr. Mompesson reading his pass, and knowing the hands of those gentlemen whose names were pretended to be subscribed, discovered the cheat, and commanded the vagrant to put off his drum, and ordered a constable to secure him ; but not long after he got clear of the constable. In April following, Mr. Mompesson's house was much disturbed with knockings and with drummings ; for an hour together a dæmon would beat Round-heads and Cuckolds, the tattoo and several other points of war, as well as any drummer. On November 5, the dæmon made a great noise in the house, and caused some boards therein to move to and fro in the day time, when there was an whole room full of people present. At his departure, he left behind him a sulphurous smell, which was very offensive. The next night, chairs walked up and down the room ; the childrens shoes were hurled over their heads. The minister of the town being there, a bedstaff was thrown at him, and hit him on the leg, but without the least hurt. In the latter end of December, 1662, they heard a noise like the jingling of money, the occasion of which was thought to be, some words spoken the night before by one in the family, who said that fairies used to leave money behind them, and they wished it might be so now. In January, lights were seen in the house, which seemed blue and glimmering, and caused a great stiffness in the eyes of them that saw them. One in the room (by what authority I cannot tell) said 'Satan, if the drummer set thee a work, give three knocks and no more;' which was done accordingly. Once, when it was very sharp severe weather, the room was suddenly filled with a noisome smell, and was very hot, though without fire. This dæmon would play some nasty and many ludicrous foolish tricks. It would empty chamber-pots into the beds; and fill porringers with ashes. Sometimes it would not suffer any light to be in the room, but would carry them away up the chimney. Mr. Mompesson coming one morning into his stable, found his horse on the ground, having one of his hinder legs in his mouth, and so fastened there that it was difficult for several men with a leaver to get it out. A smith, lodging in the house, heard a noise in the room as if one had been shoeing an horse, and somewhat come as it were with a pincers snipping at the smith's nose, most part of the night. The drummer was under vehement suspicion for a conjuror. He was condemned to transportation. All the time of his restraint and absence, the house was quiet."—See Mr. Glanvil's *Collection of Modern Relations,* p. 71, &c.

But I proceed to give an account of some other things lately hapning in New-England, which were undoubtedly præternatural, and not without diabolical operation. The last year did afford several instances, not unlike unto those which have been mentioned. For then Nicholas Desborough, of Hartford in New-England, was strangely molested by stones, pieces of earth, cobs of Indian corn, &c., falling upon and about him, which sometimes came in through the door, sometimes through the window, sometimes down the chimney; at other times they seemed to fall from the floor of the chamber, which yet was very close; sometimes he met with them in his shop, the yard the barn, and in the field at work. In the house, such things hapned frequently, not only in the night but in the day time, if the man himself was at home, but never when his wife was at home alone. There was no great violence in the motion, though several persons of the family, and others also, were struck with the things that were thrown by an invisible hand, yet they were not hurt thereby. Only the man himself had once his arm somewhat pained by a blow given him; and at another time, blood was drawn from one of his legs by a scratch given it. This molestation began soon after a controversie arose between Desborough and another person, about a chest of clothes which the other said that Desborough did unrighteously retain: and so it continued for some moneths (though with several intermissions), in the latter end of the last year, when also the man's barn was burned with the corn in it; but by what means it came to pass is not known. Not long after, some to whom the matter was referred, ordered Desborough to restore the clothes to the person who complained of wrong; since which he hath not been troubled as before. Some of the stones hurled were of considerable bigness; one of them weighed four pounds,

8

but generally the stones were not great, but very small ones.   One time a piece of clay came down the chimney, falling on the table which stood at some distance from the chimney.   The people of the house threw it on the hearth, where it lay a considerable time : they went to their supper, the piece of clay was lifted up by an invisible hand, and fell upon the table; taking it up they found it hot, having lain so long before the fire, as to cause it to be hot.

Another providence, no less remarkable than this last mentioned, hapned at Portsmouth in New-England, about the same time: concerning which I have received the following account from a worthy hand.

"On June 11, 1682, being the Lords Day, at night showers of stones were thrown both against the sides and roof of the house of George Walton: some of the people went abroad, found the gate at some distance from the house wrung off the hinges, and stones came thick about them, sometimes falling down by them, sometimes touching them without any hurt done to them; though they seemed to come with great force, yet did no more but softly touch them; stones flying about the room, the doors being shut; the glass windows shattered to pieces by stones that seemed to come not from without but within, the lead of the glass casements, window-bars, &c. being driven forcibly outwards, and so standing bent.   While the secretary was walking in the room, a great hammer came brushing along against the chamber floor that was over his head and fell down by him.   A candlestick beaten off the table.   They took up nine of the stones and marked them, and laid them on the table, some of them being as hot as if they came out of the fire; but some of those mark't stones were found flying about again. In this manner, about four hours space that night. The secretary then went to bed, but a stone came and broke up his chamber-door; being put to (not lockt), a brick was sent upon the like errand. The abovesaid stone the secretary lockt up in his chamber, but it was fetched out, and carried with great noise into the next chamber. The spit was carried up chimney, and came down with the point forward, and stuck in the back-log, and being removed by one of the company to one side of the chimney, was by an unseen hand thrown out at window. This trade was driven on the next day, and so from day to day; now and then there would be some intermission, and then to it again. The stones were most frequent where the master of the house was, whether in the field or barn, &c. A black cat was seen once while the stones came, and was shot at, but she was too nimble for them. Some of the family say, that they once saw the appearance of an hand put forth at the hall window, throwing stones towards the entry, though there was no body in the hall the while: sometimes a dismal hollow whistling would be heard; sometimes the noise of the trotting of an horse, and snorting, but nothing seen. The man went up the great bay in his boat to a farm he had there, and while haling wood or timber to the boat, he was disturbed by the stones as before at home. He carried a stirrup-iron from the house down to the boat, and there left it; but while he was going up to the house, the iron came jingling after him through the woods, and returned to the house, and so again, and at last went away, and was heard of no more. Their anchor leaped overboard several times as they were going home, and stopt the boat. A cheese hath been

8a

taken out of the press and crumbled all over the floor. A piece of iron with which they weighed up the cheese-press, stuck into the wall, and a kittle hung up thereon. Several cocks of English hay, mowed near the house, were taken and hung upon trees; and some made into small whisps, and put all up and down the kitchen, *cum multis aliis,* &c. After this manner have they been treated ever since at times; it were endless to particularize. Of late, they thought the bitterness of death had been past, being quiet for sundry dayes and nights: but last week were some returnings again; and this week (Aug. 2, 1682) as bad or worse than ever. The man is sorely hurt with some of the stones that came on him, and like to feel the effects of them for many dayes." Thus far is that relation.

I am moreover informed, that the dæmon was quiet all the last winter, but in the spring he began to play some ludicrous tricks, carrying away some axes that were locked up safe. This last summer he has not made such disturbances as formerly; but of this no more at present.

There have been strange and true reports concerning

a woman now living near the Salmon Falls in Barwick (formerly called Kittery), unto whom evil spirits have sometimes visibly appeared; and she has sometimes been sorely tormented by invisible hands: concerning all which an intelligent person has sent me the following narrative.

A brief Narrative of sundry Apparitions of Satan unto, and Assaults at sundry times and places upon, the person of Mary, the wife of Antonio Hortado, dwelling near the Salmon Falls. Taken from her own mouth, Aug. 13, 1683.

"In June, 1682 (the day forgotten), at evening, the

said Mary heard a voice at the door of her dwelling, saying, "What do you here ?" About an hour after, standing at the door of her house, she had a blow on her eye that settled her head near to the door-post ; and two or three dayes after, a stone, as she judged about half a pound or a pound weight, was thrown along the house within into the chimney, and going to take it up it was gone ; all the family was in the house, and no hand appearing which might be instrumental in throwing the stone. About two hours after, a frying-pan then hanging in the chimney was heard to ring so loud, that not only those in the house heard it, but others also that lived on the other side of the river near an hundred rods distant or more. Whereupon the said Mary and her husband going in a cannoo over the river, they saw like the head of a man new-shorn, and the tail of a white cat, about two or three foot distance from each other, swimming over before the cannoo, but no body appeared to joyn head and tail together ; and they returning over the river in less than an hours time, the said apparition followed their cannoo back again, but disappeared at landing. A day or two after, the said Mary was stricken on her head (as she judged) with a stone, which caused a swelling and much soreness on her head, being then in the yard by her house; and she presently entring into her house, was bitten on both arms black and blue, and one of her breasts scratched ; the impressions of the teeth being like mans teeth were plainly seen by many. Whereupon deserting their house to sojourn at a neighbours on the other side of the river, there appeared to said Mary in the house of her sojourning, a woman clothed with a green safeguard, a short blue cloak, and a white cap, making a profer to strike her with a fire-brand, but struck her not. The day following, the same shape appeared to her, but now arrayed with a grey gown, white apron, and white head-clothes, in appearance laughing several times, but no voice heard. Since when, said Mary has been freed from those Satanical molestations.

" But the said Antonio being returned in March last with his family, to dwell again in his own house, and on his entrance there, hearing the noise of a man walking in his chamber, and seeing the boards buckle under his feet as he walked, though no man to be seen in the chamber (for they went on purpose to look), he returned with his family to dwell on the other side of the river; yet planting his ground, though he forsook his house, he hath had five rods of good log-fence thrown down at once; the feeting of neat cattle plainly to be seen almost between every row of corn in the field, yet no cattle seen there, nor any damage done to his corn, not so much as any of the leaves of the corn cropt." Thus far is that narrative.

I am further informed, that some (who should have been wiser) advised the poor woman to stick the house round with bayes, as an effectual preservative against the power of evil spirits. This counsel was followed; and as long as the bayes continued green, she had quiet; but when they began to wither, they were all by an unseen hand carried away, and the woman again tormented.

It is observable, that at the same time three houses in three several towns should be molested by dæmons, as has now been related.

CHAPTER VI.

THAT THERE ARE DÆMONS AND POSSESSED PERSONS.

Signs of such. Some mad men are really possessed, notwithstanding many fabulous stories about witchcrafts. That there are witches proved by three arguments. That houses are sometimes troubled by evil spirits. Witchcraft often the cause of it. Sometimes by the devil without witchcraft. Ordered by Providence as punishment for sin. The disturbance in Waltons house further considered, with a parallel story That the things related in the preceding chapter were undoubtedly præternatural and diabolical.

THE Sadduces of these dayes being like unto Avicenna, and Averroes, and other atheistical philosophers in former times, say that there are no spirits, and that all stories concerning them are either fabulous or to be ascribed unto natural causes. Amongst many others, the learned Voetius (*in Disp. de operationibus Dæmonum*) has sufficiently refuted them. And as the experience of other ages and places of the world, so the things which Divine Providence hath permitted and ordered to come to pass amongst ourselves, if the Scriptures were silent, make it manifest beyond all contradiction, that there are devils infesting this lower world. Most true it is, that Satan and all his wicked angels are limited by the providence of God, so as that they cannot hurt any man or creature, much less any servant of his, without a commission from him, whose kingdom is over all. It is a memorable passage, which Chytræus relateth concerning Luther, that when he was sought after by his popish and implacable enemies (being then hid by the Duke of Saxony), they consulted with magicians that so they might find where Luther absconded, but the wizzards confessed they could not discover him. Undoubtedly the devils knew where Luther hid himself; only God would not suffer them to reveal it. Nevertheless the Lord doth, for wise and holy ends, sometimes lengthen the chain which the infernal lions are bound fast in. And as there are many tremendous instances confirming the truth hereof, so that of Satan's taking bodily possession of men is none of the least. Sometimes indeed it is very hard to discern between natural diseases and satanical possessions; so as that persons really possessed have been thought to be only molested with some natural disease, without any special finger of the evil spirit therein. Fernelius (*de Abditis Rerum Causis*, lib. 2, cap. 16) speaketh of a certain young gentleman that was taken with strange convulsions, which did surprize him at least ten times in a day. In his fits he had the use of his speech and reason free; otherwise his disease would have been judged no other than an ordinary epilepsy. Much means was used by skilful physitians for his relief, but without success for three moneths together; when all on a sudden, a dæmon began to speak out of the miserable patient; and that with not only Latin but Greek sentences, which the afflicted party himself had no knowledge of; and the dæmon discovered many secrets both of the physitians and of other persons that attended, deriding them for their vain attempts to cure a man whom he had the possession of. There are sundry authors (in special Balduinus in his cases of conscience, and Darrel in his history of the *Seven Possessed Persons in Lancashire*) who have endeavoured to describe and characterise possessed persons. And such particulars as these following are by them mentioned as signs of possession.

1. If the party concerned shall reveal secret things, either past or future, which without supernatural assistance could not be known, it argueth possession.

2. If he does speak with strange languages, or discover skill in arts and sciences never learned by him.

3. If he can bear burthens, and do things which are beyond humane strength.

4. Uttering words without making use of the organs of speech, when persons shall be heard speaking, and yet neither their lips nor tongues have any motion, 'tis a sign that an evil spirit speaketh in them.

5. When the body is become inflexible.

6. When the belly is on a sudden puft up, and instantly flat again.

These are thought to be certain arguments of an energumenical person. Some other signs are mentioned by Thyræus (*De Obsessis*, part 2, cap. 25, 26).

There are who conceive (and that as they suppose upon scripture grounds) that men may possibly be dæmoniacal, when none of those mentioned particulars can be affirmed of them. The excellently learned and judicious Mr. Mede is of opinion, that the dæmoniacks whom we read so frequently of in the New Testament, were the same with epilepticks, lunaticks, and mad men. The Turks at this day have their mad men in great veneration, supposing them to be acted by a spirit; but they (in that being themselves mad) take it to be a good when as 'tis an evil spirit that does operate in such persons. And that the Jews of old did look upon maniacks to be possessed with an evil spirit, is evident from that expression of theirs, John x, 20: "He hath a devil and is mad." Moreover, we read of one, Mat. xvii, 15, that was lunatick, and did oft fall into the fire, and oft into the water. Now that this lunatick person was a dæmoniack is clear from v. 18, where it is said that Jesus rebuked the devil, and he departed out of him. And of the same person 'tis said, in Luke ix, 39: "A spirit taketh him and teareth him." So Beza and Heinsius, in Mat. viii, 16; and xvii, 15. It has been commonly said that in Christs time more persons were possessed with evil spirits than ever was known before or since; but if that were so, the Jews, and probably some historians, would have noted it as a thing strange and extraordinary; whenas we read of no such observation to be made on those times. And saith Mr. Mede (in his Discourse on John x, 20): "If those possessed persons were not such as we now adayes conceive to be no other than mad men, the world must be supposed to be well rid of devils, which for my part I believe it is not." There is in special, a sort of melancholy madness, which is called *lycanthropia* or *lupina insania, h. e.,* when men imagine themselves to be turned into wolves or other beasts. Hippocrates relates concerning the daughters of king Prætus, that they thought themselves kine. Wierus (*de Præstigiis Dæmonum,* l. iii. c. 21) speaketh of one in Padua, that would not believe to the contrary but that he was a wolf; and of a Spaniard, who thought himself a bear. Euwichius (and from him

Horstius) writeth of a man that was found in a barn under the hay, howling and saying he was a wolf. The foolish rusticks, who surprized him, began to flay him, that so they might see if he had not hair growing on the inside of his skin. Forestus has many instances to this purpose. Heurnius saith, that it is a disease frequent in Bohemia and Hungaria. No doubt but this disease gave occasion to Pliny's assertion, that some men in his time were turned into wolves, and from wolves into men again. Hence was Ovid's fable of Lycaon, and the tale of Pausanias being ten years a wolf, and then a man again. He that would see more instances, may read Austin, *de Civ. Dei.* l. xviii, c. 5 ; Burton of *Melancholly,* page 9. They that are subject unto this malady, for the most part lye hid all the day, and go abroad in the night, barking and howling at graves and in desarts. We may suppose that Nebuchadnezzar was troubled with this disease. And that such persons are molested with a dæmon is evident from Luke viii, 27, with Mark v, 3, 4. The possessed person there spoken of was Lycanthropos.

There are that acknowledge the existence of spirits, and that the bodies of men are sometimes really possessed thereby, who, nevertheless, will not believe there are any such woful creatures *in rerum naturâ* as witches, or persons confederate with the devil. I have read of a famous wizard, whose name was William de Lure, that after he had laboured much in opposing their opinion, who think that there are men on earth joyned in an explicit confederacy with the fiends of hell, was himself convicted and condemned for that crime which he designed to make the world believe that no man was or could be guilty of.

I shall not suspect all those as guilty of witchcraft, nor yet of heresie, who call the received opinion about witches into question.   There are four or five English writers, viz. Mr. Scot, Ady, and of late, Wagstaff and Webster, and another anonymous author, who do, with great vehemence, affirm, that never any did maintain that familiarity with the evil spirits which is commonly believed.   Wierus (otherwise a judicious author) conceiveth that all those things supposed to be done by witches are done by the evil spirits themselves, without any confederates.   But he is sufficiently refuted by Bindsfieldius, Bodinus, Sennertus, and others.   True it is, that many things have been looked upon as proceeding from witchcraft when it has not been so.   The sympathies and antipathies of nature have some- times been esteemed the effects of witchcraft.   A sympa- thetical powder, made without any magical ceremonies, has done strange things, so as that the artist which used it has upon that account been suspected of witchcraft.   A man may easily, by such natural magick as is described by Porta, and by Weckerus, *De Secretis,* make the ignorant believe he is a wizard.   It is also true, that the world is full of fabulous stories concerning some kind of familiari- ties with the devil, and things done by his help, which are beyond the powers of creatures to accomplish.   What fables are there concerning *incubi* and *succubæ,* and of men begotten by dæmons!   No doubt but the devil may de- delude the fancy, that one of his vassals shall think (as the witch at Hartford did) that he has carnal and cursed com- munion with them beyond what is real.   Nor is it impos- sible for him to assume a dead body, or to form a lifeless one out of the elements, and therewith to make his witches become guilty of sodomy.   Austin saith, they are impudent who deny this. But to imagine that spirits shall really generate bodies is irrational. I am not ignorant that there have been men in the world (more than one or two) pretended to be thus begotten and born. Thus doth Niderius affirm concerning all the old inhabitants of the isle of Cyprus. The like has been reported concerning Arcturus, and concerning our British Merlin. Yea, the Gentiles believed that Homer, Æneas, Hercules, and others, were begotten by dæmons, whom, thereupon, they esteemed as *semidei*. And Olympias, the mother of Alexander the Great, supposed herself to be with child by Jupiter Hammon. When her husband, King Philip of Macedon, was absent from her, Nectanebus (an Egyptian prince, and a great magician) sent her word that Jupiter would embrace her, and that he would come to her such a night in the form of a dragon; at the time appointed, Nectanebus himself, by his magical impostures, made Olympias believe that a dragon was in the room, and so did himself do that which the deluded queen thought Jupiter had done. I doubt not but that Merlin and others, imagined to come into the world not in the usual way, were the sons of dæmons, just as Alexander was. It has been a received maxim, that though the devil may by his art produce insects and vermin (to the generation whereof a seminal vertue is not alwayes necessary), yet he cannot bring forth a *perfect animal*. How then is it consistent with reason, that he should produce a real man, who is of all animals the most perfect and noble? It is also extreamly fabulous that witches can transform themselves or others into another sort of creatures, *e. g.* into horses, wolves, cats, mice, &c. *Carminibus Circe socios mutavit Ulyssis.* A blind heathenish phansie: and yet stories of this nature

have been generally believed; and I have not without
wonderment seen grave authors relating them, as if the
things had been really so.   But it is beyond the power of
all the devils in hell to cause such a transformation : they
can no more do it than they can be the authors of a true
miracle. (See Horstius, *Inst. Med.* disp. 3, exercit. 9,
quest 9.) Though I deny not but that the devil may so
impose upon the imagination of witches, as to make them
believe that they are transmuted into beasts. Sennertus
(in *Pract. Med.* l. vi, part 9, cap. 5) reports that a noble
person, and one worthy of credit, gave him an account of
a strange passage to this purpose, which himself was particularly acquainted with.   The story is this :—

A certain woman being in prison on suspicion for
witchcraft, pretending to be able to turn herself into a
wolf, the magistrate before whom she was brought, promised her, that she should not be put to death, in case
she would then in his presence so transform herself ; which
she readily consented unto.   Accordingly she anointed
her head, neck, and arm-pits ; immediately upon which
she fell into a most profound sleep for three hours ; after
which she suddenly rose up, declaring that she had been
turned into a wolf, and been at a place some miles distant,
and there killed first a sheep and then a cow.   The
magistrate presently sent to the place, and found that
first a sheep, and then a cow, had there been killed.

Wierus and Baptista Porta have divers stories to the
same purpose.   It is then evident, that the devil himself
did that mischief ; and in the meantime the witches, who
were cast into so profound a sleep by him as they could
not by any noises or blows be awakened, had their phansies

imposed upon by dreams and delusions according to the pleasure of their master Satan. It must, moreover, be sadly confessed, that many innocent persons have been put to death under the notion of witchcraft, whereby much innocent blood hath been shed ; especiallly it hath been so in Popish times and places. Superstitious and magical wayes of trying witches have been a bloody cause of those murders. Sometimes persons have been tried for witchcraft by hot, sometimes by cold water (of which more in the eighth chapter of this Essay), sometimes by pricking them, sometimes by sticking awls under their seats, sometimes by their ability, or otherwise, to repeat the Lords Prayer.

An Irish witch, which was tried at Youghall, Sept. 11, 1661, being by the court put upon repeating the fifth petition, alwayes left out the words, "Forgive us our trespasses." Another witch, tried at Taunton, 1663, could not repeat the last petition; but though she was directed to say it after one that repeated it distinctly, would say, "Lead us into temptation," and could never repeat it right, though she tried to do it half a score times. But Judge Archer did wisely admonish the jury, that they were not in the least measure to guide their verdict by that, since it was no legal evidence.

The author of the advertisement to Mr. Glanvil's *Relations* (p. 171) saith, that his curiosity led him to examine certain witnesses at the castle in Cambridge and that the most notorious witch of them all pleaded that she was no witch because she was able to say the Lords Prayer and the Creed ; and though she was out in repeating the Creed, she said the Lords Prayer right.

But from such considerations as those which have been mentioned, Wierus and some others, not atheists, but persons of worth, have, εξ αμετριας ανθολκης, run into an extream on the other hand, so as to question whether there were any persons really confederate with the infernal spirits. Nevertheless, that there have been such the folfowing arguments do manifest.

1. The argument by many insisted on from the Scriptures is irrefragable: therein witchcrafts are forbidden. And we often read in the Scripture of metaphorical bewitchings, Nahum iii, 4; Gal. iii, 1; which similitudes are undoubtedly taken from things that have a real existence in *rerum naturâ*. Yea, the Scripture makes particular mention of many that used those cursed arts and familiarities with the devil, *e. g.* Jannes, and Jambres, Balaam, Manasseh, Simon, Elymas. Nor is the relation which the Scripture giveth of the Witch of Endor, and the reasons from thence deduced to prove the being of witches, sufficiently confuted by any of our late witch-advocates. Though (as one speaketh) some men, to elude the argument from that instance, " play more hocos-pocus tricks in the explication of that passage than the witch herself did in raising deceased Samuel." It is a poor evasion in those who think to escape the dint of this argument, by pretending that the witches and familiar spirits spoken of in the Scripture were only juglers, or men that by legerdemain would do strange feats of activity. The divine law requires that such witches should be cut off by the sword of justice; which may not be affirmed of everyone that shall, without any confederacy with the devil, play tricks of legerdemain.

2. Experience has too often made it manifest that there

are such in the world as hold a correspondence with hell.
There have bin known wizards; yea, such as have taught
others what ceremonies they are to use in maintaining
communion with devils. Trithemius his book *de Septem
Intelligentiis,* and Cornelius Agrippa's books of occult
philosophy, wherein too much of these nefandous abominations is described, are frequently in the hands of men.
Several other books there are extant which do professedly
teach the way of familiarity with dæmons; the titles
whereof, as also the names of the authors that have published them, I designedly forbear to mention, lest haply
any one into whose hands this discourse may come, should
out of wicked curiosity seek after them to the ruine of his
soul. There are famous histories of several who had their
paredri or familiar spirits, some in one likeness, some in
another, constantly attending them : thus had Apollonius
Thyanæus of old ; and of later times, Mich. Scot and
Josephus Niger. Likewise Cardanus (*de Subtilitate,* lib.
xix, p. 963) writeth, that his own father had such a familiar for thirty years together. So had Christopher Waga-
neer a familiar in the form of an ape for seven years
attending him ; so had Tolpardus, which two were at last
carried away body and soul by the devil, unto whose
service they had devoted their lives. There is also a true
(as well as a romantick) story of Faustus. The excellent
Camerarius, in his *Horæ Subsecivæ,* cent. i. cap. 70, relateth
strange things of him, which he received from those who
knew Faustus, and were eye-witnesses of his magical and
diabolical impostures. He also had a familiar devil, in
form of a monk, accompanying of him for the space of
twenty-four years. Hausdorfius and Lonicer *ad 2 præc*
p. 167, speak of Faustus. Melancthon declares that he

9

knew the man; so that Naudeus is to be convinced of vanity, in denying that ever there was such a person in the world. In a word, it is a thing known, that there have been men who would discourse in languages and reason notably about sciences which they never learned; who have revealed secrets, discovered hidden treasures, told whither stolen goods have been conveyed, and by whom; and that have caused bruit creatures, nay statues or images, to speak and give rational answers. The Jews *teraphims* oftentimes did so. *Vide* R. Sol. Jarchi *in Hos.* iii, 4; Selden *de Diis Syriis.* part i, cap. 2; Thom. *contra Gentes,* lib. iii, cap. 104. Such things as these cannot be done by the help of meer natural causes. It must needs be, then, that the practisers of them are in confederacy with Satan.

3. There have been many in the world who have, upon conviction, confessed themselves guilty of familiarity with the devil. A multitude of instances this way are mentioned by Bodinus, Codronchus, Delrio, Jacquerius, Remigius, and others. Some in this countrey have affirmed that they knew a man in another part of the world, above fifty years ago, who having an ambitious desire to be thought a wise man, whilest he was tormented with the itch of his wicked ambition, the devil came to him with promises that he should quickly be in great reputation for his wisdom, in case he would make a covenant with him; the conditions whereof were, that when men came to him for his counsel, he should labour to perswade them that there is no God, nor devil, nor heaven, nor hell; and that such a term of years being expired, the devil should have his soul. The articles were consented to: the man continuing after this to be of a very civil conversation, doing

hurt to none, but good to many; and by degrees began to have a name to be a person of extraordinary sagacity, and was sought unto far and near for counsel, his words being esteemed oracles by the vulgar. And he did according to his covenant upon all occasions secretly disseminate principles of atheism, not being suspected for a wizard. But a few weeks before the time indented with the devil was fulfilled, inexpressible horror of conscience surprized him, so that he revealed the secret transactions which had passed betwixt himself and the devil. He would sometimes, with hideous roarings, tell those that came to visit him that now he knew there was a God, and a devil, and an heaven, and an hell. So did he die a miserable spectacle of the righteous and fearful judgement of God. And every age does produce new examples of those that have by their own confession made the like cursed covenants with the prince of darkness.

In the year 1664, several who were indicted at the assizes held at Taunton in Somersetshire, confessed that they had made an explicit league with the devil; and that he did baptise pictures of wax with oyl, giving them the names of those persons they did intend mischief unto.

Anno 1678, one John Stuart, and his sister, Annibal Stuart, at the assizes held at Paysley in Scotland, confessed that they had been in confederacy with the devil; and that they had made an image of wax, calling it by the name of Sir George Maxwel, sticking pins in the sides and on the breast of it. Such an image, with pins in it, was really found in the witches houses; and upon the removal of it, the pins being taken out, Sir George had immediate ease, and recovered his health.

There is lately published (by Dr. Horneck) the *History of the Witches in Sweden;* by whose means that kingdom was fearfully plagued. Upon examination, they confessed their crime, and were executed in the year 1670.

And no longer since than the last year, viz. on Aug 25, 1682, three women, who were executed at Exon in Devonshire, all of them confessed that they had had con verses and familiarities with the devil.

But the instance of the witch executed in Hartford, here in New England (of which the preceding chapter giveth an account), considering the circumstances of that confession, is as convictive a proof as most single examples that I have met with. It is a vain thing for the patrons of witches to think that they can sham off thi argument, by suggesting that these confessions did proceed from the deluded imaginations of mad and melancholly persons. Some of them were as free from distemperature in their brains as their neighbours. That divers executed for witches have acknowledged things against themselves which were never so, I neither doubt or deny; and that a deluded phansie may cause persons verily to think they have seen and done these things which never had any existence except in their own imaginations, is indisputable. I fully concur with a passage which I find in worthy Dr. Owen's late excellent discourse about the work of the Spirit in prayer (p. 202), where he has these words :— " We find by experience that some have had their imaginations so fixed on things evil and noxious by satanical delusions, that they have confessed against themselves things and crimes that have rendred them obnoxious to capital punishment, whereof they were never really and actually guilty." This, notwithstanding that persons,

whose judgement and reason have been free from disturbance by any disease, should not only voluntarily acknowledge their being in cursed familiarities with Satan, but
mention the particular circumstances of those transactions,
and give ocular demonstratiou of the truth of what they
say, by discovering the *stigmata* made upon their bodies
by the devils hand ; and that, when more than one or two
have been examined apart, they should agree in the circumstances of their relations; and yet that all this should
be the meer effect of melancholly or phrensie, cannot,
without offering violence to reason and common sense, be
imagined. And as there are witches, so, many times, they
are the causes of those strange disturbances which are in
houses haunted by evil spirits, such as those mentioned in
the former chapter. Instances concerning this may be
seen in Mr. Glanvil's *Collections,* together with the continuation thereof, published the last year by the learned
Dr. Henry More. Sometimes Providence permits the
devil himself (without the use of instruments) to molest
the houses of some, as a punishment for sin committed,
most commonly either for the sin of murder : Plutarch
writes, that the house of Pausanias was haunted by an evil
spirit after he had murdered his wife; many like instances
have been reported and recorded by credible authors;
or else for the sin of theft. As for Walton, the Quaker
of Portsmouth, whose house has been so strangely troubled,
he suspects that one of his neighbours has caused it by
witchcraft ; she (being a widow-woman) chargeth him with
injustice in detaining some land from her. It is none of
my work to reflect upon the man, nor will I do it ; only,
if there be any late or old guilt upon his conscience, it
concerns him by confession and repentance to give glory to

that God who is able in strange wayes to discover the sins of men.

I shall here take occasion to commemorate an alike notable scene of Providence, which was taken notice of in another part of the world, at Brightling in Sussex, in England. The minister in that town (viz. Mr. Joseph Bennet) has given a faithful account of that strange Providence, which is published by Mr. Clark in his *Examples*, vol. ii, p. 593, &c. I shall relate it in his words: thus he writeth concerning it :—

"Anno Christi, 1659. There was at Brightling an amazing Providence, containing many strange passages; a wonderful hand of God, by what instrument or instruments soever: which was, a fire strangely kindled, which burnt down a mans house, and afterwards kindled in another to which the mans goods were carried, and to which himself, and his wife, and his servant girl, were removed; and several things were thrown by an invisible hand, powerfully convincing, and thereby discovering the hypocrisie and theft of the man, and for a warning to others to take heed of the like.

" November 7, in the evening, the fire first kindled in this man's milk-house; and November 9, there was dust thrown upon this man and his wife, as they lay in bed together, and there was knocking several times; and the same morning divers things were thrown about, and the fire again kindled in the milk-house, which was yet put out by the woman herself; then it kindled in the eves of the house, in the thatch, which was put out by a man which was their next neighbour. That night, as the man had a pot of beer in his hand, a stone feel into the pot; then did he set down the pot upon the table. When some men came to be with them that night, they were speaking how convenient it would be to have a tub filled with water, to stand ready, in case they should have occasion to use it; and as they were going out of the door to prepare it, the fire again kindled in the milk-house, and suddenly the whole house was on fire, but most of the goods and hous-hold-stuff were carried out and preserved. The fire was a strange fire, very white, and not singing their hands when they pulled the things out of it.

"The next day the houshold-stuff was carried to ano-ther house, wherein was a family: but those were to be in one end of the house, and the other in the other end. But before the man and his wife went to bed there was dust thrown upon them, which so troubled them that the man, having another man with them, and a candle and lanthorn in his hand, came up to me (saith my author), who was in bed and asleep; but when I was awakened, I heard him say, 'The hand of God still pursues me;' and so he intreated me to go down with him; and accordingly I and my brother went down, where we found them in the house, greatly troubled by reason of things that were thrown about, and some things were thrown presently after we came in. Hereupon we went to prayer; and as I was kneeling down, dust was thrown upon me; but afterwards all was quiet, so long as we were at prayer. When we arose from prayer, I applied myself to the reading of a portion of Scripture, which was Psal. xci, the man standing by me, and holding the candle; but pre-sently something did beat out the light; whereupon the man said that somebody else must hold it. Presently a knife was thrown at me, which fell behind me; my brother said he saw it come; then a chopping-knife was thrown

(I think at the man's wife); whereupon the man said, 'Things are thrown at others for my sake.' At length he fell upon his knees, and confessed that he had been a hipocrite and a pilfering fellow, and that he had robbed his master, &c.; and he was willing to separate the things which he had taken wrongfully from the rest, which he did accordingly: laying forth several things which he said were none of his, naming the persons from whom he had taken them; and as a great chest was carrying forth, trenchers, platters, and other things, were thrown about in so dreadful a manner, that one not much noted for religion said, 'Pray you, let us go to prayer;' and indeed that was our only refuge, so to go to God. And so we spent our time as well as we could, in prayer, reading some portions of Scripture, and singing of psalms: and though divers things were thrown, as a dish several times; so that once I had a smart blow on the cheek with a dish; and the man that lived in the house had his boots thrown at him, and a chopping-knife twice, crabs out of a tub standing in the midst of the room, a fire brand, though without fire, and an hammer thrown twice, and a Bible; the man's wife who lived in the house usually took up the things thus thrown; yet still in time of prayer all was quiet. In the morning, after I had prayed (before which prayer I was hit with a dish), my brother and I came away; and as we were coming near home, we turned aside to speak with a friend; but before we got home, we heard that the house was on fire: hereupon they sent for me again; and in the mean time they carried out their goods, pulled off the thatch, and quenched the fire; yet (as I heard) it kindled again and again, till all the man's goods were carried out: and when these people whose house was

burnt down to the ground, together with all their goods
were removed into the field, all was quiet in this second
house ; but some things were thrown in the field ; and in
the afternoon, when another minister and I went to them,
some assured us that some things had been thrown. This
was November 11. The night following, some noise was
heard among the houshold-stuff, as was testified to me.

" Thus these poor creatures were distressed. Their
house was burned down ; that to which they were removed several times fired, so that neither they nor their
goods might stay any longer there, nor durst any other
receive them : but they, with their goods, were forced to
lie in the open field for divers dayes and nights together ;
being made a sad spectacle to all sorts of people, that came
far and near to see and hear of the business. Hereupon I
sent to some neighbouring ministers, to joyn with us in
keeping a fast on November 15 ; and four spent the time
in prayer and preaching. The sermons were upon these
texts : Job xi, 13, 'If thou prepare thine heart, and
stretch out thine hands towards him ; if iniquity be in
thine hand, put it far away, and let not wickedness dwell
in thy tabernacles. For then shalt thou lift up thy face
without spot ; yea, thou shalt be stedfast, and shalt not be
afraid,' &c. Amos iii, 6, 'Shall a trumpet be blown in
the city, and the people not be afraid ? shall there be evil
in a city, and the Lord hath not done it ?' Luke xiii, 2, 3,
&c., ' Suppose ye that these Galileans were sinners above
all the Galileans, because they suffered such things ? I
tell you nay : But except ye repent, ye shall all likewise
perish : or those eighteen,' &c. Isai. xxxiii, 14, 15, 16,
' The sinners in Sion are afraid, fearfulness hath surprized
the hypocrites. Who among us shall dwell with devour-

ing fire? Who among us shall dwell with everlasting burnings? He that walketh righteously and speaketh uprightly : he that despiseth the gain of oppression, that shaketh his hand from holding bribes, that stoppeth his ears from hearing of blood, and shutteth his eyes from seeing of evil : He shall dwell on high. His place of desire shall be the munitions of rocks : Bread shall be given him, his water shall be sure.'

"The distressed persons attended diligently, and a great congregation was assembled. These providential dispensations were not ordinary ; yet there was a seeming blur cast, though not on the whole, yet upon some part of it ; for their servant girl was at last found throwing some things : and she afterwards confessed that an old woman came to her, November 7, a little before these things come to pass, and told her that her master and dame were bewitched, and that they should hear a great fluttering about their house for the space of two dayes ; she said also that the old woman told her that she must hurl things at her master and dame, and withal bad her not to tell, for if she did the devil would have her : and she confessed that she hurled the firebrand, an hammer, and an iron tack ; and said that she did it because the old woman bad her, and said to her, that if she hurled things about the house it would be the better. But besides the throwing of the things about, there were other passages of Providence very observable and remarkable. One house was at several times strangely fired, and, notwithstanding the warning they had, at last quite burned down : and another house to whom they removed, greatly molested, and at length fired. Besides the efficacy of prayer is most observable, for the encouragement of the duty, and God's omniscient and omnipotent providence wonderfully magnified, thus to discover the hypocrisie and theft of the man, and yet withal graciously and mercifully delivering them. For though they were not wholly delivered when the fast was first appointed, yet after the fast they were fully freed, and not at all any more troubled in that manner." Thus far is Mr. Bennets relation.

That the things which have been related in the chapter immediately preceding came not to pass without the operation of dæmons, is so manifest as that I shall not spend many words concerning it: though whether the afflicted persons were only possessed, or bewitched, or both, may be disputed. As for the maid at Groton, she was then thought to be under bodily possession : her uttering many things (some of which were diabolical railings) without using the organs of speech, and being able sometimes to act above humane strength, argued an extraordinary and satanical operation. Concerning the woman in Berwick : evil spirits, without being set on work by instruments, have sometimes caused the like molestation ; but commonly such things are occasioned by witchcraft. Dr. Balthasar Han (who was chief physitian to the Prince Elector of Saxony) relates concerning one of his patients, that in November 1634, she was, to the amazement of all spectators, pricked and miserably beaten by an invisible hand, so as that her body from head to foot was wounded as if she had been whipped with thorns. Sometimes a perfect sign of the cross was imprinted on her skin ; sometimes the usual configurations whereby astronomers denote the cælestial bodies, such as ♄ ♃ and their conjunctions, and oppositions by ☌ ☍ ; and the characters used by chymists, △ ☉ &c. (in which sciences, though that be not usual for those of her sex, she was versed.) These characters would remain for several weeks after the invisible hand had violently impressed them on her body ; also a needle was thrust into her foot, which caused it to bleed. Once she took the needle and put it into the fire ; and then an old woman, to whom she had given some of her wearing linnen, appeared to her with a staff in her hand, striking her with a cruel blow, and saying, " Give me my needle." At last the miserable patient, by constant attendance to prayer and other religious exercises, was delivered from her affliction. Many instances of an alike nature to this, are to be seen in the writings of those that treat upon subjects of this kind. Sometimes (as Voetius and others observe) bodily possessions by evil spirits are an effect of witchcraft. Examples confirming this are mentioned by Hierom, in the *Life of Hilarion;* Theodoret, in his *History of the Fathers;* and by Anastasius. And there are more instances in Sprenger, and in Tyræus *de Dœmoniacis.* It may be Ann Cole of Hartford might be subject to both of these miseries at the same time. Though she be (and then was) esteemed a truly pious Christian, such amazing afflictions may befall the righteous as well as the wicked in this world. The holy body of Job, that so his patience might be tried, was sorely handled by Satan. We read in the gospel of a daughter of Abraham whom Satan had bound for eighteen years, Luke xiii, 16. Mary Magdalen and several others, who had been molested and possessed by evil spirits, yet belonged to God, and are now in heaven. So might Ann Cole be a true Christian, and yet be for a time under Satan's power as hath been related. And that her malady was not meer natural disease, is past all doubt, inasmuch as in those strange *paroxysmes* where-with she was at times surprized, the tone of her discourse would sometimes be after a language unknown to her. Lemnius indeed supposeth that melancholly humors may cause persons not only to divine, but to speak with strange tongues; and Forestus (lib. x, observat. 19) does not contradict his opinion. But the unreasonableness of that phansie has been sufficiently evinced by sundry learned men. *Vide* Johnston *Thaumatograph*, sect. x, chap. 7, art. 1; La Torr, *Disp.* 27. How shall that be in the mouth which never was in the mind; and how should that be in the mind which never came there through the outward senses? This cannot be without some super-natural influence; as when things destitute of reason have given rational answers unto what hath been demanded of them, it must needs have proceeded from the operation of a supernatural agent. It is reported that one of the Popes, in way of pleasancy, saying to a parrat, "What art thou thinking of?" the parrat immediately replied, "I have considered the dayes of old, the years of ancient times;" at the which consternation fell upon the Pope and others that heard the words, concluding that the devil spake in the parrat, abusing Scripture expressions; where-upon they caused it to be killed. De La Cerda speaketh of a crow that did discourse rationally; undoubtedly it was acted by a caco-dæmon. Some write of Achilles his horse, and that Simon Magus had a dog that would discourse with him; yea, it is storied concerning the river Causus, and the keel of ship Argus, and of many statues, that they have been heard speaking. The image of Memnon in Ægypt, as the rising sun shined upon its mouth, began to speak. The image of Juno Moneta, being asked if she would be removed to Rome : replied that she would. The image of Fortune being set up, said, " *Rite me consacrastis.*" (*Valer. Maxim,* lib. i, cap. ult.) A gymnosophist in Ethiopia caused an elm, with a low and soft voice to salute Apollonius. Such things must needs be the operation of caco-dæmons. The like is to be concluded when any shall utter themselves in languages which they never learned. It is not they but a spirit which speaketh in them. The noble man whom Fernelius writeth of, was first known to be possessed by a dæmon, inasmuch as many sentences uttered by him were Greek, in which language the diseased person had no knowledge. A maid in Frankford was concluded to be possessed, is that when in her fits, she could speak the High Dutch language perfectly, though she never learned it. Manlius writeth of a possessed woman, who used to speak Latin and Greek, to the admiration of all that heard it.

I remember an honourable gentleman told me, that when he was at Somers in France a woman there was possessed with a devil. Many learned divines, both Protestants and Papists, discoursing with her, she would readily answer them, not only in the French tongue, but in Latin, Greek, or Hebrew. But when one Mr. Duncan after he had discoursed and received answer in more learned languages, spake to her in the British tongue, the dæmon made no reply ; which occasioned great wonderment, and too much sporting about a sad and serious matter.

CHAPTER VII.

CONCERNING APPARITIONS.

They are not so frequent in places where the Gospel prevaileth as in the dark corners of the earth. That good angels do sometimes visibly appear. Confirmed by several histories. That caco-dæmons oftentimes pretend to be good angels. That Satan may appear in the likeness of holy men, proved by notable instances. Concerning the appearance of persons deceased. The procuring cause thereof is usually some sin committed. Some late remarkable examples. Of mens covenanting to appear after their death. It is an heavy judgement when places are infested with such doleful spectres.

AS yet no place nor any person in New England (excepting the instances before mentioned) have been troubled with aparitions. Some indeed have given out, that I know not what spectres were seen by them; but upon enquiry I cannot find that there was any thing therein more than phansie and frightful apprehensions, without sufficient ground. Nevertheless, that spirits have sometimes really (as well as imaginarily) appeared to mortals in the world, is amongst sober men beyond controversie; and that such things were of old taken notice of, we may rationally conclude from that scripture, Luke xxiv, 37, where it is said, that the disciples "were terrified and affrighted, and supposed that they had seen a spirit." It is observable that such frightful spectres do most frequently shew themselves in places where the light of the Gospel hath not prevailed. Some hath propounded it as a question worthy the inquiring into : What should be the reason that dæmons did ordinarily infest the Gentiles of old, as also the East and West Indians of later times, and that popish countries are still commonly and grievously molested by them ; but in England and Scotland, and in the United Provinces, and in all lands where the Reformed religion hath taken place, such things are more rare ? Popish authors do acknowledge that as to matter of fact it is really thus ; and the reason which some of them assign for it is, that the devils are so sure of their interest in heretical nations, as that they pass over them, and come and molest Papists, whom they are most afraid of losing. But they should rather have attributed it to the light of the Gospel, and the power of Christ going along therewith. Justin Martyr, Tertullian, and others, observe that upon the first promulgation of the Gospel, those diabolical oracles, whereby Satan had miserably deceived the nations, were silenced ; in which respect the word of Christ, Luke x, 17, was wonderfully fulfilled. The like may be said as to Protestant being less imposed upon then Popish nations by deceitful dæmons. It is moreover, sometimes very difficult to pass a true judgement of the spectres which do appear, whether they are good or evil angels, or the spirits of deceased men. That holy angels were frequently seen in old times, we are from the Scriptures of truth assured ; and that the angelical ministration doth still continue, is past doubt, Heb. i, 14 ; but their visible appearance is less frequent than formerly. They do invisibly perform many a good office for the heirs of salvation continually. Nor is it to be questioned, but they may still appear visibly, when the work which they are sent about cannot otherwise be performed. I would not reject as fabulous all those passages which are related by judicious authors referring to this subject.

At a time when Grynæus, Melancthon, and several other learned men, were discoursing together at an house in Spyres, there came a man of very grave and goodly countenance into the house, desiring to speak with Melancthon; who going forth to him, he told him that within one hour some officers would be at that house to apprehend Grynæus, and therefore required Melancthon to advise Grynæus to flee out of that city; and having so spoken, he vanished out of sight. Melancthon returning into the room, recounted the words of this strange monitor; whereupon Grynæus instantly departed; and he had no sooner boated himself upon the Rhine, but officers came to lay hold of him. This story is mentioned by Melancthon in his commentary upon Daniel. And he concludeth that the man who had appeared to him was indeed an angel, sent in order to Grynæus his being delivered from the bloody hands of them that sought his life. Many instances like to this I could mention. But I shall only take notice of a strange providence which came to pass of late years; the particulars whereof are known to some who I suppose may be still living.

I find the history of the matter I intend in Mr. Clark's *Examples*, vol. ii, page 18, 19. It is in brief as followeth :—

One Samuel Wallas of Stamford in Lincolnshire, having been in a consumption for thirteen years, was worn away to a very skeleton, and lay bed-rid for four years. But

10

April 7, 1659, being the Lords Day, about 6 h. P.M. finding himself somewhat revived, he got out of the bed ; and as he was reading a book entituled, *Abraham's Suit for Sodom,* he heard somebody knock at the door ; whereupon (there being none then in the house but himself) he took a staff in the one hand, and leaning to the wall with the other, came to the door, and opening it, a comely and grave old man of a fresh complexion, with white curled hair, entred ; and after walking several times about the room, said to him, "Friend, I perceive you are not well ; " to whom Wallas replied he had been ill many years, and that the doctors said his disease was a consumption and past cure, and that he was a poor man, and not able to follow their costly prescriptions ; only he committed himself and life into the hands of God, to dispose of as he pleased. To whom the man replied, " Thou sayest very well ; be sure to fear God, and serve him, and remember to observe what now I say to thee : to-morrow morning go into the garden, and there take two leaves of red sage, and one of blood-wort, and put those three leaves into a cup of small beer, and drink thereof as oft as need requires ; the fourth morning cast away those leaves, and put in fresh ones ; thus do for twelve dayes together ; and thou shalt find e're these twelve dayes be expired, through the help of God, thy disease will be cured, and the frame of thy body altered." Also he told him that after his strength was somewhat recovered, he should change the air, and go three or four miles off ; and that within a moneth he should find that the clothes which he had on his back would then be too strait for him : having spoken these things, he again charged Samual Wallas to remember the directions given to him, but above all things to fear

God and serve him. Wallas asked him if he would eat any thing; unto whom he answered, "No, friend, the Lord Christ is sufficient for me. Seldom do I drink any thing but what cometh from the rock." So wishing the Lord of heaven to be with him, he departed. Samuel Wallas saw him go out of the door, and went to shut the door after him, at which he returned half way into the entry again, saying, " Friend, remember what I have said to you, and do it; but above all, fear God, and serve him." Wallas beheld the man passing in the street, but none else observed him, though some were then standing in the doors opposite to Wallas his house; and although it rained when this grave person came into the house, and had done so all that day, yet he had not one spot of wet or dirt upon him. Wallas followed the directions prescribed, and was restored to his health within the dayes mentioned. The fame of this strange Providence being noised abroad, sundry ministers met at Stamford, to consider and consult about it, who concluded that this cure was wrought by a good angel, sent from heaven upon that errand. However, it is not impossible but that holy angels may appear, and visibly converse with some. Yet for any to desire such a thing is unwarrantable, and exceeding dangerous; for thereby some have been imposed upon by wicked dæmons, who know how to transform themselves into angels of light.

Bodinus hath a strange relation of a man that prayed much for the assistance of an angel; and after that, for above thirty years together, he thought his prayer was heard : being often admonished of his errors by a cælestial monitor, as he apprehended, who once appeared visibly in

10a

the form of a child, otherwhile in an orb of light; would sometimes speak to him when he saw nothing. Yet some fear that his spirit which he took to be his good genius was a subtle caco-dæmon. Plato writeth concerning Socrates, that he had a good genius attending him, which would still admonish him if he were about to do any thing that would prove ill or unhappy.

The story of the familiarity which was between Dr. Dee and Kelly, with the spirits which used to appear to them, is famously known. Those dæmons would pretend to discover rare mysteries to them, and at times would give good advices in many things, so that they verily thought they had extraordinary communion with holy angels, whenas it is certain they were deceived by subtile and unclean devils, since the spirits they conversed with did at last advise them to break the seventh commandment of the moral law. Satan, to insinuate himself and carry on a wicked design, will sometimes seem to perswade men unto great acts of piety.

Remigius (and from him others) write of a young man whose name was Theodore Maillot, unto whom a dæmon appearing, advised him to reform his life, to abstain from drunkenness, thefts, uncleanness, and the like evils; and to fast twice a week, to be constant in attendance upon publick worship, and to be very charitable to the poor. The like pious advice did another dæmon follow a certain woman with, unto whom he appeared. Could a good angel have given better counsel? But this was Satans policy, hoping that thereby he should have gained an advantage to take silly souls alive in his cruel snare.

Like as thieves upon the road will sometimes enter into religious discourse, that so their fellow-travellers may have good thoughts of them, and be the more easily dispoyled by them. And as the evil spirit will speak good words, so doth he sometimes appear in the likeness of good men, to the end that he may the more effectually deceive and delude all such as shall be so unhappy as to entertain converses with him. No doubt but that he knows how to transform himself into the shape of not only an ordinary saint, but of an Apostle, or holy prophet of God, 2 Cor. xi, 13, 14. This we may gather from the sacred history of dead Samuel's appearing to Saul. Some are of opinion that real Samuel spake to Saul, his soul being by magical incantations returned into his body; so divers of the fathers and school-men; also Mendoza, Delrio, and other Popish authors. Of late M. Glanvil and Dr. Windet do in part favour that notion. But Tertullian, and the author of the *Quest.* and *Respons.*, which pass under the name of Justin Martyr, are of the judgement that a lying dæmon appeared to Saul in Samuel's likeness. Our Protestant divines generally are of this judgment. It was customary amongst the Gentiles for magicians and necromancers to cause dead persons to appear, and they would bring whomsoever they were desired to call for. Thus did a wizard by Pompeys command call a dead souldier, whom he enquired of the event of the Pharsalic war, *vide* Lucan, lib. 6. Many examples to this purpose are recorded in the histories of former times, and mentioned by the old poets. Those apparitions were cacodæmons, which feigned themselves to be the spirits of men departed. I see no cogent reason why we should not conclude the like with respect unto Samuel's appearing unto Saul.   Most certain it is, that the souls of holy men departed are not under power of the devils, much less of magicians to bring them hither when they please.   As for those that are gone into the other world, there is a gulf fixed, that if men would they cannot pass into this world again without leave, Luke xvi, 26.   If Dives could not bring Lazarus his soul out of Abraham's bosome, how the witch of Endor should be able to bring Samuel's soul from thence, I know not.   Lyra (and from him others) pretends that God then interposed and sent real Samuel as he unexpectedly appeared to Baalam, when imployed about his magical impostures.   But I dare not believe that the holy God or the true Samuel would seem so far to countenance necromancie or psycomancy as this would be, should the soul of Samuel really return into the world when a witch called for him, Saul desiring that it might be so.   This opinion establisheth necromancy, the main principal upon which that cursed and lying art is built, being this, that it is possible for men to cause the souls of dead persons to be brought back again.   This seeming Samuel did not at all ascribe his appearance to the extraordinary providence of God, but rather to the devil, since he complained that Saul had by the witch disquieted him.   The appearing Samuel was seen ascending out of the earth, whenas the true Samuel would rather have appeared as descending from heaven. Moreover, the words of the witches Samuel, when he said, "Tomorrow thou and thy sons shall be with me," 1 Sam. xxix, 18, are hardly consistent with truth.   Nor is it likely that the true Samuel would preach nothing but desperation to Saul, without so much as once exhorting him in a way of repentance, to endeavour that his peace might be made with that God, whom he had provoked by his sins; *v.* P. Martyr, in 1 Sam. xxviii, p. 161, 162, and Voet. *de Spectris*, page 1006. This instance, then, doth sufficiently prove that Satan may appear in the shape of an holy man. Some acknowledge that he may do so as to persons that are dead, but that he cannot personate good and innocent men who are still living. It is by some reported, that Mr. Cotton did once deliver such a notion. Nothing is more frequent than for the judgment of worthy men to be misrepresented after they are gone, and not capable of clearing themselves. I know Mr Cotton was a man of great reading, and deep judgment I shall therefore rather suppose that they who relate Mr. Cotton's opinion did themselves mistake him, then believe that a man so learned and wise would express himself as some say he did. Sure I am, that authentick historians mention examples to the contrary.

Memorable is that which Lavater (*de Spectris*, part i, cap. 19, p. mihi 86) hath testified, *sc.* that the præfect of Zurick, travelling abroad with his servant betimes in the morning, they saw an honest citizen committing nefandous villany; at the which being astonished, they returned back, and knocking at the citizens door, they found him in his own house, nor had he been abroad that morning; so that what the præfect and his servant beheld, appeared to be nothing else but a diabolical illusion: a spiteful dæmon designing to blast the credit and take away the life of an innocent man. It is also reported by Albertus Granzius (lib. iv, cap. 5), that Kunegund the empress was for some time thought to be guilty of adultery, by reason that a noble person was frequently seen going out of her chamber; but after it appeared that the suspected noble person had not been there, only a dæmon in his shape. I concern not myself with the authentickness of that relation. The matter in hand is sufficiently confirmed by a thing that hapned more lately, and nearer home; for if any of the old Puritans, who lived in Colchester in England fifty years ago, be yet surviving, they can doubtless remember the strange things which hapned to one Mr. Earl, a young man, in those dayes. The devil did then frequently appear to him in the shape of some of his acquaintance, and would perswade him to three things: 1, that he should abstain from praying; 2, that he should not frequent church-meetings; 3, that he should never marry. But he did not hearken to these suggestions. The night wherein he was married, soon after he and his wife were bedded, the devil came into the room, and pulled two of his teeth out of his head, which put him to great pain; whereupon he cried out, and when his friends came in, they found his mouth bloody, and used means to ease his pain. This Mr. Earl was afterwards for the space of ten years, ever and anon assaulted by the devil, who under many appearances of his friends, did endeavour to seduce him. There were then two famous men, ministers of those parts, viz. Mr. John Rogers of Dedham (who was father to the late eminent Mr. Nathaniel Rogers of Ipswich in New England), and Mr. Liddal of Colchester. With these Mr. Earl did converse for comfort and instruction, but chiefly with Mr. Liddal, than whom there was not a man more eminent for godliness. It fell out once that the devil came to Mr. Earl in Mr. Liddal's shape, and, as Mr. Earl's custom was, he did propose to the seeming Mr. Liddal his cases of conscience; but found that Mr. Liddal did not discourse after his ordinary rate, which made him suspect whether he was not imposed upon by a deceitful dæmon. The next day, going to Mr. Liddal's house, he enquired whether he was with him the day before ; Mr. Liddal told him that he was not ; " Then," said Mr. Earl, " it was my enemy in your shape. What a miserable man am I, that know not when I speak with my enemy or with my friend ! " To which Mr. Liddal replied : " If you would know when you speak with a spirit or with a man, remember and follow the advice of Christ ; who, when he appeared to his disciples after his resurrection, and they thought he had been a spirit, and were therefore troubled, he said to them, ' Handle me and see, for a spirit hath not flesh and bones as you see me have.' Luke xxiv, 39." This advice Mr. Earl followed ; for not long after the devil coming to him in Mr. Liddal's shape, he went to take hold on his arms, but could feel no substance, only a vanishing shadow. It seems that this Mr. Earl was once an atheist, that did not believe that there was either God or devil, and would often walk in solitary and dismal places, wishing for the sight of a spirit ; and that he was first assaulted by a devil in a church-yard. And though God mercifully gave him repentance, yet he was miserably haunted with an evil spirit all his dayes. I find that Mr. Clark in his first volume of *Examples*, chap. civ, p. 510, hath some part of this strange Providence, but he mentions not Mr. Earl's name. A gentleman worthy of credit affirmed this relation to be most certainly true, according to the particulars which have been declared ; I have thought it, therefore, not unworthy the publication.

There is another remarkable passage to this purpose, which hapned of later years, wherein the Turkish Chaous, baptized at London, January 30, A.D. 1658, was concerned.

This Chaous being alone in his chamber, 3h P.M. a person in the likeness of Mr. Dury, the minister with whom he did most ordinarily converse, came and sat by him. This seeming Mr. Dury told him, that he had waited with a great deal of patience as to the matter of his baptism ; and that himself had endeavoured by all means possible to procure it to be performed with publick countenance ; and to that effect, had dealt with Richard, and several of his counsel, but that now he perceived that it was in vain to strive or wait longer ; and therefore advised him not to be much troubled at it ; but, setting his mind at rest, to leave these thoughts, and take up his resolution another way. When the Chaous heard this discourse, being much perplexed in his spirit, he lifted up his hands and eyes to Heaven, uttering words to this effect : " O my Lord Jesus Christ, what a miserable thing is this, that a true Christian cannot be owned by other Christians ; that one who believeth on thee cannot be baptized into thy name." When he had so spoken, looking down he saw nobody, the appearance of Mr. Dury being vanished, which was at first an amazement to him ; but recollecting himself, he began to rejoyce, as hoping that Satan would be disappointed of his plot. About 8h. at night, the true Mr. Dury met with the Chaous, who acquainted him with what had hapned to him, so did he more fully understand how he had been imposed upon by Satan. The mentioned instances are enough to prove that the devil may possibly appear in the shape of good men, and that not only of such as are dead, but of the still living. It might, as a further confirmation of the truth we assert, have been here noted, that the devil doth frequently amongst the Papists visibly appear, pretending to be Christ himself, as their own authors do acknowledge. They affirm that he came in the shape of Christ to Pachomius and to St. Martin. So hath he often appeared in the form of the Virgin Mary, whereby miserable souls have been seduced into gross idolatries. It is likewise reported, that when Luther had spent a day in fasting and prayer, there appeared to him one seeming to be Christ; but Luther said to him, " Away, thou confounded devil, I will have no Christ but what is in my Bible," whereupon the apparition vanished.

As for the spirits of men deceased, it is certain they cannot reassume their bodies, nor yet come to men in this world when they will, or without a permission from Him, in whose hand they are. Chrysostom, in his second sermon concerning Lazarus, saith the dæmons would oftentimes appear, falsely pretending themselves to be the souls of some lately dead. He saith, that he himself knew many dæmoniacks; that the spirits in them would feign the voice of men lately killed, and would discover the secrets of such persons, professing that they were the souls of those very men. But those were no other then devilish lies. Upon which account men had need be exceeding wary what credit they give unto, or how they entertain communion with, such spectres. I do not say that all such apparitions are diabolical; only that many of them are so. And as yet I have not met with any τεκμηρια, whereby the certain appearance of a person deceased may be infallibly discerned from a meer diabolical illusion. The rules of judging in this case, described by Malderus, are very fallible.

As for the moving and procuring cause of such apparitions, commonly it is by reason of some sin not discoverable in any other way; either some act of injustice done or it may be some murder committed. Platina, Nauclerus, and others, relate that Pope Benedict VIII did after his death appear sitting upon a black horse before a bishop of his acquaintance, declaring the reason to be, in that he had in his lifetime nefariously consumed a great sum of money which belonged to the poor. And there are fresh examples to this purpose lately published in the second edition of Mr. Glanvil's *Sadducismus Triumphatus.* He there speaks of a man in Guildford, unto whom belonged some copyhold land which was to descend to his children; he dying, leaving no child born, his brother took possession of the estate. So it hapned that the deceased man's wife conceived with child but a little before her husbands death, which after she perceived, by the advice of her neighbours, she told her brother-in-law how matters were circumstanced; he railed upon her, calling her whore, and said he would not be fooled out of his estate so. The poor woman went home troubled, that not only her child should lose the land, but which was worse, that she should be thought an whore. In due time she was delivered of a son. Some time after which, as her brother-in-law was going out of the field, his dead brother (the father of the injured child) appeared to him at the stile, and bid him give up the land to the child, for it was his right. The brother being greatly affrighted at this spectre, ran away, and not long after came to his sister, saying, she had sent the devil to him, and bid her take the land; and her son is now possessed of it.

The same author relates that the wife of Dr. Bretton of

Deptford (being a person of extraordinary piety) did appear after her death. A maid of hers, whose name was Alice (for whom in her lifetime she had a great kindness), married a near neighbour. As this Alice was rocking her infant in the night, some one knocking at the door, she arose and opened it, and was surprized by the sight of a gentlewoman not to be distinguished from her late mistriss. At the first sight she expressed great amazement and said, " Were not my mistriss dead I should conclude you are she." The apparition replied, " I am she which was your mistriss ;" and withal added, that she had a business of great importance to imploy her in, and that she must immediately go a little way with her. Alice trembled, and entreated her to go to her master, who was fitter to be employed than she. The seeming mistriss replied that she had been in the chamber of him who was once her husband, but he was asleep ; nor had she any commission to awake him. Alice then objected that her child was apt to cry vehemently, and should she leave it, some hurt might come to him. The apparition replied, "The child shall sleep until you return." Seeing there was no avoiding it, Alice followed her over the style into a large field, who said, " Observe how much of this field I measure with my feet ;" and when she had took a good large leisurly compass, she said, " All this belongs to the poor, it being gotten from them by wrongful means ;" and charged her to go and tell her brother, whose it was at that time, that he should give it up to the poor again forthwith, as he loved her and his deceased mother. This brother was not the person that did this unjust act, but his father. She added, that she was the more concerned, because her name was made use of in some writing that related to this land.   Alice asked her how she should satisfie her brother that this was no cheat or delusion of her phansie ? She replied, "Tell him this secret, which he knows that only himself and I am privy to, and he will believe you."   Alice promised her to go on this errand. She entertained her the rest of the night with divine discourse and heavenly exhortations ; but when the twilight appeared, the spectre said, "I must be seen by none but yourself," and so disappeared.   Immediately, Alice makes hast home, being thoughtful for her child, but found it, as the spectre said, fast asleep in the cradle. That day she went to her master the doctor, who, amazed at the account she gave, sent her to his brother-in-law. He at first hearing of Alice's story, laughed at it heartily, supposing her to be troubled with strange whimsies ; but then she told him of the secret which her appearing mistriss, the gentleman's sister, had revealed ; upon which he presently changed his countenance, and told her he would give the poor their own, which accordingly he did, and they now enjoy it.   Dr. Bretton himself (being a person of great sincerity) gave a large narrative of his wives apparition to several, and, amongst others, to Dr. Whichcot ; and this narrative was attested unto by Mr. Edward Fowler, Feb. 16, 1680.   See Mr. Glanvil's *Collection of Relations,* p. 197.

In the same book, p. 243, he relates concerning one Francis Taverner, that in September, 1662, riding late at night from Hilbrough in Ireland, there appeared to him one in the likeness of James Haddock, formerly an inhabitant in Malone, where he died five years before. Taverner asked him who he was ; the spectre replied, I am James

Haddock; you may call me to mind by this token, that about five years ago, I and two other friends were at your fathers house, and you by your fathers appointment brought us some nuts, therefore be not afraid; and told him if he would ride along with him he would acquaint him with a business he had to deliver to him. Which Taverner refused to do : upon his going from the spectre, he heard hideous scrieches and noises, to his great amazement. The night after there appeared again to him, the likeness of James Haddock, telling him, that the woman who had been his wife, when living, was now married unto one Davis in Malone; and that the said Davis and his wife wronged the son of James Haddock; and that the will of Haddock, who had given a lease to his son, was not fulfilled; and therefore he desired Taverner to acquaint them therewith, and to see his son righted. Taverner neglected to deliver his message, whereupon the spectre appeared again unto him in divers formidable shapes, threatning to tear him in pieces, if he did not do as he was required. This made him leave his house where he dwelt in the mountains and remove to the town of Belfast, where it appeared to him again in the house of one Pierce, severely threatning of him. Upon which Taverner, being much troubled in his spirit, acquainted some of his friends with his perplexity. They take advice from Dr. Downs, then minister in Belfast, and Mr. James South, chaplain to the Lord Chichester, who went with Taverner to the house of Davis, and in their presence he declared to her, that he could not be quiet for the ghost of her former husband James Haddock, who threatened to tear him in pieces, if he did not tell her she must right John Haddock her son by him, in a lease wherein she and Davis her now husband had wronged him. Two nights after, the spectre came to him again, looking pleasantly upon him, asking if he had done the message? He answered, he had. Then he was told, he must do the like to the executors. The day following Dr. Jeremie Taylor, bishop of Down, Connor, and Dromore, being to keep court at Dromore, ordered his Secretary (Thomas Alcock) to send for Taverner, who accordingly came, and was strictly examined. The bishop advised him, the next time the spectre appeared to him, to ask him these questions: " Whence are you? Are you a good or bad spirit? where is your abode? what station do you hold? How are you regimented in the other world? And what is the reason that you appear for the relief of your son in so small a matter, when so many widows and orphans are oppressed in the world, and none of their relations appear as you do to right them?" That night Taverner lodged at my Lord Conways, where he saw the spectre coming over a wall; and approaching near to him, asked if he had done his message to the executor also? He replied, he had, and wondered that he should be still troubled. The apparition bid him not be afraid, for it would not hurt him, nor appear to him any more, but to the executor, if the orphan were not righted. Taverners brother being by, put him in mind to propound the bishops questions to the spirit; which he did; but the spectre gave no answer to them; only seemed to crawl on his hands and feet over the wall again, and vanished with a melodious harmony. The persons concerned about the lease (much against their wills) disposed of it for the use of Haddock's son, only for fear lest the apparition should molest them also. Thus concerning this. Before

I pass to the next relation, I cannot but animadvert upon
what is here expressed, concerning the questions which
the bishop would needs have propounded to, and resolved
by this spectre. I am perswaded that the Apostle Paul,
who speaks of a mans intruding into those things which he
hath not seen, Col. ii, 18, would hardly have given such
counsel as the bishop did. One of his questions (viz.
" Are you a good or a bad spirit?") seems to be a needless
and impertinent enquiry ; for good angels never appear in
the shape of dead men ; but evil and wicked spirits have
oftentimes done so. His other queries savour too much of
vain curiosity ; they bring to mind what is by that great
historian, Thuanus (lib. cxxx, page 1136), reported concerning Peter Cotton the Jesuit, who, having a great
desire to be satisfied about some questions which no man
living could resolve him in, he applied himself to a maid
who was possessed with a devil, charging the spirit in her
to resolve his proposals ; some of which were relating to
this world, *e.g.*, he desired the devil, if he could, to tell
him when Calvinism would be extinguished ? and what
would be the most effectual means to turn the kingdome
of England from the Protestant to the Popish religion ?
what would be the issue of the wars and great designs
then on foot in the world ? Other of his enquiries
respected the old world: *e.g.* How Noah could take the
living creatures that were brought into the ark ? who
those sons of God were who loved the daughters of men
whether serpents went upon feet before Adam's fall ? &c.
Some of his questions respected *the other world*. He
would have the spirit to resolve him, How long the fallen
angels were in heaven before they were cast down from
thence? And what is the most evident place in the

11

Scripture to prove that there is a purgatory? Who are the seven spirits who stand before the throne of God? Who is the king of the arch-angels? Where Paradise is? Now, let the reader judge whether Dr. Taylor's questions, when he would have the spectre resolve him, "Where is your abode? What station do you hold? How are you regimented in the other world" &c. be not as curious as some of these of the Jesuits. Wise men thought it tended much to the disreputation of Peter Cotton, when, through his incogitant leaving the book wherein his enquiries of the dæmon were written with a friend, the matter came to be divulged. I cannot think that Dr. Taylor's secretary his publishing these curiosities of his lord hath added much to his credit amongst sober and judicious persons.

There is a tragical passage related in the story of the dæmon, which for three moneths molested the house of Mr. Perreaud, a Protestant minister in Matiscon. One in the room would needs be propounding needless questions for the devil to answer, though Mr. Perreaud told him of the danger in it. After a deal of discourse, the devil said to him, "You should have hearkened to the ministers good counsel, who told you that you ought not to ask curious questions of the devil; yet you would do it, and now I must school you for your pains." Presently upon which, the man was by an invisible hand plucked up by his thumb, and twirled round, and thrown down upon the floor, and so continued in most grievous misery. I hope, then, that none will be emboldened from the bishops advice, to enquire at the mouth of devils or of apparitions, until such time as they know whether they are devils or no. But to pass on.

That the ghosts of dead persons have sometimes

appeared, that so the sin of murder (as well as that of theft) might be discovered, is a thing notoriously known. I shall only mention two or three examples for this; and the rather because some who are very unapt to believe things of this nature, yet have given credit to those relations. Two of the stories are recited by Mr. Webster in his *Book of Witchcraft.* He saith (p. 297) :—

"That about the year 1623, one Fletcher, of Raskelf, a town in the North Riding of Yorkshire, a yeoman of a good estate, married a woman from Thornton Brigs, who had formerly been naught with one Ralph Raynard, who kept an inn within half a mile from Raskelf, in the high road betwixt York and Thirsk, his sister living with him. This Raynard, continuing in unlawful lust with Fletcher's wife, and not being content therewith, conspired the death of Fletcher; one Mark Dunn being made privy, and hired to assist in the murther; which Raynard and Dunn accomplished upon May Day, by drowning him, as they were travelling all three together from a town called Huby, and acquainted the wife with the deed; she gave them a sack therein to convey his body, which they did, and buried it in Raynard's back side, or croft, where an old oak had been stubbed up, and sowed mustard-seed in the place, thereby to hide it. They then continued their wicked course of lust and drunkenness; and the neighbours did much wonder at Fletchers absence; but his wife excused it, and said, 'he was only gone aside, for fear of some writs being served upon him;' and so it continued till about July 7 after, when Raynard going to Topcliff fair, and setting up his horse in the stable, the spirit of Fletcher, in his usual shape and habit, did appear unto him, and said, 'O Ralph! repent! repent! for my revenge is at hand!'

11a

and ever after, until he was put in the gaol, the spirit
seemed continually to stand before him, whereby he became
sad and restless ; and his own sister, overhearing his confession and relation of it to another person, did, through
fear of losing her own life, immediately reveal it to Sir
William Sheffield, who lived in Raskelf; whereupon Raynard, Dunn and the wife, were all three apprehended, and
sent to the gaol at York, where they were condemned and
executed, near the place where Raynard lived and Fletcher
was buried; the two men being hung up in chains, and
the woman burned under the gallows. I have recited this
story punctually, as a thing that hath been very much
fixed on my memory (being then but young), and a certain
truth, I being (with many more) an ear-witness of their
confessions, and eye-witness of their executions, and likewise saw Fletcher when he was taken up, where they had
buried him in his clothes, which were a green fustian
doublet pinckt upon white, and his walking boots, and
brass spurs, without rowels."   Thus Mr. Webster.

Again the same author (p. 298) relates—

"That about the year 1632, there lived one Walker,
near Chester, who was a yeoman of a good estate, and a
widower; he had a young kinswoman to keep his house,
who was by the neighbours suspected to be with child, and
was sent away one evening in the dark with one Mark
Sharp, a collier, and was not heard of, nor little notice
taken of her, till a long time after, one James Grayham,
a miller, who lived two miles from Walker's house, being
one night alone very late in his mill, grinding corn, about
twelve a clock at night, the doors being shut, there stood
a woman in the midst of the floor, with her hair hanging
down all bloody, and five large wounds in her head.   He

was very much frighted, yet had the courage to ask her
who she was, and what she wanted? To whom she
answered, 'I am the spirit of such a woman, who lived
with Walker; and being got with child by him, he promised to send me to a private place, where I should be
well lookt to till I was brought a bed and well, and then
I should come again and keep his house; and, accordingly'
(said the apparition), 'I was one night late sent away with
one Mark Sharp, who upon a moor' (naming a place which
the miller knew) 'slew me with a pick such as men dig
coals withal, and gave me these five wounds, and after
threw my body into a coal pit hard by, and hid the pick
under the bank; and his shoes and stockins being bloody,
he endeavoured to wash them, but seeing the blood would
not wash off, he left them there.' And the apparition
further told the miller, that he must be the man to
reveal it, or else she must still appear and haunt him.
The miller returned home very sad and heavy, but spake
not one word of what he had seen, yet eschewed as much
as he could to stay in the mill in the night without company, thinking thereby to escape the seeing this dreadful
apparition. But, notwithstanding, one night when it
began to be dark, the apparition met him again, and
seemed very fierce and cruel, and threatning him, that if he
did not reveal the murder she would continually pursue
and haunt him; yet, for all this, he still concealed it,
until St. Thomas Eve before Christmas, when being, soon
after sunset, walking in his garden, she appeared again,
and then so threatned and affrighted him, that he promised faithfully to reveal it the next morning. In the
morning he went to a magistrate and discovered the whole
matter, with all the circumstances; and, diligent search

being made, the body was found in a coal-pit, with five wounds in the head, and the pick and shoes and stockins, yet bloody, and in every circumstance as the apparition had related to the miller. Whereupon Walker and Mark Sharp were both apprehended, but would confess nothing. At the assizes following (I think it was at Durham) they were arraigned, found guilty, and hanged; but I could never hear that they confessed the fact. It was reported that the apparition did appear to the judge, or the foreman of the jury, but of that I know no certainty. There are many persons yet alive that can remember this strange murder; and I saw and read the letter which was sent to Serjeant Hutton about it from the judge before whom they were tried, which maketh me relate it with greater confidence."

Thus far we have Mr. Webster's relations.

It is also credibly attested, that a thing no less remarkable than either of the former hapned but nine years ago at another place in England. The sum of the story, as it is published in Mr. Glanvil's *Collection of Relations*, p. 172, is this :—

On the 9th of November, 1674, Thomas Goddard, of Marlborough, in the county of Wilts, as he was going to Ogborn, about 9h. A.M. he met the apparition of his father-in-law, Edward Avon, who had been dead about half a year. He seemed to stand by the stile which Goddard was to go over. When he came near, the spectre spake to him with an audible voice, saying, " Are you afraid ?" to whom he answered, " I am thinking of one who is dead and buried, whom you are like." To which the apparition replied, " I am he : come near me, I will do you no harm." To which Goddard replied, "I trust in Him who hath bought my soul with his precious blood, you shall do me no harm." Then the spectre said, "How stand cases at home?" Goddard asked, "What cases?" Then it asked him, "How doth William and Mary?" meaning belike, his son William and his daughter Mary, whom this Goddard had married. And it said, "What? Taylor is dead!" meaning, as Goddard thought, one of that name in London, who had married another of Avon's daughters, and died in September before this. The spectre offered him some money, desiring it might be sent to his daughter, that was lately become a widow; but Goddard answered, "In the name of Jesus Christ I refuse all such money." Then the apparition said, "I perceive you are afraid; I will meet you some other time." So it went away. The next night about 7h. it came and opened his shop-window, and looked him in the face, but said nothing; and the next night after, as Goddard went into his back-side, with a candle light in his hand; but he, being affrighted, ran into his house, and saw it no more at that time. But on Thursday, November 12, as he came from Chilton, the apparition met him again, and stood (about eight foot) directly before him, and said with a loud voice, "Thomas, bid William Avon take the sword which he had of me, which is now in his house, and carry to the wood as we goe to Alton, to the upper end of the wood by the wayes side; for with that sword I did wrong above thirty years ago and he never prospered since twas his. And do you speak with Edward Lawrence, and I desire you to pay him twenty shillings out of the money which you received of James Eliot at two payments; for I borrowed so much money of Edward Lawrence, and said that I had paid him, but I did not pay it him." This money was received of James Eliot on a bond due to Avon, and Goddard had it at two payments after Avon had been dead several moneths. Lawrence saith that he lent Avon twenty shillings in money about twenty years ago, which was never paid him again. November 23, Goddard did, by order from the mayor of the town, go with his brother-in-law, William Avon, with the sword to the place where the apparition said it should be carried. And coming away thence, Goddard looking back saw the same apparition, whereupon he called to his brother-in-law and said, " Here is the apparition of your father !" William replied, " I see nothing." Then Goddard fell upon his knees, and said, " Lord, open his eyes that he may see." But William said, " Lord, grant that I may not see it, if it be thy blessed will." Then the ghost did, to Goddard's apprehension, becken with his hand. To whom Goddard said, " What would you have me to do ?" The apparition replied, " Take up the sword and follow me." To which he said, " Should both of us come, or but one of us ?" The spectre replied, " Thomas, do you take up the sword." So he took it up, and followed the apparition about ten poles into the wood. Then the spectre coming towards Goddard, he stept back two steps ; but it said to him, " I have a permission to you, and a commission not to touch you." Then it took the sword, and went to the place at which before it stood, and pointed the top of the sword into the ground, and said, " In this place was buried the body of him whom I murdered in the year 1635, but it is now rotten and turned to dust." Whereupon Goddard said, " For what cause did you murder him ?" The seeming Avon replied, " I took money from the man, and he contended with me, and so I murdered him." Then Goddard said, "Who was confederate with you in the murder?" The spectre answered, "None but myself." "What," said Goddard, "would you have me do in this thing?" The apparition replied, "Only to let the world know that I murdered a man, and buried him in this place, in the year 1635." Then the spectre laid down the sword on the bare ground there, whereupon grew nothing, but seemed to Goddard to be as a grave sunk in. All this while William Avon remained where Goddard left him, and said he saw no apparition, only heard Goddard speak to the spectre, and discerned another voice also, making reply to Goddard's enquiries, but could not understand the words uttered by that voice. The next day the mayor caused men to dig in the place where the spectre said the body was buried, but nothing could be found.

These examples then, show that the ghosts of dead men do sometimes appear, and that for such causes as those mentioned. There have been some in the world so desperate as to make solemn covenants with their living friends to appear unto them after their death; and sometimes (though not alwayes) it hath come to pass. It is a remarkable passage which Baronius relates concerning Marsilius Ficinus and his great intimate, Michael Mercatus. These two, having been warmly disputing about the immortality of the soul, entered into a solemn vow, that if there were truth in those notions about a future state in another world, he which died first should appear to his surviving friend. Not long after this Ficinus died. On a morning when Mercatus was intent upon his studies, he heard the voice of Ficinus his friend at his window, with a loud cry, saying, "O Michael! Michael! *Vera, vera sunt illa:* O, my friend Michael, those notions about the souls of men being immortal, they are true! they are true!" Whereupon Mercatus opened his window, and saw his friend Marsilius Ficinus, whom he called unto, but he vanished away. He presently sent to Florence to know how Ficinus did, and was informed that he died about the hour when his ghost appeared at Mercatus his window.

There are also later instances, and nearer home, not altogether unlike to this; for in Mr. Glanvil's late *Collection of Relations* (which we have had occasion more than once to mention), it is said that Dr. Farrar and his daughter made a compact, that the first of them which died, if happy, should after death appear to the surviver, if possible: his daughter with some difficulty consenting to the agreement. Some time after, the daughter, living then near Salisbury, fell in labour; and, having by an unhappy mistake a noxious potion given to her instead of another prepared, suddenly died. That very night she appeared in the room where her father then lodged, in London, and opening the curtains looked upon him. He had before heard nothing of her illness, but upon this apparition confidently told his servant, that his daughter was dead, and two dayes after received the news.

Likewise, one Mr. Watkinson, who lived in Smithfield, told his daughter (taking her leave of him, and expressing her fears that she should never see him more), that should he die, if ever God did permit the dead to see the living, he would see her again. Now, after he had been dead about half a year, on a night when she was in bed but could not sleep, she heard musick, and the chamber grew lighter and lighter; she then saw her father by the bed side, who said, " Mall, did not I tell thee that I would see thee again?" He exhorted her to be patient under her afflictions, and to carry it dutiful towards her mother; and told her that her child that was born since his departure should not trouble her long; and bid her speak what she would speak to him now, for he must go, and she should see him no more upon earth. *Vide* Glanvil's *Collections*, pp. 189—192. Sometimes the great and holy God hath permitted, and by his providence ordered, such apparitions, to the end that atheists might thereby be astonished and affrighted out of their infidelity.

Nam primus timor fecit in orbe Deos.

Remarkable and very solemn is the relation of the appearance of Major Sydenham's ghost mentioned in the book but now cited (p. 181): it is in brief this:—Major George Sydenham of Dulverton in Somerset, and Captain William Dyke of Skillgate in that county, used to have many disputes about the being of God, and the immortality of the soul; in which point they continued unresolved. To issue their controversies, they agreed that he that died first should, the third night after his funeral, between the hours of twelve and one, appear at a little house in the garden. After Sydenham was dead, Captain Dyke repairs to the place appointed between them two. He acquainted a near kinsman, Dr. Thomas Dyke, with his design, by whom he was earnestly disswaded from going to that place at that time; and was told that the devil might meet him and be his ruine, if he would venture on in such rash attempts. The captain replied that he had solemnly engaged, and nothing should discourage him. Accordingly, betwixt twelve and one he went into the garden-house, and there tarried two or three hours without seeing or hearing any thing more than what was usual. About six weeks after, Captain Dyke rides to Eaton, to place his son a scholar there. The morning before he returned from thence, after it was light, one came to his bed-side, and, suddenly drawing back the curtains, calls, "Cap! Cap!" (which was the term of familiarity which the major when living used to call the captain by). He presently perceived it was his major, and replieth, "What, my major!" On the table in the room there lay a sword which the major had formerly given to the captain. After the seeming major had walked a turn or two about the room, he took up the sword, and drew it out, and not finding it so bright and clean as it ought, "Cap! Cap!" said he, "this sword did not use to be kept after this manner when it was mine." He also said to the captain, "I could not come to you at the time appointed; but I am now come to tell you that there is a God, and that he is a very just and a terrible God, and if you do not turn over a new leaf you will find it so." So did he suddenly disappear. The captain arose and came into another chamber (where his kinsman, Dr. Dyke, lodged); but in a visage and form much differing from himself, his hair standing, his eyes staring, and his whole body trembling, telling with much affection what he had seen. The captain lived about two years after this, but was much altered in his conversation, the words uttered by his majors ghost ever sounding in his ears. Thus of that remarkable providence.

I have not mentioned these things, as any way approving of such desperate covenants; there is great hazard attending them. It may be, after men have made such agreements, devils may appear to them, pretending to be their deceased friends, and thereby their souls may be drawn into woful snares. Who knoweth whether God will permit the persons, who have thus confederated, to appear in this world again after their death? and if not, then the surviver will be under great temptation unto atheism; as it fell out with the late Earl of Rochester, who (as is reported in his Life, p. 16, by Dr. Burnet) did, in the year 1665, enter into a formal ingagement with another gen tleman, not without ceremonies of religion, that if either of them died, he should appear and give the other notice of the future state, if there were any. After this the other gentleman was killed, but did never appear after his death to the Earl of Rochester, which was a great snare to him during the rest of his life. Though when God awakened the earl's conscience upon his death-bed, he could not but acknowledge that one who had so corrupted the natural principles of truth as he had, had no reason to expect that such an extraordinary thing should be done for his conviction. Or, if such agreement should necessitate an apparition, how would the world be confounded with spectres; how many would probably be scared out of their wits; or what curious questions would vain men be proposing about things which are (and it is meet they should be) hid from mortals! I cannot think that men who make such covenants (except it be with very much caution, as I have heard that Mr. Knewstubs and another eminent person did) are duely mindful of that Scripture, Deut. xxix, 29, "The secret things belong to the Lord; but those things which are revealed belong to us." Moreover, such sights are not desirable; for many times they appear as forerunners of notable judgements at hand. I could instance out of approved history, how particular families have found that things of this nature have come to them as the messengers of death.   Lavater, in his book *de Spectris,* and Goulartius, in his *Select History,* say, that spectres are the harbingers of publick mutations, wars, and calamitous times. Voetius, in his disputation, *de Peste,* sheweth that sometimes the plague or strange diseases follow after such appearances.   There was lately a very formidable apparition at Meenen. We are advised, that there did appear in that place a person all in white, with a mitre on his head, being followed with two more in black ; after him came four or five squadrons, who drew up as if they intended to storm the town. The souldiers there refused to stand their centry, having been so affrighted as that some of them fell down in their posts. These spectres appeared every night in June, 1682. How it is there since that, or what events have followed in that place, I know not; but I find in credible authors, that oftentimes mischief and destruction unto some or other hath been the effect of apparitions. Luther tells us of a shepherd (of whom also he speaketh charitably) that, being haunted with a spirit, the apparition told him, that after eight dayes he would appear to him again, and carry him away and kill him ; and so it came to pass. The ministers whom the poor man acquainted with his sorrowful estate, advised him not to despair of the salvation of his soul, though God should suffer the devil to kill his body. I have read of threescore persons all killed at once by an apparition. George Agricola giveth an account of twelve men, that as they were digging in the mines, a spectre slew them. Some have been filled with such anxiety at the appearance of a spectre, that in one nights time the hair of their heads has turned white. Lavater speaketh of a man, who one night meeting with an apparition, the terror of it caused such a sudden change in him, as that when he came home his own children did not know him. We may then conclude that the witlings of this drolling age know not what they do, when they make themselves sport with subjects of this nature. I shall only add this further here, that from the things which have been related, it is evident that they are mistaken who suppose devils cannot appear to men except with some deformities whereby they are easily discovered. The nymphs which deluded many of old, when the world was buried under heathenism, were dæmons, presenting themselves in shapes very formose. *Vide Martinii Lexic. in verbo Nymphæ.*

CHAPTER VIII.

SEVERAL CASES OF CONSCIENCE CONSIDERED.

That it is not lawful to make use of herbs or plants to drive away evil spirits; nor of words or characters. An objection answered. Whether it be lawful for persons bewitched to burn things, or to nail horse-shoes before their doors, or to stop urin in bottles, or the like, in order to the recovery of health. The negative proved by several arguments. Whether it be lawful to try witches by casting them into the water. Several reasons evincing the vanity of that way of probation. Some other superstitions witnessed against.

THE preceding relations about witchcrafts and diabolical impostures give us too just occasion to make enquiry into some cases of conscience, respecting things of this nature. And in the first place the *quære* may be:

Whither it is lawful to make use of any sort of herbs or plants to preserve from witchcrafts, or from the power of evil spirits? The answer unto which is: That it is in no wise lawful, but that all attempts of that nature are magical and diabolical, and therefore detestable superstition; as appears—1. In that if the devils do either operate or cease to do mischief upon the use of such things, it must needs be in that they are signs which give notice to the evil spirits what they are to do. Now, for men to submit to any of the devils sacraments is implicitly to make a covenant with him. Many who practise these

176

nefarious vanities little think what they do. They would not for the world (they say) make a covenant with the devil; yet, by improving the devils signals, with an opinion of receiving benefit thereby, they do the thing which they pretend to abhor. For, 2. Angels (bad as well as good) are by nature incorporeal substances. There are some authors, who by a corporeal substance intend no more but a real being; so that the term is by them used in opposition to meer phantasms in that sence; none but Sadduces will deny angels to be corporeal; and in that respect the antient doctors, Tertullian and others, call them *corpora*. But commonly a body is set in opposition to a meer spiritual substance, Mat. x, 28; Heb. xii, 13; and thus it is certain that dæmons are incorporeal, Eph. vi, 12. They are frequently, not only by authors, but in the Holy Scripture, stiled spirits, because of their being incorporeal. And thence it is that they are not visible or palpable, or any way incurring the outward sences, Luke xxiv, 39. Homer saith, that when the ghost of Anticlea appeared to Ulysses, he attempted three times to embrace that image, but could feel nothing, for it had not σαρκας και οστεα, but, as Virgil expresseth it, *tenues sine corpore vitas.* Cajetan and Vasquez affirm that apparitions can at no time be felt. It is not to be doubted but that spirits may make use of vehicles that are subject to the outward senses; nevertheless, a meer spirit cannot be touched by humane hands. Moreover, we read of a legion of dæmons possessing one miserable body, Luke viii, 30. A legion is at least 6000; now, if they were corporeal substances, it could not be that so many of them should be in the same person at the same time; and if they are incorporeal substances, then it is not possible that herbs or any sensible

12

objects should have a natural influence upon them as they have upon elementary bodies. This argument is of such weight, as that of Porphyrius and other heathenish authors, who affirm that dæmons are affected with smells, and with blood, &c. suppose them to have aereal bodies; so do some Talmudical and cabalistical writers; they hold that there are a middle sort of devils made of fire and air, who live upon the liquidity of the air and the smoke of fire, &c. These are called שׁדׁים. Munster, in his notes on Lev. xvii, does, out of R. Abraham, cite many passages to this purpose; but such Jewish fables are so foolish as that they need no confutation. And as the argument we have mentioned is a sufficient refutation of them that imagine a natural vertue to be in herbs, whereby evil spirits are driven away; so may it be improved against their superstition, who suppose that fumes are of force to expel dæmons. The author of the book of Tobit, chap. vi, tells a tale that the heart and liver of a fish, if a smoke be made therewith, the devil will smell it, and then be forced to flee away from any one that shall be troubled with an evil spirit; and that Tobit following the counsel which Raphael gave him about these matters, the devil was fain to run for it as far as to the utmost parts of Ægypt, chap. viii, ver. 2, 3. This passage is so far from being divine as that indeed it is prophane and magical; whereas the author saith, that whoever is troubled with an evil spirit shall by that means find relief; he does expressly contradict the Son of God, who has taught otherwise, Matt. xvii, 21; Mark ix, 28. And his ascribing such vertue to the heart of a fish is as true as what Cornelius Agrippa saith, who affirms that the gall of a black dog will drive away evil spirits, and free from witchcrafts. And there is as much credit to be given to these things as to another Jewish fable, viz, that the clapping of a cocks wings will make the power of dæmons to become ineffectual; yet that this fable hath obtained too much credit in the world is evident by words of Prudentius, who saith—

> Ferunt vagantes Dæmonas,
> Lætos tenebros noctium
> Gallo canente exterritos
> Sparsim timere et cedere.

3. God, in his Holy Word, has forbidden his people to imitate the heathen nations. He requires that those who profess his Name should not learn the way of the heathen, nor do after their manners, Lev. xx, 23; Jer. x, 2. But to attempt the driving away of evil spirits by the use of herbs, fumes, &c. is an heathenish custom. Whoso shall read Proclus his book, *de Sacrificio et Magia*, will see how the Ethnicks taught that smells and smokes would cause dæmons to depart; and the like they believed (and practised accordingly) with respect unto several sorts of herbs. See Sennertus *Med. Pract.* l. vi, part 9, cap. 7. Dioscorides, being deceived with the doctrine of that great magician, Pythagoras, saith, that the sea-onion being hung in the porch of an house will keep evil spirits from entring therein. In that book which passeth under the name of Albertus Magnus *de Mirabilibus Mundi* (though Picus Mirandula, in his disputation about magick, is so favourable as to think Albertus was not the author of it, but that the true author has abusively prefixed Albertus his name), there are many superstitious vanities of this nature, which, in times of Popish darkness, were received from the Arabians and other heathenish worshippers of the devil. It is true that the Jews did some of them practise this kind

of magick. Josephus (*Antiq.* lib. viii, cap. 2) confesseth, that those of their nation (in special, one whose name was Eleazar), did, by holding an herb (viz. that called " Solomon's seal") to the noses of dæmoniacks, draw the devils out of them. He speaketh untruly in saying that they learned such nefarious arts from Solomon, for they had them from the heathen, who received them from the devil himself; as is evident from another passage in the mentioned Josephus. In his *History of the Wars with the Jews.* lib. vii, cap. 25, he says, that there is a root, by the Jews called *baaras,* which if a man pluck it up he dieth presently; but to prevent that, they make bare the root, and then tye it with a string to a dog, who, going away to follow his master, easily plucks up the root, whereupon the dog dieth; but his master may then, without danger handle the root, and thereby fright the devils out of persons possessed with infernal spirits; whom he (in that also following the heathen) supposes to be the spirits of wicked men deceased. And that the Jews received these curious or rather cursed arts from Ethnics, is manifest, inasmuch as Pliny taught that the herb called Aglaophotis had power to raise the gods (so did they call the devils whom they served). Now that was the same herb with *baaras;* for as Delacampius, Rainold, and others have observed, both names have the same signification. So then the making use of herbs to fright away devils, or to preserve from the power of witches, is originally an heathenish custome, and, therefore, that which ought to be avoided and abhorred by those that call themselves Christians.

It is no less superstitious when men endeavour by characters, words, or spells, to charm away witches, devils, or diseases. Such persons do (as Fuller speaks) fence themselves with the devils shield against the devils sword. Agrippa, in his book, *de Occulta Philosophia*, has many of these impious curiosities. But in his book of *The Vanity of Sciences*, chap. xlviii, he acknowledgeth that he wrote his other book of *Occult Philosophy* when he was a young man, and bewails his iniquity therein, confessing that he had sinfully mispent precious time in those unprofitable studies. There is also an horrid book full of conjurations and magical incantations, which the prophane author hath ventured to publish under the name of *King Solomon*. There cannot be a greater vanity than to imagine that devils are really frighted with words and syllables : such practices are likewise of diabolical and heathenish original. They that have read subjects of this nature are not ignorant of what is related concerning the strange things done by the incantations of that famous wizard, Apollonius. The like has been also noted of the Brackmanes of old, who were much given to such unlawful arts. It is still customary amongst the heathenish Africans, by incantations, to charm serpents ; which, when they are in that way brought to them by the devil, they use with the blood of such serpents to anoint their weapons, that so they may become the more mortiferous. And that the like incantations were practised among the Gentiles of old, is evident from that verse of Virgil in his 8th *Eclog.*,

> Frigidus in pratis cantando rumpitur anguis.

As also by that of Ovid in *Metam.* lib. vii,

> Viperias rumpi verbis et carmina fauces.

Yea, the Holy Scriptures intimate, that such diabolical practices were used by some in the dayes of old : those words of David, Psalm lviii, 4, 5, imply no less, as our excellent

Rainold has, with great learning and judgement, evinced. It must be acknowledged that the notion which many have from Austin taken up, as if serpents, to avoid the power of charms would lay one ear to the ground, and with their tails stop the other ear, is to be reckoned amongst vulgar errors; nevertheless, that there were then charmers in the world, the mentioned (as well as other) scriptures notifie. Moreover, those inchanters had their *formulæ*, whereby they did imprecate the persons whom they designed hurt unto; and the devil (when the great and holy God saw meet to permit him) would, upon the using of those words, go to work and do strange things. Hence Livy speaks of the *devotaria carmina* used by wizards. The truth of this is also manifest from some passages in Æschines his *Oration* against Ctesiphon. And of this nature were Balaam's curses, desired by Baalak, as enchantments against Jacob, Numb. xxii, 6, and xxiii, 23. If it had not been a thing famously known, that Balaam (a black wizard) did mischief others by his incantations, the king of Moab would never have sent to him for that end. And as witchcrafts of this kind were frequent among the Gentiles who knew not God, so, in a more especial manner, amongst the Ephesians, before they were enlightened by the Gospel of Jesus Christ. Upon their conversion to the Christian faith, as many as had used *curious* (*i.e.* as the Syriac translation rightly interprets *magical*) arts, brought their books together, and burned them before all men, Acts xix, 19; which sheweth that Ephesus did once abound with these heathenish superstitions. They pretended that they could by certain words cure diseases, eject devils, &c. Hence, it became a proverbial phrase to say Εφέσια γραμματα, when magical spells and incantations were intended. Hesychius mentions some of those charms being obscure and barbarous words; such as ασκι, κατα κι, αιξ, τετραξ, &c. These words they would sometimes carry about with them, fairly written ; and then they were a sacrament for the devil to operate by. That insignificant word, *Abrodacara*, is by Sammonicus mentioned as a magical spell; which hobgoblin word the late miracle-monger or Mirabilarian stroaker in Ireland, Valentin Greatrix, attempted to cure an ague by. Porphyrius saith that the Egyptians had symbols which Serapis appointed them to use in order to the driving away dæmons. Now, he whom the Egyptians called Serapis, is by the Greeks called Pluto, and by the Jews Belzebub ; and, as the heathen learned such things from Belzebub, so have the Papists (who are called Gentiles in the Scripture, Rev. xi, 2; and well they may be so, since as to all manner of idolatry and superstition they gentilize) from them learned to cure diseases, and drive away evil spirits by words and spells, exorcizations, &c. Matthiolus reports that he knew a man that would, and that without seeing the persons wounded, by charms heal those that were stung with deadly serpents; and Fernelius saith that he has seen some curing a feaver only by muttering words, without the use of any natural means. Not only possessed heathen, but Papists, have, by reciting certain verses, been wont to cure other diseases; yea, they have practised to free persons from the epilepsie, by mentioning the names of the three kings of Colon (as the wise men which came from the East are usually called). Hence are those celebrated verses :—

> Hæc tria qui secum portabit nomina regum
> Solvitur a morbo Christi pietate caduco.

It is too well known that Popish countries do still
abound with such superstitious vanities as these mentioned. And as Voetius (in his dissertation, *de Exorcismo*)
truly tells them, the exorcizations of the Papists are as like
those of the heathen as milk is like to milk, or as one egg
is like to another. I know that some Popish authors (who
are more ingenious) write against attempting the cure of
diseases by words or charms.   Fernelius, Benevenius, and
(as I remember) Valesius, disapprove of it; but few (if
any) of them are against conjuring away evil spirits by
words, and I know not what formulæ of their own, or
rather of the devils inventing. One of them (viz.
Hieronymus Mengus), having published a book filled with
conjurations, entituleth it *The Scourge of Devils*. It adds
to the abomination when men shall not only break the
first and second commandment, but the third also, by
making use of any of the sacred names or titles belonging
to the glorious God, or to his Son Jesus Christ, as
charms; then which nothing is more frequent amongst
Romanists.   To conclude, God in his word doth with the
highest severity condemn all such practices, declaring not
only that enchanters and charmers are not to be tolerated
amongst his people, but that all who do such things are an
abomination to him, Deut. xviii, 10, 11, 12.   The Jews
are wont to be extreamly charitable towards those of their
own nation, affirming, "That every Isrealite shall have a
part in the world to come;" only they except such as
shall by incantations heal diseases.   There are some that
practise such things in their simplicity, not knowing that
therein they gratifie the devil. Voetius, in his disputation,
de Magia, p. 576, speaks of one that, according to the
vain conversation received by tradition from forefathers,

would sometimes attempt things of this nature; but upon Voetius his instructing him concerning the sin and evil which was therein, the man durst never more do as formerly. If this discourse fall into the hands of any whose consciences tell them they have been guilty of the same iniquity, God grant that it may have the same effect on them. It is a marvelous and an amazing thing, that in such a place as New England, where the Gospel hath shined with great power and glory, any should be so blind as to make attempts of this kind; yet some such I know there have been. A man in Boston gave to one a sealed paper as an effectual remedy against the tooth-ach, wherein were drawn several confused characters, and these words written, "*In nomine Patris, Filii, et Spiritus Sancti,* preserve thy servant (such an one)." Bodinus and others write of a convicted witch, whose name was Barbary Dore, that confessed she had often cured diseases by using the like words unto those mentioned. Not long since a man left with another in this town, as a rare secret, a cure for the ague, which was this : five letters viz. *κ*, *α*. &c. were to be written successively on pieces of bread, and given to the patient; on one piece he must write the word *Kalendant*, and so on another the next day; and in five dayes (if he did believe) he should not fail of cure. These considerations have made me the more willing a little to inlarge upon the argument in hand.

But before I proceed to handle the next case it may not be amiss to answer that which seems the most considerable allegation against the arguments thus far insisted on. It is then by some objected that musick driveth away evil spirits ; for when David took an harp and played with his hand the evil spirit departed from Saul, 1 Sam. xvi, 23 ;

so that it seems the devils are driven away by sounds, and why not then by words, or fumes, or herbs?

Ans. 1.   It is confessed that Satan does take great advantage from the ill humors and diseases which are in the bodies of men, greatly to molest their spirits.   Especially it is true concerning melancholly, which has therefore been called *Balneum Diaboli*—the devils bath, wherein he delights to be stirring.

2. When bodily diseases are removed by the use of natural means, the matter upon which the evil spirit was wont to operate being gone, he does no more disturb and disquiet the minds of men as before that he did. The passive disposition in the body ceasing, the active affliction caused by the devil ceaseth also. Rulandus writes of possessed persons who were cured by emetic medicines, clearing them of those melancholly humors by means whereof the evil spirit had sometimes great advantages over them. This also Pomponatius does by many instances confirm. Sennertus likewise has divers passages to the same purpose. Also we see, by frequent experience, persons strangely hurried by Satan, have, by the blessing of God upon the endeavour of the physitian, been delivered from those woful molestations. Serrarius, Delrio, Burgensis, and others, commenting on 1 Sam. xvi, conceive that the ingress and egress of evil spirits depends upon the humors and dispositions of the body ; which assertion is not universally true ; for sometimes the devil hath laughed at the physitians, who have thought by medicinal applications to dispossess him. Examples for this may be seen in Fernelius and Codronchus ; wherefore Voetius, in his disputation, *de Emergumenis*, p. 1025, speaketh cautiously and judiciously, in asserting that we

may not suppose that the devils taking bodily possession of this or that person depends wholly upon corporeal dispositions; nevertheless that natural distempers sometimes are an occasion thereof.

3. It is also true that musick is of great efficacy against melancholly discomposures. This notwithstanding, there is no reason to conclude with Mendozo, Bodin, and others, that musick is so hateful to the devil, as that he is necessitated to depart when the pleasant sound is made. If that were so, how comes it to pass that appearing dæmons do sometimes depart with a melodious sound? or that in the conventicles of witches there is musick heard? But La Torr has notably confuted such imaginations. Indeed, the sweetness and delightfulness of musick has a natural power to lenisie melancholly passions. They say that Pythagoras by musick restored a frantick man to his wits again. Thus was Saul's pensive spirit refreshed by David's pleasant harp; and when he was refreshed and well, the evil spirit, which took advantage of his former pensiveness, upon his alacrity departed from him. So that it remains still a truth, that corporeal things have no direct physical influence upon infernal spirits; and that, therefore, for men to think that they shall drive away dæmons by any such means is folly and superstition. I shall add no more in answer to the first *quære* proposed.

A second case which we shall here take occasion to enquire into, is, Whether it be lawful for bewitched persons to draw blood from those whom they suspect for witches; or, to put urin into a bottle, or, to nail an horse-shoe at their doors, or the like, in hopes of recovering health thereby?

Ans. There are several great authors who have discovered and declared the evil of all such practices. In special, Voetius, Sennertus, and our Perkins, disapprove thereof. There is another question, much what of the same nature with this, viz. Whether a bewitched person may lawfully cause any of the devils symbols to be removed, in order to gaining health? As, suppose an image of wax, in which needles are fixed, whereby the devil doth, at the instigation of his servants, torment the diseased person, whether this, being discovered, may be taken away, that so the devils power of operation may cease, and that the sick person may in that way obtain health again? The affirmative of this question is stiffly maintained by Scotus, Cajetan, Delrio, Malderus, and by Popish authors generally. Yet, amongst them, Hesselius, Estius, and Sanchez, hold the negative; and so do all our Protestant writers, so far as I have had occasion to observe. And although some make light of such practices, and others undertake to justifie them, yet it cannot justly be denied but that they are impious follies.

For, 1. They that obtain health in this way have it from the devil. The witch cannot recover them but by the devils help. Hence, as it is unlawful to entreat witches to heal bewitched persons, because they cannot do this but by Satan, so is it very sinful by scratching, or burnings, or detention of urin, &c. to endeavour to constrain them to unbewitch any; for this is to put them upon seeking to the devil. The witch does neither inflict nor remove the disease but by the assistance of the devil; therefore, either to desire or force thereunto, is to make use of the devils help. The person thus recovered cannot say, "The Lord was my healer," but "The devil was my healer." Certainly, it were better for a man to remain sick all his dayes, yea (as Chrysostom speaks), " He had better die than go to the devil for health."

Hence, 2. Men and women have, by such practices as these mentioned, black commerce and communion with the devil. They do (though ignorantly) concern and involve themselves in that covenant which the devil has made with his devoted and accursed vassals ; for, whereas it is pleaded that if the thing bewitched be thrown into the fire or the urin of the sick stopped in a bottle, or an horse shoe nailed before the door, then, by vertue of the compact which is between the devil and his witches, their power of doing more hurt ceaseth. They that shall for such an end so practise, have fellowship with that hellish covenant. The excellent Sennertus argueth solidly in saying, " They that force another to do that which he cannot possibly do but by vertue of a compact with the devil, have themselves implicitly communion with the diabolical covenant." And so is the case here. Who was this art of unbewitching persons in such a way first learned of ? If due enquiry be made, it will be found that magicians and devils were the first discoverers. Porphyrie saith, it was by the revelation of the dæmons themselves that men came to know by what things they would be restrained from, and constrained to this or that: *Euseb. Præp. Evan.* l. v, c. 7 ; Dr. Willet in Ex. vii, quest. 9. To use any ceremonies invented by Satan, to attain a supernatural end, implies too great a concernment with him ; yea, such persons do honour and worship the devil, by hoping in his salvation. They use means to obtain health which is not natural, nor was ever appointed by God, but is wholly of the devils institution ; which he is much pleased with, as being highly honoured thereby; nay, such practices do imply an invocation of the devil for relief, and a pleading with him the covenant which he hath made with the witch, and a declaration of confidence that the father of lies will be as good as his word; for the nefandous language of such a practice is this: "Thou, O devil, hast made a covenant with such an one, that if such a ceremony be used, thou wilt then cease to torment a poor creature that is now afflicted by thee. We have used that ceremony, and therefore now, O Satan, we expect that thou shouldest be as good as thy word, which thou hast covenanted with that servant of thine, and cease tormenting the creature that has been so afflicted by thee." Should men in words speak thus, what horrid impiety were it! Therefore, to do actions which import no less, is (whatever deluded souls think of it) great and heinous iniquity.

3. Let such practitioners think the best of themselves, they are too near a kin to those creatures who commonly pass under the name of "white witches." They that do hurt to others by the devils help are called "black witches:" but there are a sort of persons in the world that will never hurt any; but only by the power of the infernal spirits they will un-bewitch those that seek unto them for relief. I know that by Constantius his law, black witches were to be punished, and white ones indulged; but M. Perkins saith, that the good witch is a more horrible and detestable monster than the bad one. Balaam was a black witch, and Simon Magus a white one. This later did more hurt by his cures than the former by his curses. How persons that shall un-bewitch others, by putting urin into a bottle, or by casting excrements into the fire, or nailing of horse-shoes at men's doors can wholly clear

themselves from being white witches I am not able to understand.

4. Innocent persons have been extreamly wronged by such diabolical tricks ; for sometimes (as is manifest from the relation of the Groton maid, mentioned in the fifth chapter of this essay) the devil does not only himself inflict diseases upon men, but represent the visages of innocent persons . to the phansies of the diseased, making them believe that they are tormented by them, when only himself does it ; and in case they follow the devils direction, by observing the ceremonies which he has invented, he will inflict their bodies no more. So does his malice bring the persons accused by him (though never so innocent) into great suspicion ; and he will cease afflicting the body of one, in case he may ruin the credit of another, and withal endanger the souls of those that hearken to him.

5. If the devil, upon scratchings, or burnings, or stoppings of urin, or the nailing of an horse-shoe, &c. shall cease to afflict the body of any, he does this either as being compelled thereto, or voluntarily. To imagine that such things shall constrain the evil spirit to cease afflicting, whether he will or no, is against all reason ; but if he does this voluntarily, then, instead of hurting their bodies, he does a greater mischief to souls : εχθρων αδωρα δωρα. The devil heals the body that he may wound the soul; he will heal them with all his heart, provided that he may but thereby draw men to look unto him for help, instead of seeking unto God alone, in the use of his own means, and so receive that honour (the thing that he aspires after) which is the Lords due. How gladly will that wicked spirit heal one body, upon condition that he may entangle many souls with superstition ! and if men and women

(especially in places of light) will hearken to him, it is a righteous thing with God to suffer it to be thus. It is past doubt that Satan, who has the power of death, Heb. ii, 14, has also (by Divine permission) power to inflict, and consequently to remove, diseases from the bodies of men. In natural diseases he has many times a great operation, and is willing to have them cured rather by the use of superstitious than of natural means. It is noted in the *Germanic Ephemeris*, for the year 1675, that a man troubled with a fistula, which the physitians by all their art could no way relieve, a person that was esteemed a wizard undertook to cure him ; and applying a powder to the wound, within a few dayes the sick party recovered. The powder was some of the ashes of a certain woman who had been burnt to death for a witch. This was not altogether so horrid as that which is by authors worthy of credit reported to have come to pass in the days of Pope Adrian VI; when, the plague raging in Rome, a magician (whose name was Demetrius Spartan) caused it to be stayed by sacrificing a bull to the devil. See P. Jovius *Histor.* lib. xxi. Such power hath the righteous God given unto Satan over the sinful children of men ; yea, such a ruler hath he set over them as a just punishment for all their wickedness. His chief design is to improve that power which, by reason of sin, he hath obtained to seduce into more sin ; and the Holy God, to punish the world for iniquity, often suffers the enemy to obtain his desire this way. What strange things have been done, and how have diseases been healed, by the sign of the cross many times, by which means Satans design in advancing staurolatry to the destruction of thousands of souls, has too successfully taken place ! And this iniquity did he early and gradually advance amongst Christians. I have not been able without astonishment to read the passages related by Augustin, *de Civitate Dei*, lib. xxii, cap. 8. He there speaks of one Innocentia, whom he calls a most religious woman, who, having a cancer in her breast, the most skilful physitians doubted of the cure; but in her sleep she was admonished to repair unto the font where she had been baptized, and there to sign that place with the sign of the cross; which she did, and was immediately healed of her cancer. In the same chapter he reports that a friend of Hesperius did from Jerusalem send him some earth that was taken out of the place where our Lord Christ had been buried; and that Hesperius had no sooner received it but his house, which before had been molested with evil spirits, was rid of those troublesome guests. He giveth an account also of strange cures wrought by the reliques of the martyrs. It was not (he saith) known where the bodies of Protasius and Gervas (holy martyrs) were buried; but Ambrose had it revealed to him in his sleep; and a blind man approaching near unto the bodies, instantly received his sight. Another was cured of blindness by the reliques of the martyr Stephen. And a child playing abroad, a cartwheel run over him, and bruised him, so that it was thought he would immediately expire; but his mother carrying him unto the house that was built to honour the memory of St. Stephen, life and health were miraculously continued. Many other wonderful cures doth Augustin there mention as done by Stephen's reliques. But who seeth not that the hand of Joab was in all things? For by this means Satan hath filled the world with superstition. The cross is worshipped; the reliques of martyrs are adored; the honour due to God alone is given to the creature.

The same method has the grand enemy observed, that so he might bring that superstition of iconolatry or image worship, which is so provoking to the jealous God, into repute amongst Christians. It would be endless to enumerate how many in Popish countries have been cured of diseases, which for their sins God hath suffered the devil to punish them with, by touching the image of this or that saint; nay, some whose bodies have been possessed with evil spirits, have in that way of superstition found relief; in a more especial manner, when the image of the Virgin Mary hath been presented before persons possessed, the devil in them hath cried out and shrieked after a fearful manner, as if he had been put to horrible torture at the sight of that image, and so hath seemed to depart out of the miserable creature molested by him; and all this that so deluded Papists might be hardened in their superstitious opinion of that image. Many such devices hath Satan to ensnare and ruin the souls of men. Some report that the bodies of excommunicates in the Greek churches at this day are strangely handled by the devil after death hath taken hold of them. M. Ricaut, in his relation of the present state of the Greek Churches, page 279, &c., saith that a grave Kaloir told him that, to his own certain knowledge, a person who fell under their church-censure, after he had been for some time buried, the people where his corps lay interred were affrighted with strange apparitions, which they concluded arose from the grave of the accursed excommunicate, which thereupon was opened, and they found the body uncorrupted, and replete with blood, the coffin furnished with grapes, nuts, &c. brought thither by infernal spirits. The Kaloirs resolved to use the common remedy in those cases, viz. to cut the body in several parts, and to boyl it in wine, as the approved means to dislodge the evil spirit; but his friends intreated rather that the sentence of excommunication might be reversed, which was granted. In the mean time prayers and masses and offerings were presented for the dead; and whilst they were performing these services, on a sudden was heard a rumbling noise in the coffin of the dead party; which being opened, they found the body consumed and dissolved into dust, as if it had been interred seven years. The hour and minute of this dissolution being compared with the date of the patriarchs release when signed at Constantinople, was found exactly to agree with that moment. If there be truth in this relation, 'tis a dreadful evidence of Satans reigning amongst a superstitious people, who nevertheless, call themselves Christians; and that he does by such means as these keep them under chains of darkness still. The devil hath played such reax as these are, not only amongst Christians, but amongst the Gentiles of old; for Titus Latinus was warned in his sleep that he should declare unto the senate that they must reniew their stage plays. He neglecting to deliver his message, was again by the same dæmon spoken unto in his sleep, and severely reproved for his omission, and his son died. Still persisting in his omission, the dæmon again cometh to him, so that he was surprized with an acute and horrible disease. Hereupon, by counsel of his friends, he was carried in his bed into the senate; and as soon as he had declared what he had seen, his health was restored, that he returned home upon his feet. The issue was, stage plays were more in fashion than ever before. Augustin, *de Civitate Dei*, lib. iv, cap. 26. Learned men are not ignorant that strange cures were effected amongst the heathen by the use of talismans or images; of which inventions, Zoroaster (the father of magicians) is supposed to be the first author. It is reported that Virgil made a brazen fly, and a golden horse-leach, whereby flies were hindred from coming into Naples, and the horse-leaches were all killed in a ditch. Thus doth Beelzebub draw miserable men into superstition.

And although I am upon a serious subject, and my design in writing these things is, that so I might bear witness against the superstition which some in this land of light have been found guilty of, and that (if God shall bless what has been spoken to convince men of the error of their way) the like evils may no more be heard of amongst us; this notwithstanding it may not be improper here to recite some facetious passages which I have met with in Hemmingius his discourse *de Superstitione Magica,* since they are to my present purpose, as discovering what delight the infernal spirits take in drawing men to make use of superstitious means for the recovery of health unto their bodies. The learned author mentioned reports, that as he was instructing his pupils in the art of logic, he had occasion to recite a couple of verses consisting of nine hobgoblin words, *fecana, cajeti, daphenes,* &c. adding, by way of joke, that those verses would cure a feaver, if every day a piece of bread were given to the sick person with one of these words written upon it. A simple fellow that stood by thought Hemmingius had been in earnest in what he spoke; and not long after, having a servant that fell sick of a feaver, he gave him the first day a bit of bread, with a paper wherein *fecana* was written, and so on for six dayes until he came to the word *gebali;* and then, on a sudden, his servant was well again. Others seeing the efficacy of the amulet, did the like, and many were cured of feavers thereby.

In the same chapter, page 908, Hemmingius writeth of a knavish scholar, that a certain women repairing to him for help, who was exceedingly troubled with sore eyes, promising him a good reward for his cure, the knave, though he had no skill, yet for lucre sake, he promised to effect a cure; and, in order thereto, taketh a piece of paper, and maketh therein characters, unto which he never saw the like before, only then devised them, and writeth in great letters these abominable words: *Diabolus eruat tibi oculos, et foramina stercoribus impleat.* (The Papists say that their Saint Francis caused the devil to depart out of a possessed person by using an alike brutish expression.) He folded up the paper in a cloth, requiring the diseased party to wear it about her neck ; which she did, and her disease was healed. After two years, being desirous to know what was in the paper, she caused it to be opened and read; and being greatly offended and inraged at this indignity, cast the paper away, immediately upon which her sore eyes returned again. Without doubt, then, the devils design in this cure was to encourage the prophane impostor to endeavour the removal of diseases by like superstitious and wicked practices, whereby his own and the souls of others, unto whom he should impart the mystery, would be endangered. The like is to be affirmed concerning attempts to heal diseases by scratching suspected witches, or stopping urin in bottles, nailing of horse-shoes, &c. It may be the time will come when they that have been thus foolish will feel their own consciences smiting them for what they have done. Let them remember the example of that gracious and famous gentlewoman,

Mrs. Honeywood; the occasion of whose sorrowful and doleful desertion was, in that having a child sick, she asked counsel of a wizard about its recovery. Certainly it is better for persons to repent of sin, the procuring cause of all affliction, and by the prayer of faith to betake themselves to the Lord Jesus, the great Physitian both of body and soul; and so to wait for healing in the use of lawful means, until God shall see meet to bestow that mercy on them; I say this is better than to follow such dark methods as those declared against, wherein, if they have found any success, they may fear it is in wrathful judgment unto them or theirs. Some observe, that persons who receive present healing in such unlawful wayes, usually come to unhappy ends at last. Let me, then, conclude the answer unto the case propounded with the words which the angel bid the prophet Elijah speak to Ahaziah's messengers, 2 Kings i, 3, "Is it because there is no God in Israel that you go to Baalzebub the god of Ekron?"

There is another case of conscience which may here be enquired into, viz. "Whether it be lawful to bind persons suspected for witches, and so cast them into the water, in order to making a discovery of their innocency or guiltiness; so that if they keep above the water, they shall be deemed as confederate with the devil; but if they sink they are to be acquitted from the crime of witchcraft?" As for this way of purgation, it cannot be denied but that some learned men have indulged it. King James approveth of it in his *Discourse of Witchcraft*, b. iii, ch. 6, supposing that the water refuseth to receive witches into its bosom, because they have perfidiously violated their covenant with God, confirmed by water in baptism. Kornmannus and Scribonius do, upon the same ground, justifie this way of tryal. But a worthy casuist of our own giveth a judicious reply to this supposal, viz. that all water is not the water of baptism, but that only which is used in the very act of baptism. Moreover, according to this notion the *proba* would serve only for such persons as have been baptized. Wierus and Bodinus have written against this experiment; so hath Hemmingius, who saith that it is both superstitious and ridiculous. Likewise that learned physitian, John Heurnius, has published a treatise, which he calls, *Responsum ad supremam curiam Hollandiæ, nullum esse æquæ innatationem lamiarum indicium:* that book I have not seen, but I find it mentioned in Meursius his *Athenæ Batavæ.* Amongst English authors, Dr. Cotta hath endeavoured to shew the unlawfulness of using such a practice; also, Mr. Perkins is so far from approving by this probation by cold water, as that he rather inclines to think that the persons who put it in practice are themselves, after a sort, practisers of witchcraft. That most learned, judicious, and holy man, Gisbertus Voetius, in his forementioned exercitation *de Magia,* p. 573, endeavours to evince that the custom of trying witches by casting them into the water is unlawful, a tempting of God, and indirect magic. And that it is utterly unlawful I am by the following reasons convinced:

1. This practice has no foundation in nature, nor in Scripture. If the water will bear none but witches, this must needs proceed either from some natural or some supernatural cause. No natural cause is, or can be, assigned why the bodies of such persons should swim rather than of any other. The bodies of witches have not lost their natural properties: they have weight in them as well as others. Moral changes and viciousness of mind

make no alteration as to these natural proprieties which
are inseparable from the body. Whereas some pretend
that the bodies of witches are possessed with the devil,
and are on that account uncapable of sinking under the
water. Malderus his reply is rational, viz. that the allegation has no solidity in it, witness the Gadarens hoggs,
which were no sooner posssessed with the devil but they
ran into the water and there perished. But if the experiment be supernatural, it must either be divine or diabolical. It is not divine, for the Scripture does no where
appoint any such course to be taken to find out whether
persons are in league with the devil or no. It remains,
then, that the experiment is diabolical. If it be said that
the devil has made a compact with wizards, that they
shall not be drowned, and by that means that covenant
is discovered, the reply is, we may not in the least build
upon the devils word. By this objection, the matter is
ultimately resolved into a diabolical faith. And shall
that cast the scale when the lives of men are concerned?
Suppose the devil saith, these persons are witches, must
the judge, therefore, condemn them?

2. Experience hath proved this to be a fallacious way
of trying witches, therefore it ought not to be practised.
Thereby guilty persons may happen to be acquitted, and
the innocent to be condemned. The devil may have power
to cause supernatation on the water in a person that never
made any compact with him; and many times known
and convicted wizards have sunk under the water when
thrown thereon. In the *Bohemian History* mention is
made of several witches, who being tried by cold water,
were as much subject to submersion as any other persons.
Delrio reports the like of another witch. And Godel-

mannus speaks of six witches in whom this way of trial failed. Malderus saith, it has been known that the very same persons being often brought to this probation by water, did at one time swim and another time sink; and this difference has sometimes hapned according to the different persons making the experiment upon them; in which respect one might with greater reason conclude that the persons who used the experiment were witches, then that the persons tried were so.

3. This way of purgation is to be accounted of, like other provocations or appeals to the judgement of God, invented by men; such as camp-fight, explorations by hot water, &c. In former times it hath been customary (and I suppose tis so still among the Norwegians) that the suspected party was to put his hand into scalding water, and if he received no hurt thereby then was he reputed innocent; but if otherwise, judged as guilty. Also, the trial by fire ordeal has been used in our nation in times of darkness. Thus Emma, the mother of King Edward the Confessor, was led barefoot and blindfold over certain hot irons, and not hapning to touch any of them, was judged innocent of the crime which some suspected her as guilty of. And Kunegund, wife to the Emperour Henry II, being accused of adultery, to clear herself, did in a great and honourable assembly take up seven glowing irons one after another with her bare hand, and had no harm thereby. These bloody kind of experiments are now generally banished out of the world. It is pity the ordeal by cold water is not exploded with the other.

4. This vulgar probation (as it useth to be called) was first taken up in times of superstition, being (as before

was hinted of other magical impostures) propagated from Pagans to Papists, who would (as may be gathered from Bernards 66 *Serm. in Cantica*) sometimes bring those that were under suspicion for heresie unto their purgation in this way. We know that our ancestors, the old Pagan Saxons, had amongst them four sorts of ordeal (*i.e.*, trial or judgement, as the Saxon word signifies), whereby, when sufficient proof was wanting, they sought (according as the prince of darkness had instructed them) to find out the truth concerning suspected persons, one of which ordeals was this, the persons surmised to be guilty, having cords tied under their arms, were thrown with it into some river, to see whether they would sink or swim : so that this probation was not originally confined to witches, but others supposed to be criminals were thus to be tried; but in some countries they thought meet thus to examine none but those who have been suspected for familiarity with the devil. That this custom was in its first rise superstitious, is evident from the ceremonies of old used about it. For the *proba* is not canonical, except the person be cast into the water with his right hand tied to his left foot. Also, by the principle which some approvers of this experiment alledge to confirm their fansies, their principle is, *Nihil quod per necromantian fit, potest in aqua fallere aspectum intuentium.* Hence William of Malmsbury, lib. ii, p. 67, tells a fabulous story (though he relates it not as such) of a traveller in Italy that was by a witch transformed into an asse, but retaining his humane understanding, would do such feats of activity as one that had no more wit than an asse could not do ; so that he was sold for a great price ; but breaking his halter, he ran into the water, and thence was instantly unbewitched, and turned into a man again. This is as true as Lucian's relation about his own being by witchcraft transformed into an asse ; and I suppose both are as true as that cold water will discover who are witches. It is to be lamented that Protestants should in these dayes of light either practise or plead for so superstitious an invention, since Papists themselves have of later times been ashamed of it. Verstegan in his *Antiquities*, lib. iii. p. 53, speaking of the trials by ordeal, and of this by cold water in particular, has these words : " These aforesaid kinds of ordeals the Saxons long after their Christianity continued ; but seeing they had their beginnings in paganism, and were not thought fit to be continued amongst Christians, at the last, by a decree of Pope Stephen II, they were abolished." Thus he. Yea, this kind of trial by water was put down in Paris A.D. 1594, by the supream court there. Some learned papists have ingenuously acknowledged that such probations are superstitous. It is confessed that they are so by Tyræus, Binsfeldius, Delrio, and by Malderus *de Magia*, tract x, cap 8, dub. 11, who saith that they who shall practise this superstition, and pass a judgement of death upon any persons on this account, will (without repentance) be found guilty of murder before God.

It was in my thoughts to have handled some other cases of the like nature with these insisted on ; but upon further consideration, I suppose it less needful, the practices which have given occasion for them being so grosly superstitious, as that they are ashamed to show their heads openly. The Chaldæans, and other magicians amongst the heathen nations of old, practised a sort of divination by sieves (which kind of magic is called *coscinomantia*). The like superstition has been frequent in Popish countries, where they have been wont to utter some words of Scripture and the names of certain saints over a sieve, that so they might by the motion thereof know where something stollen or lost was to be found. Some also have believed that if they should cast lead into the water, then Saturn would discover to them the thing they enquired after. It is not Saturn but Satan that maketh the discovery, when any thing is in such a way revealed. And of this sort is the foolish sorcery of those women that put the white of an egg into a glass of water, that so they may be able to divine of what occupation their future husbands shall be. It were much better to remain ignorant than thus to consult with the devil. These kind of practices appear at first blush to be diabolical, so that I shall not multiply words in evincing the evil of them. It is noted that the children of Israel did secretly those things that are not right against the Lord their God, 2 Kings xvii, 9. I am told that there are some who secretly practice such abominations as these last mentioned, unto whom the Lord in mercy give deep and unfeigned repentance and pardon for their grievous sin.

CHAPTER IX.

DEAF AND DUMB PERSONS.

A strange relation of a woman in Weymouth in New England that has been dumb and deaf ever since she was three years old, who, nevertheless, has a competent knowledge in the mysteries of religion, and is admitted to the sacrament. Some parallel instances. Of wayes to teach those that are naturally deaf and dumb to speak. Another relation of a man in Hull in New England, under whose tongue a stone bred. Concerning that petrifaction which humane bodies are subject unto. That plants and diverse sorts of animals have sometimes bred in the bodies of men.

AVING dispatched the disgression which the things related in some of the preceding chapters did necessarily lead us into, I now proceed in commemorating some other remarkables, which it is pity but that posterity should have the knowledge of. I shall in this chapter only take notice of two particulars amongst ourselves, with some parallel instances which have hapned in other parts of the world. I am informed that there is now at Weymouth in New England a man and his wife who are both of them deaf, that the woman had been so from her infancy; and yet she understands as much concerning the state of the countrey, and of particular persons therein, and of observable occurrences, as almost any one of her sex; and (which is more wonderful), though she is not able to speak a word, she has by signs made it appear that she is not

ignorant of Adam's fall, nor of man's misery by nature, nor of redemption by Christ, and the great concernments of eternity, and of another world, and that she herself has had experience of a work of conversion in her own soul. I have made enquiry about this matter of some that are fully acquainted therewith, and have from a good hand received this following account :—" Matthew Prat, aged about fifty-five years, was in his minority by his godly parents educated religiously, and taught to read. When he was about twelve years old, he became totally deaf by sickness, and so hath ever since continued. After the loss of his hearing he was taught to write. His reading and writing he retaineth perfectly, and makes much good improvement of both ; but his speech is very broken and imperfect, not easily intelligible ; he maketh use of it more seldom, only to some few that are wonted to it ; he discourseth most by signs, and by writing. He is studious and judicious in matters of religion ; hath been in church-fellowship, a partaker of all ordinances near thirty years ; hath approved himself unto good satisfaction therein, in all wayes of church communion, both in publick and private, and judged to be a well-wrought convert and real Christian. Sarah Prat, his wife, being about forty-three years old, was also quite deprived of hearing by sickness, when about the third year of her age, after she could speak, and had begun to learn letters ; having quite lost hearing, she lost all speech (doubtless all remembrance and understanding of words and language); her religious parents being both dead, her godly brother, Ephraim Hunt (yet surviving), took a fatherly care of her ; she also happily fell under the guardianship and tuition of the Reverend Mr. Thomas Thacher, who laboured with design to teach her to understand speech or language by writing, but it was never observed that any thing was really effected ; she hath a notable accuracy and quickness of understanding by the eye ; she discourseth altogether by signs; they that are able to discourse with her in that way will communicate any matter much more speedily (and as full) as can be by speech, and she to them. Her children sign from the breast, and learn to speak by their eyes and fingers sooner than by their tongues. She was from her childhood naturally sober, and susceptible of good civil education, but had no knowledge of a Deity, or of any thing that doth concern another life and world ; yet God hath of his infinite mercy revealed Himself, his Son, and the great mysteries of salvation, unto her by an extraordinary and more immoderate working of his spirit (as tis believed), in a saving work of conversion. An account of her experiences was taken from her in writing by her husband ; upon which she was examined by the elders of the church, they improving her husband and two of her sisters, intellectual persons, and notably skill'd in her artificial language, by whose help they attained good satisfaction that she understandeth all the principles of religion : those of the unity of the divine essence, trinity of persons, the personal union, the mystical union, they made most diligent enquiry about, and were satisfied that her knowledge and experience was distinct and sound, and they hoped saving. She was under great exercise of spirit, and most affectionately concerned for and about her soul, her spiritual and eternal estate ; she imparted herself to her friends, and expressed her desire of help; she made use of the Bible and other good books, and remarkt such places and passages as suited her condition, and that with tears. She did once in her exercise write with a pin upon a trencher three times over, 'Ah, poor soul!' and therewithal burst forth into tears before divers of her friends. She hath been wont to enquire after the text, and when it hath been shewed to her, to look and muse upon it; she knoweth most, if not all, persons names that she hath acquaintance with; if Scripture names, will readily turn and point to them in the Bible. It may be conceived, that although she understands neither words, letters, nor language, yet she understands things hieroglyphically; the letters and words are unto her but signs of the things, and as it were hieroglyphicks. She was very desirous of church communion in all ordinances, and was admitted with general and good satisfaction, and hath approved herself to the best observation a grave and gracious woman. They both attend publick worship with much reverence and constancy, and are very inoffensive, and (in divers respects) exemplary in their conversation." Thus far is that narrative, written June 27, 1683.

I suppose no one that rightly considers the circumstances of this relation will make a scruple about the lawfulness of admitting such persons to participate in the holy mysteries of Christ's kingdom. All judicious casuists determine, that those who were either born, or by any accident made, deaf and dumb, if their conversation be blameless, and they able by signs (which are analogous to verbal expressions) to declare their knowledge and faith, may as freely be received to the Lords supper as any that shall orally make the like profession. Of this judgement was Luther, and Melancthon *in Consil.* part i, page 268; Gerhard *Loc. Com.* tom. v. Thess. 226; Alting, *Loc. Com.* part i, page 90; Voetius *Disp. Select.* part ii, *in Appendice*

de Surdis.   Balduinus, in his *Cases of Conscience*, lib. ii,
c. 12, does confirm this, by producing several instances
of dumb persons admitted to the communion.   It is certain that some such have been made to understand the
mysteries of the Gospel, so as to suffer martyrdome on that
account.

In the year 1620, one that was deaf and dumb, being
solicited by the Papists to be present at masse, chose
rather to suffer death.   It is also a thing known, that men
are able by signs to discourse, and to communicate their
sentiments one to another.   There are above thirty mutes
kept in the Ottoman court for the Grand Seignior to sport
with ; concerning whom, Mr. Ricaut, in his *History of the
Present State of the Ottoman Empire* (p. 62) reports that
they are able by signs not only to signifie their sence in
familiar questions, but recount stories, and understand
the fables of the Turkish religion, the laws and precepts of
the Alcoran, the name of Mahomet, and what else may be
capable of being expressed by the tongue.   This language
of the mutes is so much in fashion in the Ottoman court,
that almost every one can deliver his sense in it.   And
that deaf persons have been sometimes able to write, and
to understand what others say to them by the very motion
of their lips is most certain.   Camerarius tells us of a
young man and a maid, then living at Noremberg, who,
though deaf and dumb, could read and write and cypher,
and by the motion of a mans lips knew his meaning.
Platerus speaketh of one deaf and dumb born, that yet
could express his mind in a table-book, and understood
what others wrote therein ; and was wont to attend upon
the ministry of Oecolampadius, understanding many things
by the motion of the lips of the preacher.   Mr. Clark, in

14

his *Examples* (vol. i, chap. 33), saith, that there was a woman in Edinburgh in Scotland (her name was Gennet Lowes), who being naturally deaf and dumb, could understand what people said meerly by the moving of their lips. It is famously known, that Mr. Crisp of London could do the like. Borellus giveth an account of one that lost his hearing by a violent disease when he was five years old, yet if they did but whisper to him, he could by their lips perceive what they said. There is one now living (or that not many years since was so) in Silesia, in whom that disease of the small-pox caused a total deafness, who, nevertheless, by exact observing the motion of mens lips, can understand what they say; and if they do but whisper, he perceives what they say better than if they vociferate never so loudly; he attends upon publick sermons, being able to give an account of what is delivered, provided he may but see the preacher speaking, though he cannot hear a word. It is consistent with reason that mutes should understand what others say by the motion of their lips, since it is evident that the lips are of great use in framing speech. Hence Job calls his speech, " the moving of his lips," chap. xvi, ver. 5; and we know that tongueless persons, by the help of their lips and other organs of speech, have been able to speak. Ecclesiastical story informs us of several confessors of the truth, who after their tongues were cut out by bloody persecutors, could still bear witness to the truth. Honorichus (that cruel king of the Vandals) caused the tongues of many to be violently pluckt out of their mouths, who after that could speak as formerly; only two of them, when they became guilty of the sin of uncleanness, were able to speak no more. This has been attested by three credible witnesses who knew the persons : see Mr. Baxter's *Church History*, p. 130.   There is lately published (in Latin) a very strange relation of a child in France (his name was Peter Durand) who being visited with the small-pox when he was about six years old, his tongue putrified, and was quite consumed ; after which (the *uvula* in his mouth being longer than it was before) he could, by the help of the other organs of speech, discourse as plainly as if he had never lost his tongue.   These things are marveilous : and yet I have lately met with a passage more strange than any of these related.   There is (or was in the year 1679) living, near Kerchem in Germany, a man (his name is John Algair) who suddenly lost the use of his speech : the case has been so with him, that fourteen years together he can never speak but one hour of the day ; just as the sun cometh to the meridian, he has the liberty of his speech for an hour and no more, so that he knoweth exactly when it is twelve a clock, because then he can speak, and not a minute before that, nor a minute after one.   This is related in the *Germanic Ephemerides of Miscellaneous Curiosities* for the year 1679 (observat. 188).   It is evident that the sun has a marvelous influence as to some diseases which the bodies of men are subject unto ; for in Egypt, though the plague rage the day before, on that very day when the sun enters into Leo it ceaseth, when also the floods of Nilus abate, as geographers inform us.

Moreover, it is possible by art to teach those that are by nature deaf and dumb to speak.   The *Dactylogy* of Beda is pretty, whereby men speak as nimbly with the fingers as with the tongue ; taking five fingers of the one hand for vowels, and the several positions of the other for consonants.   But that deaf persons may learn to speak

14*a*

happy experience hath proved, and that by many instances.
A. Castro has given an account of the method by him successfully observed in teaching a boy to speak that was
born deaf.   After the use of some purgative medicines, he
caused the hair to be shaven off from his head, over the
coronal suture, and then frequently anointed the shaven
place with a mixture of *aqua vitæ, saltpeter, oyl of bitter
almonds*, &c.   Having done this, he began to speak to the
deaf person (not at his ear, but) at his *coronal suture ;* and
there, after the use of unctions and emunctions, the sound
would pierce, when at his ears it could not enter ; so did he
by degrees teach him to speak.   (*Vide Ephem. German.*
anno 1670, observat. 35.)   But others have, with good
effect, followed another kind of method.   There was a
Spanish nobleman (brother to the constable of Castile),
who being born deaf, and consequently dumb, from his
infancy, physitians had long in vain tried experiments for
his relief.   At last a certain priest undertook to teach
him to speak.   His attempt was at first laughed at ; but
within a while the gentleman was able (notwithstanding
his deafness still remained) to converse and discourse with
any friend.   He was taught to speak by putting a cord
about his neck, and straitning or losening the same, to
advertise him when to open or shut his mouth, by the
example of his teacher.   Nor was there any difference
found between his speech and that of other men, only that
he did not regulate his voice, speaking commonly too high.
(*Vid. Conferences of Virtuosi*, p. 215).   Not long since,
Fran. Mercur. Helmont, designing to teach a deaf man
to speak, concluded it would be more easily practicable if
the experiment were made with an eastern wide-mouthed
language, which does remarkably expose to the eye the

motions of the lips, tongue, and throat. Accordingly he tried with the Hebrew tongue, and in a short time his dumb schollar became an excellent Hebrician. Others have lately been as successful in their attempts to cause deaf persons to speak and understand the European languages. We need not go out of our own nation, for there we find living instances. In the *Philosophical Transactions* for the year 1670, numb. 61, an account is given concerning Mr. Daniel Whaley, of Northampton, in England, who, by an accident, lost his hearing when he was about five years of age, and so his speech, not at once, but by degrees in about half a years time. In the year 1661, the learned and ingenious Dr. Wallis, of Oxford, undertook to teach the deaf gentleman to speak and write. Nor did the doctor fail in attaining his end ; for in the space of one year the dumb man had read over great part of the English Bible, and had attained so much skill as to express himself intelligibly in ordinary affairs, to understand letters written to him, and to write answers to them. And when foreigners, out of curiosity, came to visit him, he was able to pronounce the most difficult words of their language (even Polish itself) which any could propose unto him. Nor was this the only person on whom the doctor showed his skill, but he has since done the like for another (a gentleman of very good family), who did from his birth want his hearing. Likewise, Dr. Holder, in his late book about the natural production of letters, giveth rules for the teaching of the deaf and dumb to speak.

I have the rather mentioned these things, for that there are several others in this countrey who are deaf and dumb, when, as if they had an ingenious instructor, I am abundantly satisfied that they might be taught to speak, their deafness notwithstanding. Nor is this more difficult than it is to learn those that are blind to write; which, though some may think it impossible and incredible, there is (or, at least, three years ago there was) a living instance to convince them; for, in the *Weekly Memorials for the Ingenious*, lately published at London (in page 80), I find an observable passage, which I shall here cause to be transcribed and inserted, from the *Journal des Scavans*, set forth March 25, 1680 :—

An Extract of a Letter written from Lyons, by M. Spon, M.D., &c., concerning a remarkable Particular.

"Esther Elizabeth van Waldkirk, daughter of a merchant of Shaffhausen, residing at Geneva, aged at present nineteen years, having been blind from two moneths old, by a distemper falling on her eyes, nevertheless hath been put on to the study of learning by her father, so that she understands perfectly, French, High-Dutch, and Latin; she speaks ordinarily Latin with her father, French with her mother, and High-Dutch with the people of that nation; she hath almost the whole Bible by heart, is well skill'd in philosophy, plays on the organs and violin, and, which is wonderful in this condition, she hath learned to write, by an invention of her fathers, after this manner :—

"There was cut for her upon a board, all the letters of the alphabet, so deep as to feel the figures with her fingers, and to follow the traces with a pencil, till that she had accustomed herself to make the characters. Afterwards they made for her a frame, which holds fast her paper when she will write, and which guides her hand to make straight lines; she writes with a pencil rather than with ink, which might either foul her paper, or, by falling, might cause her to leave words imperfect. 'Tis after this manner that she writes often in Latin to her friends, as well as in the other two languages."

But this much may suffice to be spoken about mutes, and the possibility of their being taught intelligibly to express themselves, though their deafness should still remain. I now proceed unto things of another nature : and the next remarkable which we shall take notice of, is concerning one now in Hull in New England (viz. Lieutenant Collier), who, about sixteen years ago, being sensible of pain in his throat, made use of the common remedies in that case, but to little effect. At last the pain about those parts became very extream, especially when he drank any beer, nor was he able to swallow without much difficulty, so that he lived upon water and liquid substances. After he had been for some time in this misery, a stone appeared under his tongue, which, though visible to the eye, continued there for some dayes before it was taken out ; and at last of itself fell into his mouth (and so into his hands) leaving an hole behind it at the roof of his tongue. This stone I have by me, whilest I write this, only some part of it is broken away ; that which remains weighs twelve grains. The person concerned affirms that it was first of a yellowish colour, but now it is white, not being an inch in length, in shape somewhat resembling a mans tongue. But that which made the matter the more strange, was, that when he had occasion to void urin, he was in as much pain as if the stone had been in his bladder or kidney; for when his urin passed from him he was usually put into a sweat with pain and anguish, the eason whereof I shall leave unto the more curious inquisitors into nature to determine.   There are lapideous humors in the bodies of men, occasioned, sometimes by colds, sometimes by ill diet, which are apt to become stones.   It is related by the late *German. Curiosi*, that in the year 1655 a person of quality in Dantzick was much afflicted with a painful tumor in his tongue; a skilful chirurgeon, perceiving a stone there, cut it out, upon which the patient recovered, the stone being as big as a small olive.   The like hapned to another in the year 1662. Again in the year 1678, a gentlewoman in Grunberg, having been for several years in the spring and in the fall afflicted with a pain in her tongue, at last the pain became intollerable, untill a stone as big as a filberd-nut came out of her tongue, upon which she had ease.   In the *Philo-sophical Transactions* for the year 1672, page 4062, an account is given of a man in England who had a stone breeding under his tongue, occasioned by his suffering much cold in a winter sea voyage.   Not long after his landing he found an hard lump in the place where the stone was generated.   There were eight years between the time of the stones first breeding and its being taken away. Upon a fresh cold-taking he suffered much pain; but when his cold was over his pain ceased.   At last it caused a swelling about his throat, especially at the first draught of beer at meals.   The last summer of his affliction the stone caused him to be vertiginous; and some dayes before its excision such an abundance of rheume and spittle flowed out of his mouth as would presently wet all the bed about him.   The stone weighed but seven grains, being much of the shape of our ordinary horse-beans.   This stone was by judicious observators judged to be one of those tumors called *atheroma*, and therefore the name they

would have it called by is *lapis atheromatis.* Stones
have been taken out of the joynts of many gouty persons,
some cold imposthumes arising in their joynts before.
Sennertus, Platerus, Bartholinus, Skenckius, and other
learned men, have observed that humane bodies are subject
to petrification in every part of them; and many notable
instances to this purpose are mentioned in the *Philosophical Transactions* at London, and by the *Curiosi* in
forreign countries. I presume it will not be unacceptable
unto such as have not those books for me to relate some
examples out of them to our present purpose. There was
then a man, who being troubled with a catarrh and
obstruction of urin, when a vein was opened, there came
four stones out of it. Again, a person that was much
afflicted with a distillation of rhume, and another that was
continually imployed in preparing lime, small stones bred
in their lungs, many of which (as big as peas) were
coughed up. A stone as big as a gooses egg was found
adhering to the liver of the Countess of Nadasti. One
that died by a violent pain in his head, there was found a
stone therein between the *dura* and the *pia mater.* A
woman that died by nephretick pains, the physitian found
her left kidney to be filled with large stones; as for the
right kidney, the substance of it was converted into a perfect stone. In the same year, there was an ox near Padua
in Italy, which could by no means be made fat, but was
observed to be strangely stupid, and to hold down his
head after an unusual manner; they that killed him found
that his brains were petrified, being as hard as marble.
The like hapned to another ox in Suecia.

Nor are humane bodies wholly free from the like petrification; for anatomists of good credit affirm that they

have known several dissected by them, whose brains were
in part petrified; nay, the heart itself is not exempted from
this misery.   There were three stones found in the heart
of the Emperour Maxmilian II. It is no less strange
that bones should be generated in the lungs, heart, and
other bowels.   Nothing in nature seems more mysterious
than that which hapned to the brother of the illustrious
Caspar Horwath, a baron in the kingdom of Hungaria,
who having been for some years consumptive, after his
death the physitians opened him, and found in the midst
of his heart (which was very much dried) a bone like an
almond, perfectly expressing the genuine effigies of the
dead gentleman, representing his very beard, and all the
features of his face so exactly, as that it was not possible
for any artist to have drawn a picture more like the person
than nature had performed in this bone. (*Vide Germ.
Ephem.* an. 1671, observ. 40, p. 72.) Moreover, credible
histories report, that in Africa the bodies of men (and of
other animals) have been turned into perfect stones. Nor
is that much less prodigious which Albosius reports concerning a tailors wife (her name was Columba Chatry),
who having conceived with child, the usual time for deli-
very being come, was in great pain, and other symptoms
of birth appeared, yet she was never delivered, but lived
twenty-eight years in much misery, still retaining her
burden. After her death the physitians found that the
child within her was turned into a stone. (*Vide* Sennert.
Pract. Med. liv. iv, part 2, cap. 8, *de Lythopædia.*)
Thuanus hath another instance like unto this. And within
a few years there hapned a thing as prodigious and astonishing (though without any lapidification) as any of the former
relations; for in the year **1652**, the wife of John Puget,
at Tolouse in France, being with child, and come to her

full time, was in travailing pains, but no child followed.
For the space of twenty years she perceived the child to
stir, with many troublesome symptoms accompanying; but
for the last six years of her life she perceived it not to move.
Falling sick, she requested a chirurgeon to open her after
she was dead: that being done, a child was found in her
body, neither putrified nor yet petrified; all the inward
parts of the child were discoloured with a blackishness,
except the heart, which was red, and without any issuing
blood. This infant weighed eight pound averdupoise. The
mother died June 18, 1678, being about the sixty-fourth
year of her age. I should hardly give credit to a story so
stupendous and incredible, were it not mentioned in the
Philosophical Transactions (No. 139, p. 979), as a thing
most undoubtedly true. But to conclude the discourse
we are upon, I shall only add here, that it is not so strange
for stones to breed in all parts of the bodies of men, as for
plants and diverse sorts of animals to be formed therein;
yet many authors have attested to this; and a late writer
affirms that there was not long since a woman, who having
drunk stagnating water out of a pond where frogs used to
keep, grew cachectical, and swelled so as that she was
thought to be hydropical. One evening, walking near the
pond where the frogs croked, she perceived frogs to croke
in her belly. Acquainting a physitian, he gave her a strong
cathartick, whereupon she cast up two living frogs,
pretty large, green on their back, and yellow under their
bellies, and voided three dead by siege, with a great deal
of greenish serum; after which she was well disposed.
Again, in the year 1680, a man, living near Lyons in
France, voided a worm seven ells long, scaly like a serpent,
and hairy. See the *Weekly Memorials for the Ingenious*,
pp. 67, 82, 100.

CHAPTER X.

OF REMARKABLE TEMPESTS, Etc. IN NEW ENGLAND.

A remark upon the hurricane, anno 1635. A remarkable accident by a sudden freezing of rain in the year 1659. A strange whirl-wind in Cambridge, 1680. Another in New Haven Colony, 1682. Another at Springfield. Some parallel instances. Of earthquakes in this countrey. Land wonderfully removed. Parallel stories. Of remarkable floods this year, not only in New England, but in other parts of the world. An account of a prodigious flood in France five years ago, with conjectures concerning the natural reason of it.

OTHER remarkables, besides those already mentioned, have hapned in this countrey, many of which I cannot insert, as not having received a full and clear account concerning them. Nevertheless, such particulars as I have by good and credible hands been informed of, I shall further add. And let it be here recorded, that we have seen diverse tempests in New-England which deserve to have a remark set upon them, in respect of some notable circumstances wherewith they have been attended. I have not heard of any storm more dismal than the great hurricane which was in August, 1635, the fury whereof threw down (either breaking them off by the bole or plucking them up by the roots) thousands of great trees in the woods. Of this some account is given by Mr.

220

Thacher, in the first chapter of our present collection. And I must confess, I have peculiar reason to commemorate that solemn providence, inasmuch as my father and mother and four of my brethren were then in a vessel upon the coast of New-England, being at anchor amongst the rocks at the Isles of Sholes when the storm began; but their cables broke, and the ship was driving directly upon a mighty rock, so that all their lives were given up for lost; but then in an instant of time, God turned the wind about, which carried them from the rock of death before their eyes. This memorable providence is mentioned in my fathers life, both in that edition published in this countrey, page 21, 22, and also in that published by Mr. Clark in his last volume of lives, page 131; wherefore I shall not here further enlarge upon it. In the year 1659, near the town of Concord in New-England, there hapned that which is somewhat rare, and therefore to be reckoned amongst remarkable accidents. In the moneth of February, it having rained a great part of the day, at night it froze extreamly, so as that many limbs were broken off from many trees by the weight of the ice, caused by the sudden friezing of the rain upon the boughs. It was somewhat formidable to hear the crackings made a good part of the night, by the falling of so much wood (thousands of cords) as was by that means occasioned. Of later years several places in this countrey have been visited with strange and awful tempests. That was very remarkable which hapned in Cambridge in New-England, July 8, 1680; the persons who were witnesses of that very amazing providence have declared what themselves observed about it; the history whereof I shall here insert, a worthy person having furnished me with the following narrative :—"Samuel Stone of Cambridge in New-England does declare and testifie, that July, 1680, about two of clock in the afternoon, he being with his young son in the field, the wind then southerly, he observed a cloud in the north-west in opposition to the wind, which caused a singing noise in the air; and the wind increased till the whirl-wind came, which began in the meadow near where he was, though then it was not so violent as it proved afterwards. As it passed by him it sucked up and whirled about the hay that was within the compass of it; it passed from him towards his house over an hill, tearing down several trees as it went along; and, coming to his barn, carried off a considerable part of the roof (about twenty-four foot one way, and thirty the other), fell near the dwelling-house where people were, yet could not its fall be heard by them (yet it was so great that it was heard by some a mile off) by reason of the great rushing noise of the wind. Afterwards, as it pressed towards Matthew Bridge's house, it tore down some trees and Indian corn, and there rose up into the air for the space of a quarter of a mile; afterwards it came down upon the earth in a more violent manner; the effects whereof he saw not, but it may be known by the following relation.

" Matthew Bridge, who was an eye-witness of what happened, declares that he observed a thick cloud coming along his fathers field before his house, as to appearance very black; in the inside of the cloud, as it passed over him, there seemed to be a light pillar, as he judged about eight or ten foot diameter, which seemed to him like a screw or solid body. Its motion was continually circular, which turned about the rest of the cloud. It passed along upon the ground, tearing all before it, bushes by the roots, yea the earth itself, removing old trees as they lay along on the earth, and stones of a great magnitude, some of which could not be found again. Great trees were twisted and torn down, and carried a distance from the place where they were; branches of trees, containing about a load of wood, were blown from their bodies, and carried forty yards or more. The cloud itself was filled with stones, bushes, boughs, and other things that it had taken up from the earth, so that the top and sides of the cloud seemed like a green wood. After it went from him, it went a mile and half before it scattered, bearing down the trees before it above a mile in breadth; passing through a thick swamp of spruce pine and other young trees (which was about half a mile through), it laid all flat to the ground, yet the trees, being young, are since risen up. It was observable, as it passed through a new-planted orchard, it not only pulled up some of the young trees by the roots, but broke off some of them in the bodies, about two or three foot high, as if they had been shot off, not hurting the stocks. Moreover, there was such a great noise made by the storm, that other considerable noises at the same time, as falling of very great trees very near one, could not be heard. The above-said Matth. Bridge, and a boy with him, endeavoured to run to the house, but were prevented by the storm, so that they were necessitated to ly flat upon the ground behind some bushes, and this thick cloud and pillar passed so near them as almost to touch their feet, and with its force bent the bushes down over them, and yet their lives were preserved. John Robbins, a servant man, was suddenly slain by this storm, his body being much bruised, and many bones broken by the violence thereof." Thus concerning that.

The last year was attended with sundry remarkable tempests in several parts of this countrey. One of which hapned in New-Haven Colony, June 10, 1682, concerning which I have received from a good hand the following account:—This storm began about 2 h. P.M., and continued two hours. It reached Stratford, Milford, Fairfield, New-Haven, and it was very violent in every one of these places, especially at Milford, where three barns were blown down by it, and one house new built, that was forty foot in length, well inclosed, was moved from the foundation at one corner, near two foot and an half. But the greatest strength of the storm was about six miles above Stratford, as is evident by the great havock that is there made: for the compass of half a mile in breadth, scarce a tree left standing, which is not shaken by the storm; the strongest oaks are torn up by the roots, some two foot, some three foot and more, over; young saplins that were not so big as a mans middle, were broken off in the midst. The storm came out of the west, and the wind did before the end somewhat vere towards the north; it was attended with a violent rain: the very noise of the wind in the woods was such, as that those that were in it could not hear the fall of a tree a few rods from them. Great limbs of trees were carried like feathers in the air an incredible distance from the trees they were broken from; many that were at work in the woods were in great danger, and had no way to preserve themselves but by running into open plains, where there were no trees. The strength of the storm passed along east and by south, over Stratford river, and between Milford and New-Haven, and there it passed away into the sound towards Long-Island. Many thousands of trees were blown down both above and below the place before specified; but in the compass of that half mile the greatest strength of the storm was; for here almost there was an universal destruction of all the trees, leaving the place upon hills so naked that very few trees are found standing. Thus of that tempest.

Also, on June 26, 1682, there were the most amazing lightnings that have been known in New-England, a great part of the night being thereby made as light as the day. In some places grievous hail fell with the lightning, breaking the windows of some houses. But at Springfield it was most dreadful, where great pieces of ice, some seven, some nine inches about, fell down from the clouds with such violence that the shingles upon some houses were broken thereby, and holes beaten into the ground that a man might put his hand in. Several acres of corn (both wheat and Indian) were beat down and destroyed by the hail. Yet this hail-storm (though terrible) was not comparable to that which hapned three years ago in another part of the world, viz., at the town of Blois in France, where the people were by the amazing fury of a prodigious tempest affrighted out of their sleep, and forced to rise out of their beds, that they might save their lives. Several houses and two (churches) meeting-houses, were beat down to the ground. This tempest was likewise accompanied with a most prodigious hail, many thousand stones being found as big as a mans fist. This unusual artillery of Heaven broke all the slates wherewith the houses were covered, and the glass-windows, all over the town, as if they had been beaten in a morter. Without the town eight whole parishes with the fields adjacent, were wholly ruined by that hail, in such a terrible manner, that it seemed as if no corn had been sown, or vines planted there.   Four other parishes were much endamaged, multitudes of chimneys beaten down, so that the damage thereby, with the breaking of the windows and tyles, were valued to be above two hundred thousand crowns; and the harm in the vineyards and corn-fields invaluable. The Divine Providence was very much seen, in that, man, woman, nor child, were killed in this fearful desolation, The reader may see a more full relation of this prodigious hail-storm in Mr. Burton's *Surprising Miracles of Nature,* pages 180, 181.   As for those sudden gusts wherewith part of Cambridge and several towns near New Haven in New England were alarmed, the like hapned at a place in England, fourteen years ago, the account whereof may be seen in the *Philosophical Transactions,* number 17, page 2156, which I shall here insert.   It is that which followeth.

Octob. 30, 1669, betwixt five and six of the clock in the evening, the wind westerly, at Ashley in Northamptonshire hapned a formidable hurricane, scarce bearing sixty yards in its breadth, and spending itself in about seven minutes of time.   Its first discerned assault was upon a milk-maid, taking her pail and hat from off her head, and carrying it many scores of yards from her, where it lay undiscovered some dayes.   Next it storm'd the yard of one Sprigge, dwelling in Westthorp (a name of one part of the town), where it blew a wagon-body off of the axel-trees, breaking the wheels and axel-trees in pieces, and blowing three of the wheels so shattered over a wall; the wagon stood somewhat cross to the passage of the wind. Another wagon of Mr. Salisburies marched with great speed upon its wheels against the side of his house, to the astonishment of the inhabitants. A branch of an ash-tree, of that bigness that two lusty men could scarce lift it, blew over Mr. Salisburies house without hurting it, and yet this branch was torn from a tree an hundred yards distant from that house. A slate was found upon a window of the house of Samuel Templer, Esq., which very much bent an iron bar in it, and yet tis certain that the nearest place the slate was at first forced from was near two hundred yards. Not to take notice of its stripping of several houses, one thing is remarkable, which is, that at Mr. Maidwells, senior, it forced open a door, breaking the latch, and thence marching through the entry, and forcing open the dairy door, it overturned the milk vessels, and blew out three panes or lights in the window; next it mounted the chambers, and blew out nine lights more; from thence it proceeded to the parsonage, whose roof it more than decimated; thence crosseth the narrow street, and forcibly drives a man headlong into the doors of Tho. Brigges. Then it passed with a cursory salute at Thomas Marstones, down to Mr. George Wignils, at least a furlongs distance from Marstones, and two furlongs from Sprigges, where it plaid notorious exploits, blowing a large hovel of peas from its supporters, and settling it cleaverly upon the ground, without any considerable damage to the thatch. Here it blew a gate-post, fixed two foot and an half in the ground, out of the earth, and carried it into the fields many yards from its first abode.

Thus much concerning remarkable tempests.

Earthquakes deserve to be mentioned amongst Remarkable providences, since Aristotle himself could say, that the man is stupid and unreasonable who is not affected

with them.   This part of the world hath not been altogether free from such tremendous accidents, albeit (through
the gracious providence of God) there never was yet any
harm done amongst us thereby, so far as I have heard.
The year 1638 was attended with a considerable
earthquake.   There are who affirm that they heard a
strange kind of noise before the earth began to tremble.
Another earthquake was observed in some parts of New
England, A.D. 1658.   Also in the year 1662, on the 26,
27, and 28 of January, the earth was shaken at least six
times in the space of three dayes.   I remember that upon
the first approach of the earthquake the things on the
shelves in the house began to move.   Many people ran
out of their houses with fear and amazement; but no
house fell, nor was any damage sustained.   There was
another earthquake, April 3, 1668.   We in Boston were
sensible of it, but some other parts of the countrey were
more terribly shaken.   The Indians say that the
earthquake this year did stop the course of a considerable
river.   It is also reported, that amongst the French in
Nova Scotia there hapned an earthquake which rent an
huge rock asunder to the centre, wherein was a vast
hollow of an immeasurable depth.   Concerning earthquakes which have lately hapned in remoter parts of the
world, I shall not here insert any thing, having mentioned
them in my *Discourse on Comets,* printed the last year;
only therein I have not taken notice of that memorable
earthquake, May 12, 1682, having received information
concerning it more lately.   Such readers as are inquisitive
into things of this nature may see that earthquake described and discoursed on in the *Weekly Memorials for
the Ingenious,* page 125, &c.   Remarkable was that which

hapned A.D. 1670, at a place called Kenebunck, in the Province of Main in New England, where not far from the river side a piece of clay ground was thrown up over the top of high oakes that grew between it and the river, into the river, stopping the course thereof, and leaving an hole forty yards square, wherein were thousands of clay bullets like musket bullets. It is also remarkable that the like to this hapned at Casco (twenty miles to the eastward of the other place) much about the same time. Whether the removal of this ground did proceed from an earthquake, or by the eruption of mineral vapors, or from some other cause, may be disputed; they that would give a probable conjecture concerning the natural cause must first know whether a great drought, or much rain, or both successively did not precede, of which I am not informed. The like memorable accidents have hapned in several places in England, both in the former and in this present age; which it may be twill be pleasing and edifying to some readers for me here to commemorate.

To proceed. The like to what hath been related fell out (1571) in Herefordshire. Marcley Hill, in the east part of the shire, with a roaring noise, removed itself from the place where it stood, and for three dayes together travelled from its old seat. It began first to take its journey February 17, being Saturday, at six of the clock at night, and by seven of the clock next morning, it had gone forty paces, carrying with it sheep in their cotes, hedge-rows and trees, whereof some were overturned, and some that stood upon the plain are firmly growing upon the hill; those that were east were turned west, and those in the west were set in the east. In this remove it over-threw Kinnaston chappel, and turned two highwayes near an hundred yards from their old paths.   The ground that thus removed was about twenty-six acres, which opening itself with rocks and all, bore the earth before it for four hundred yards space, without any stay, leaving pasturage in the place of the tillage, and the tillage overspread the pasturage.   Lastly, overwhelming its lower parts, it mounted to an hill of twelve fathom high, and there rested, after three dayes travel.

Again, on the third of January, A.D. 1582, at Hermitage in Dorsetshire, a place of ground of three acres removed from its old place (as is testified by Stow in his *Summary*), and was carried over another closure, where alders and willows grew, the space of forty rod or perches, and stopped the highway that led to Cerne; and the hedges that it was inclosed with inclose it still, and the trees stand bolt upright; and the place where this ground was before, is like a great pit.

Also, on the fourth of August, 1585, at Motingham in Kent, after a very violent tempest of thunder and rain, the ground suddenly began to sink, and three great elms growing upon it were carried so deep into the earth, that no part of them could any more be seen.   The hole left is in compass eighty yards, and a line of fifty fathom plummed into it finds no bottom.

Also, December, 18, 1596, a mile and a half from Westerham, southward (which is not many miles from Motingham), two closes lying together, separated with an hedge of hollow ashes, there was found a part thereof, twelve pearches long, to be sunk six foot and an half deep; the next morning fifteen foot more; the third morning eighty foot more at the least; and so daily, that great trench of ground, containing in length about eighty pearches, and in breadth about twenty-eight, began, with the trees and hedges on it, to lose itself from the rest of the ground lying round about it, and withal to move and shoot forward day and night for eleven dayes. The ground of two water-pits, the one six foot deep of water, the other twelve at the least, and about four pearches over in breadth, having sundry tufts of alders and ashes growing in the bottoms, with a great rock of stone under them, were not only removed out of their places, and carried towards the south, at least four pearches a pieces, but withal mounted aloft and become hills, with their sedge, flags, and black mud upon the tops of them, higher than the face of the water which they had forsaken by three foot; and in the place from which they are removed, other ground which lay higher, is descended, receiving the water which lies upon it. Moreover, in one piece of the plain field, there is a great hole made by sinking of the earth to the depth of thirty foot at the least, being in breadth in some places two pearches over, and in length five or six pearches. Also there, an hedge, thirty pearches long, carried southward with his trees seven pearches at the least; and sundry other sinkings there be in divers places, one of sixty foot, another of forty-seven, and another of thirty-four foot, by means of which confusion is come to pass; that where the highest hills were, there be the deepest dales, and the lowest dales are become the highest ground. The whole measure of breaking was at the least nine acres.

One instance more I find to the like purpose in Mr. Childrey his *Britannia Baconica*, p. 131, where speaking of the natural rareties of Cheshire, he thus writeth: "July 1, 1657, about 3h, in the Parish of Bulkley, was heard a very great noise, like thunder afar off, which was much wondred at, because the sky was clear, and no appearance of a cloud. Shortly after, a neighbour comes to me (saith the author of this relation), and told me I should see a very strange thing, if I would go with him; so coming into a field, called the Lay-field, we found a very great bank of earth, which had many tall oaks growing on it, quite sunk under the ground, trees and all. At first we durst not go near it, because the earth for near twenty yards round about is exceeding much rent, and seems ready to fall in; but since that time, myself and some others, by ropes, have ventured to see the bottom, I mean, to go to the brink, so as to discern the visible bottom, which is water, and conceived to be about thirty yards from us, under which is sunk all the earth about it for sixteen yards round at least. Three tall oaks, a very tall awber, and certain other small trees, and not a sprigg of them to be seen above water: four or five oaks more are expected to fall every moment, and a great quantity of land is like to fall, indeed never ceasing more or less; and when any considerable clod falls, it is much like the report of a canon. We can discern the ground hollow above the water a very great depth, but how far hollow, or how far deep, is not to be found out by man. Some of the water was drawn out of this pit with a bucket, and they found it to be as salt as sea water; whence some imagine that there are certain large passages there, into which the sea flows under ground; but I rather think that this salt water is no more but that which issues from those salt springs about Nant-wich and other places in this shire. But of this no more at present."

Some remarkable land floods have likewise hapned in New England. Nor is that which came to pass this present year to be here wholly passed over in silence. In the spring time, the great river at Connecticut useth to over-flow, but this year it did so after Midsummer, and that twice ; for, July 20, 1683, a considerable flood unexpect-edly arose, which proved detrimental to many in that colony. But on August 13, a second and a more dreadful flood came: the waters were then observed to rise twenty-six foot above their usual boundaries: the grass in the meadows, also the English grain, was carried away before it; the Indian corn, by the long continuance of the waters, is spoiled, so that the four river towns, viz. Windsor, Hartford, Weathersfield, Middle-town, are extream suf-ferers. They write from thence, that some who had hun-dreds of bushels of corn in the morning, at night had not one peck left for their families to live upon. There is an awful intimation of Divine displeasure remarkable in this matter, inasmuch as August 8, a day of public humiliation, with fasting and prayer, was attended in that colony, partly on the account of Gods hand against them in the former flood, the next week after which the hand of God was stretched out over them again in the same way, after a more terrible manner than at first. It is also remarkable that so many places should suffer by inundations as this year it hath been ; for at the very same time when the flood hapned at Connecticut, there was an hurricane in Virginia, attended with a great exundation of the rivers there, so as that their tobacco and Indian corn is very much damnified. Moreover, we have received information this summer, that the mighty river Danow (the biggest in Europe) hath overflowed its banks, by means whereof many have lost their lives. Also, near Aix in France, there lately hapned an unusual flood, whereby much harm was done ; and had the waters continued rising but one hour longer, the city had probably been destroyed thereby. There was likewise a sudden and extraordinary flood in Jamaica, which drowned many (both men and beast), and was very detrimental to some plantations there. They that came lately from thence assure us, that the waters in some places arose an hundred and fifty foot, such mighty streams did the heavens suddenly pour down upon them. Thus doth the great God, " who sits King upon the floods for ever," make the world see how many wayes he hath to punish them, when it shall seem good unto him. Many such things are with him. There are who think that the last comet, and those more rare conjunctions of the superiour planets hapning this year, have had a natural influence into the mentioned inundations. Concerning the flood at Connecticut, as for the more immediate natural cause, some impute it to the great rain which preceded ; others did imagine that some more than usual cataracts did fall amongst the mountains, there having been more rain than what now fell sometimes when no such flood has followed. It is not impossible but that the wind might be a secondary cause of this calamity. Judicious observators write concerning the river Dee in Cheshire in England, that though much rain do fall, it riseth but little ; but if the south wind do beat vehemently upon it, then it swells and overflows the grounds adjoyning extreamly ; the reason of which is, that the river being broad towards the sea, when the rain falls it hath a quick and easie passage, but the south wind brings the sea in, and doth somewhat stop the free passage of the river into the sea. Whether there might not be some such natural reason of the great flood in Connecticut at this time, the ingenious upon the place, who

know best how things are there circumstanced, may consider. With us in Boston it was then at first an Euro-
clydon; but in the afternoon the wind became southerly,
when it blew with the greatest fierceness. If it were so
at Connecticut, it seems very probable that the fury of the
wind gave a check to the free passage of the river, which
caused the sudden overflowing of the waters. It has,
moreover, been by some observed, that the breaking forth
of subterraneous waters has caused very prodigious floods.
Since the dayes of Noah, when the fountains of the great
deep were opened, no history mentions a more surprizing
and amazing inundation than that which hapned five years
ago at Gascoyn in France, proceeding (as tis probably
judged) from the irruption of waters out of the earth. Concerning which remarkable accident a judicious account is
given in the late *Philosophical Collections*, published by
Mr. Robert Hook, page 9. There being but one of these
books in the countrey, the ingenious will not blame me if I
here insert what is there related, which is as followeth:—

"In the beginning of the moneth of July, 1678, after
some gentle rainy dayes, which had not swelled the waters
of the Garonne more than usual, one night this river
swelled all at once so mightily, that all the bridges and
mills above Toulouse were carried away by it. In the
plains which were below this town, the inhabitants who
had built in places, which by long experience they had
found safe enough from any former inundation, were by
this surprised ; some were drowned, together with their
cattle; others had not saved themselves but by climbing
of trees, and getting to the tops of houses ; and some
others, which were looking after their cattle in the field,
warned by the noise which this horrible and furious torrent

of water, rowling towards them with a swiftness like that of the sea (in Britain he means) made at a distance, could not scape without being overtaken, though they fled with much precipitation: this, nevertheless, did not last many hours with this violence. At the same time exactly, the two rivers only of Adour and Gave, which fall from the Pyrænean hills, as well as the Garonne, and some other small rivers of Gascoyn, which have their source in the plain, as the Gimone, the Save, and the Ratt, overflowed after the same manner, and caused the same devastations. But this accident hapned not at all to the Aude, the Ariege, or the Arise, which come from the mountains of Toix, only that they had more of the same than those of the Conseraut, the Comminge, the Bigorre. Those who have heard talk of those inundations at a distance were not at all astonished at it, believing it to proceed from the violent rains of some tempests which had suddenly filled these rivers, or that they had caused a sudden thaw of the snow of the Pyræneans, which had swelled the rivers that were near.

"Monsieur Martel of Montaubon, advocate of the Parliament, an inquisitive and learned man, hath searched after this cause of this deluge (by the order of Monsieur Foucault, Intendant de Justice en la Généralité de Montauban, one not less seeing and understanding in ingenious sciences, than expert and exact in the performance of his charge and imployment), understanding that this overflowing could not be produced by either of the forementioned causes, and being assured that it must have had one more extraordinary than all these.

"And first he grounded his thoughts upon the report of the people of the place who were witnesses of this prodigy;

nd above all, of those, who being in the highest valleys
f the Pyrenæans, at the very source, had either seen or
cnown all circumstances ; for they all agreed that it had
·ained indeed, but that the rain was neither so great, nor
.asted so long, as to swell the rivers to that excess, or to
melt the snow off the mountains. But the nature of these
waters, and the manner of their flowing from the mountains, confirmed him perfectly in his sentiments. For—

1. The inhabitants of the Lower Pyrenæans observed that
the waters overflowed with violence from the entrails of the
mountains, about which there were opened several channels,
which forming so many furious torrents, tore up the trees,
the earth, and great rocks, in such narrow places where
they found not a passage large enough. The water which
also spouted from all the sides of the mountain in innu-
merable jets, which lasted all the time of the greatest
overflowing, had the taste of minerals.

" 2. In some of these passages, the waters were stinking
(as when one stirs the mud at the bottom of mineral water),
in such sort that the cattle refused to drink of it; which
was more particularly taken notice of at Lombez, in the
overflowing of the Save (which is one of the rivers), where
the horses were eight hours thirsty before they would
endure to drink it.

" 3. The Bishop of Lombez having a desire to cleanse
his gardens, which the Save passing through by many
channels by this overflowing, had filled with much sand
and mud, those which entred them felt an itching like to
that which one feels when one bathes in salt water, or
washes oneself with some strong lixivial, these waters have
caused the same kind of itching risings in the skin. This
last observation is not less strong than both the others to

prove that this overflowing was not either caused by the rains, or by the meltings of the snows, because this itching could not be produced by either of the said waters, which are not at all of this nature, but by some mineral juice, either vitriotic or aluminious, which the waters had dissolved in the bowels of the mountains, and had carried along with it in passing through those numerous crannies. And tis for this reason that Monsieur Martel believes he had found out the true cause of this overflowing to be nothing else but the subterraneous waters; for if the heavens have not supplied his prodigious quantity of waters neither by the rain, nor the melting of the snow, it cannot come else where than from the bowels of the earth, from whence, passing through divers channels, it had contracted and carried along with it that stinking and pungent quality."

But thus much concerning late remarkable floods.

CHAPTER XI.

CONCERNING REMARKABLE JUDGEMENTS.

Quakers judicially plagued with spiritual judgements. Of several sad instances in Long Island and in Plimouth Colony. That some of the Quakers are really possessed with infernal spirits proved by a late won derful example of one at Balsham, near Cambridge in England. Of several who imprecated vengeance upon themselves. The woful end of drunkards ; and of those that have designed evil against the churches of Christ in New England.

THOSE memorable judgements which the hand of Heaven has executed upon notorious sinners are to be reckoned amongst Remarkable Providences. *Lubricus hic locus et difficilis.* He undertakes a difficult province that shall relate all that might be spoken on such a subject, both in that it cannot but be gravaminous to surviving relations when such things are published, also in that men are apt to misapply the unsearchable judgements of God, which are a great deep, as Job's friends did ; and wicked Papists have done the like with respect to the untimely death of famous Zuinglius. We may not judge of men meerly by outward accidents which befal them in this world, since all things happen alike unto all, and no man knoweth either love or hatred by all that is before them. We have seen amongst ourselves that the Lords faithful servants have sometimes been the subjects of very dismal dispensations. There hapned a most awful providence at Farmington in

Connecticut colony, Dec. 14, 1666, when the house of Serjeant John Hart taking fire in the night, no man knows how (only it is conjectured that it might be occasioned by an oven), he and his wife and six children were all burned to death before the neighbours knew any thing of it, so that his whole family had been extinguished by the fatal flames of that unhappy night had not one of his children been providentially from home at that time. This Hart was esteemed a choice Christian, and his wife also a good woman. Such things sometimes fall upon those that are dear unto God, to intimate, " If this be done to the green tree, what shall be done to the dry ? that is, fit for nothing but the fire." Nevertheless, a judgement may be so circumstanced as that the displeasure of Heaven is plainly written upon it in legible characters ; on which account it is said, " That the wrath of God is revealed from heaven against all ungodliness and unrighteousness of men," Rom. i, 18. Sundry learned men have published whole volumes profitable to be read, on this subject, *e.g.* Goulartius his *Historical Collections ;* Honsdorsius, in his *Historical Theater*, which is inlarged by Lonicerus. Chassalion, his memorable *Histories of the Judgements of God.* And amongst our English writers, Dr. Beard, in his *Theater of Gods Judgements*, with Dr. Taylor's additions ; and Mr. Clark, in his two volumes of *Examples*, have said enough to convince atheists that there is a God, and that there is a judgement ; yea, the Divine Providence, in remarkable punishments inflicted upon very wicked men, has been so conspicuous and glorious as that the Gentiles of old could not but take notice of it. The poet could say, " *Raro antecedentem scelestum deseruit pede pœna claudo.*" And whereas Epicures did object that evil men sometimes escape punishment a long time; Plutarch (whose works Beza esteemed to be amongst the most excellent of humane writings) has a notable treatise, the design whereof is to vindicate Divine Justice in this matter. Many remarkable examples to our present purpose have hapned in New England, and more than I shall at present take notice of. All wise men that are acquainted therewith observe the blasting rebukes of Providence upon the late singing and dancing Quakers in signal instances, two or three of which may be here recorded, that so others may hear and fear, and do no more so wickedly.

The first instance shall be that which concerns the unhappy man that was murdered in Long Island, of which a good hand in those parts, in a letter bearing date Decemb. 12, 1681, writes as follows:—"There went down about a moneth since three mad Quakers, called Thomas Case's crew, one man named Denham, belonging to Newer-snicks, and two women with him belonging to Oyster Bay; these went down to South-hold, where they meet with Samuel Banks of Fairfield, the most blasphemous villain that ever was known in these parts. These joyning together with some other inhabitants of South-hold of the same spirit, there went into their company a young merchant named Thomas Harris, who was somewhat inclining to the Quakers before (he belonged to Boston); they all go about him, and fell a dancing and singing, according to their diabolical manner. After some time the said Harris began to act like them, and to dance and sing, and to speak of extraordinary raptures of joy, and to cry out upon all others as devils that were not of their religion; which also they do frequently. When the said Harris manifested these signs of conversion, as they accounted

16

it, they solemnly accepted of him as one of their company, and Banks or Denham (for I have forgotten which of the two) gave him this promise, 'that henceforth his tongue should be as the pen of a ready writer, to declare the praises of their Lord.' After this, the young who was sober and composed before, ran up and down, singing joy, and calling such devils as should say anything in way of opposition, and said his father was a devil that begat him. Quickly after he went from the town of South-hold, to a farm belonging to that town, to the house of a Quaker of the same spirit, and went to bed before the rest of the family; and when a young man of the same house went to go to bed to him, he told him that he must get up, and go to South-hold that night, where he had left Banks, and the rest; the young man endeavoured to perswade him to lie still till day, but he would not, but gat up, and went away; after some time he was missed, and enquiry made for him, but he could not be heard of, only his hat and gloves and neckcloth was found in the road from the farm to the town. And two dayes after, Banks looking into a Bible, suddenly shut it again, crying out, his friend Harris was dead; the next day he was found by the sea-side, about a quarter of a mile from the place, where his hat and other things were found, but out of the road, with three holes like stabs in his throat, and no tongue in his head, nor the least sign thereof, but all was clear to his neck-bone within, his mouth close shut, one of his eyes hanging down upon his cheek out of his head, the other sunk so deep in his head that at first it seemed quite out, but was whole there. And Mr. Joshua Hobart, who was one of them to view his dead body, told me that there was no sign of any tongue left in his mouth: 'Such was the end of that tongue which had the promise of being as the pen of a ready-writer.' Further, the night after he was buried, Captain Young (who is high sheriff, and chiefly concerned in looking after the business), as he told me himself, being in bed, in the dead of the night, was awakened by the voice of this Harris calling to his window very loud, requiring him to see that justice was done him. This voice came three times in that night. The next night, when he was asleep, it came into his house, close to his bed-side, and called very loud, asking him if he heard him, and awaked him." Thus concerning that tragical story.

An intelligent and credible person living upon that island, in a letter dated September 4, 1683, adds as follows :—

"There was about four years since, by some of the same crew, another attempt made amongst us, which was also attended with the like providence, though not so fatal an issue. There was a young woman, a daughter of a Quaker among us, who was howled into their society, as Harris was, and quickly fell to railing on others, and then to raving, being in a dreadful condition, so that several persons of their gang watched with her ; and she was made wonderfully strong to outstrive them, and to break away from them. One of their own party newly in favour with them, told me that he was by in the night when they watched with her, and in the very darkness of the night they heard a very doleful noise, like the crying of a young child in the yard or field near the house, which filled the auditors with some fearful apprehensions, which when the young woman heard, she violently brake from her attendance, saying, ' The Lord calls me, and I must go ;' so in

16*a*

the dark she got from them, to the cry-ward as they supposed, and it was a good space of time before they could find her, and then she was as one affrighted and bereaved of understanding, and continued so a space of time, sometimes ridiculous to behold, sometimes very awful, till such time as Justice Wood of Huntington, by the use of means, recovered her, which her quaking friends, notwithstanding their brags, could not do; so that I heard her husband say, that he was convinced that the devil was among them. This providence was at that time fearful among us, yet since, both that woman and her husband are railing Quakers, and do hum and revile as the rest of them, though several forsook their society upon this account." Thus hee.

That which was perpetrated by this woful generation of Quakers, no longer since than this last summer in Plimouth colony, is horrid to be related; yet, inasmuch as the publication of it will make appear unto all mankind that Quakers are under the strong delusions of Satan, I think myself bound to acquaint the world, that not many moneths ago, a man, passing under the name of Jonathan Dunen (*alias* Singleterry) a singing Quaker, drew away the wife of one of Marshfield to follow him; also, one Mary Ross, falling into their company, was quickly possessed with the devil, playing such frentick and diabolical tricks as the like hath seldom been known or heard of; for she made herself naked, burning all her clothes, and, with infinite blasphemy, said that she was Christ, and gave names to her apostles, calling Dunen by the name of Peter, another by the name of Thomas, declaring that she would be dead for three dayes, and then rise again; and, accordingly, seemed to die. And while she was pretendedly dead her apostle Dunen gave out that they should see glorious things after her resurrection; but that which she then did was, she commanded Dunen to sacrifice a dog. The man and the two women Quakers danced naked together, having nothing but their shirts on. The constable brought them before the magistrates in Plimouth, where Ross uttered such prodigious blasphemy as is not fit to be mentioned; Dunen fell down like a dead man upon the floor, and so lay for about an hour, and then came to himself. The magistrates demanding the reason of his strange actings, his answer was, that Mary Ross bid him, and he had no power to resist. Thus, when men will not receive the truth in the love of it, the righteous judgement of God sends upon them the efficacy of error, that they shall believe a lie. That the Quakers are some of them undoubtedly possessed with evil and infernal spirits, and acted in a more than ordinary manner by the inmates of hell, is evident, not only from the related instances, but by other awful examples which might be mentioned. They are indeed to be pitied, in that they themselves know not that an evil spirit doth possess and act them; yet others should, from that consideration, dread to come among such creatures, lest haply the righteous God suffer Satan to take possession of them also.

Memorable and marvelous is that relation, published the last year by Dr. Henry More, in his addition to Mr. Glanvil's *Collections*, p. 58, &c. wherein a true and faithful account is given of a man whose name is Robert Churchman, living at Balsham in Cambridgeshire, who was for some time inveigled in Quakerisme, and then an infernal spirit spake in him, pretending to be an angel of light. Inasmuch as there is (so far as I have heard) but one of those books in this countrey, I suppose it will be a service for the truth, and may (if the Lord please to add his blessing) tend to reclaim some from the error of their way and to deterr those from Quakerisme who have, through the temptations of Satan, any inclinations thereunto, if that notable history should be more divulged ; I shall therefore here insert it : and thus it was :—

Dr. Templar (the minister in Balsham) perceiving that Robert Churchman was in danger of being poysoned and seduced by the papers which the Quakers had been dispersing in that place, desired him, that when any of their books came to his hands, he might have the perusal of them ; which, being granted, he suggested that it would be very convenient that the person who had given him that book should be present when they considered it together. This also was consented to. When the Quaker came, a special subject of the discourse was, "Whether the Scripture is to be owned as a rule." This the Quaker denied, asserting that the rule was within them. Hereupon Dr. Templar desired Churchman to take notice that the Quakers did not own the Scriptures to be their rule, which before this conference he would not believe concerning them. The next time he met with his brother, Thomas Churchman, he acquainted him with the conference which had been in Dr. Templars house, and said, for his part, he would not be of that religion which did disown the Scripture to be the rule. Not long after, the wife of the forementioned Quaker, coming to his house to visit his wife, he met her at the door, and told her she should not come in, intimating that her visit would make division betwixt them. After some parley, the Quaker's wife spake unto him in these words : " Thou wilt not believe unless thou see a sign, and thou mayest see some such." Within a few nights after, Robert Churchman had a violent storm upon the room where he lay, when it was very calm in all other parts of the town, and a voice within him, as he was in bed, spake to him, and bid him "Sing praises; sing praises;" telling him, that he should see the glory of the New Jerusalem; about which time a glimmering light appeared all about the room. Toward the morning the voice commanded him to go out of his bed naked, with his wife and children. They all standing upon the floor, the spirit making use of his tongue, bid them to lie down and put their mouthes in the dust, which they did accordingly. It likewise commanded them to go and call his brother and sister that they might see the New Jerusalem, to whom he went naked about half a mile. When he had delivered his message, that which spake within him to denounce wrath against them, and declare that fire and brimstone would fall upon them, as it did upon Sodom and Gomorrah if they did not obey; and so he returned to his own house, where upon the floor of a low room he stood about three or four hours. All that while he was acted in a very unusual manner; sometimes the spirit within forced him to sing, sometimes to bark like a dog. When his brother and sister, who followed him, were very importunate with him to resist it, it bid him to kill them, making use of these words: "These my enemies, which would not that I should reign over them, bring them, and slay them before my face." It made him to utter with great readiness many places of Scripture which he had no knowledge of before. The drift of what was spoken was to perswade him to comply with the Quakers; and it named some which lived in the neighbouring towns. About three or four hours being thus spent, he came to himself, and was able to give a perfect account of what had befallen him.

Several nights after, the same trouble returned upon him : his wife was tortured with extraordinary pains ; the children which lay in the room complained that their mouthes were stopped with wool as they were in bed. The disturbance was so great, that he had thoughts of leaving his house for a time, and made it his desire to be at Dr. Templars, who prevailed with him not to be so sudden in his removal, but to make some further trial. It pleased God, upon a continuation with him in prayer every day in the house, that he was at last perfectly free from all molestation. The Quakers, hearing of his condition, gave it out that the power of God would come upon him again, and that the wound was but skinned over by the priest, which made Dr. Templar the more importunate with him to keep close to the publick worship of God, and to have nothing to do with them or their writings; which direction he followed till November 1661, and then perusing one of their books, a little after, upon the tenth day of that moneth, his troubles returned : a voice within him began to speak to him after the former manner. The first sentence which it uttered was : "Cease thou from man, whose breath is in his nostrils, for wherein is he to be accounted ?" The design which he discerned it did aim at, was to take him off from comeing to the church (where he had been that day), and from hearing the Word of God. It suggested several other Scriptures, in order to the perswading of him to a compliance with the Quakers, and told him that it would strive with him, as the angel did with Jacob, until the breaking of the day ; at which time it left him. The two next nights it gave him the same molestation, saying, it must be with him as it was with David, who " gave no sleep to his eyes, nor slumber to his eye-- lids, until he found a place for the Lord, an habitation for the mighty God of Jacob." Upon Wednesday at night he was very peremptory in his resisting of it. When it began to solicit him, he replied, that he saw it was a spirit of delusion, which he would not obey ; upon which the spirit denounced a curse against him in these words, "Go, ye cursed, into everlasting fire ;" and so left him with a very great heat in his body. After this, he was, in his own apprehension, in a very comfortable condition ; and while he was considering what had hapned, a voice within him spake to him, saying, " That the spirit which was before upon him was a spirit of delusion, but now the true spirit of God was come into him." It acquainted him that the doctrine of the Trinity was true ; and that God had an elect people ; and that those whom the Father elected the Son hath redeemed ; and when Christ redeemeth the Holy Ghost sanctifieth ; and told him that the minister of the town would further instruct him about the truth of these things. Upon Thursday morning, about break of day, it set him upon his knees as he was in bed, and bid him farewel. The same day it came upon him in the field, as he was going to and coming from the market, and pressed upon him to believe that it was the good spirit which he was acted with, which he still doubted of. One night that week, amongst many arguments which it used to that purpose, it told him, if he would not believe without a sign, he might have what sign he would. Upon that, Robert Churchman desired, if it was a good spirit, that a wier candlestick, which stood upon the cupboard, might be turned into brass, which the spirit said he would do. Presently there was a very unsavoury smell in the room, like that of the snuff of a candle newly put out ; but nothing else was done towards the fulfilling of the promise. Upon the Lords Day following, he then attending the publick worship of God, it came upon him ; when the chapters were named, he turned to them in his Bible, but was not able to read ; when the psalm was sung, he could not pronounce a syllable. Upon Monday morning his speech was wholly taken away from him. When the minister in that place came to him, and asked him how it was with him, he moved his head towards him, but was not able to speak. The minister waited an hour or two in the room, hoping that his speech might have returned unto him, and that he might have gained from him some account of his condition ; but finding no alteration, he desired those who were present to joyn with him in prayer. As they were praying, Churchman's body was with much violence thrown out of bed ; and then with great vehemency he called to the minister, Dr. Templar, to hold his tongue. When prayer was done, his tongue was bound as before, till at last he broke out into these words : " Thine is the kingdom ! Thine is the kingdom !" which he repeated (as was judged) above an hundred times. Sometimes he was forced into extream laughter, sometimes into singing ; his hands were usually imployed in beating his breast : all of them who stood by could discern unusual heavings in his body. This distemper did continue towards the morning of the next day, and then the voice within him signified to him that it would leave him, bidding him get upon his knees in order to that end, which he did, and then presently he had a perfect command of himself.

When Dr. Templar came to him, he gave a sober

account of all the passages of the day before having a distinct remembrance of what the spirit forced him to do, and what was spoken to him by those that stood by; in particular, he told the doctor that he was compelled to give him that disturbance in prayer before mentioned; the spirit using his limbs and tongue as it pleased, contrary to the inclination of his own mind.

Upon the Thursday following, the spirit began to rage after its former manner; as Dr. Templar was at prayer with him, it was very discernable how it wrought upon his body, forced him to grate his teeth and draw his mouth awry. He told the minister after he had done, that it bid him to denounce woe against him. It pleased God, upon continuance in prayer with him, at last to release him of all his trouble, and so far to make it advantagious to him and to his wife and some others, which were too much byassed with the principles of the Quakers, that now they have a perfect dislike that way, and do diligently attend upon the publick worship of God.

Thus concerning this strange but true relation. We may by this judge whose servants the singing Quakers are, and what spirit doth powerfully breath in and act those miserable and deluded enthusiasts.

But I shall say no more to the Quakers at present; only pray that such of them as have not "sinned unto death" may have their eyes opened, and (if possible) be delivered out of the snares of Satan, "by whom they are taken captive at his will."

It hath been by many observed, that men addicted to horrid cursings and execrations have pulled down the imprecated vengeance of Heaven upon themselves. Sundry very awful examples of this kind have lately hapned : I shall here mention one or two.

The hand of God was very remarkable in that which came to pass in the Narraganset countrey in New-England, not many weeks since ; for I have good information, that on August 28, 1683, a man there (viz. Samuel Wilson) having caused his dog to mischief his neighbours cattle, was blamed for his so doing. He denied the fact with imprecations, wishing that he might never stir from that place if he had so done. His neighbour being troubled at his denying the truth, reproved him, and told him he did very ill to deny what his conscience knew to be truth. The atheist thereupon used the name of God in his imprecations, saying, "He wished to God he might never stir out of that place, if he had done that which he was charged with." The words were scarce out of his mouth before he sunk down dead, and never stirred more ; a son-in-law of his standing by and catching him as he fell to the ground.

A thing not unlike to this hapned (though not in New-England) yet in America, about a year ago ; for in September 1682, a man at the Isle of Providence, belonging to a vessel, whereof one Wollery was master, being charged with some deceit in a matter that had been committed to him, in order to his own vindication, horribly wished "that the devil might put out his eyes if he had done as was suspected concerning him." That very night a rhume fell into his eyes, so as that within a few dayes he became stark blind. His company being astonished at the Divine hand which thus conspicuously and signally appeared, put him ashore at Providence, and left him there. A physitian being desired to undertake his cure, hearing how he came to lose his sight, refused to meddle with him

This account I lately received from credible persons, who knew and have often seen the man whom the devil (according to his own wicked wish) made blind, through the dreadful and righteous judgment of God.

Moreover, that worse than brutish sin of drunkenness hath been witnessed against from heaven by severe and signal judgements. It was a sign of the fearful wrath of God upon that notorious drunkard at a place called Seatucket in Long Island; who, as he was in drink, fell into the fire (the people in the house then being in bed and asleep), and so continued for some considerable time, until he received his death wound. At his first awakening he roared out, "Fire! Fire!" as if it had been one in hell, to the great astonishment of all that heard him. One in the house flung a pail of water on him to quench his clothes, but that added to his torment; so he continued yelling after an hideous manner, "Fire! Fire!" and within a day or two he died in great misery. And though this drunkard died by fire, it is remarkable that many of those who have loved drink have died by water, and that at the very time when their understandings have been drowned by drink. It is an awful consideration that there have been at several times above forty persons in this land whom death hath found in that woful plight, so that their immortal souls have gone out of drunken bodies to appear before God the judge of all.

That remarkable judgement hath first or last fallen upon those who have sought the hurt of the people of God in New-England, is so notorious as that it is become the observation of every man. This Israel in the wilderness hath eat up the nations his enemies ; he hath broke their bones, and pierced them through with his arrows. Some adversaries have escaped longer unpunished than others ; but then their ends have been of all the most woful and tragical at last. I shall instance only in what hath lately come to pass with respect unto the heathen who rose up against us, thinking to swallow us up quick when their wrath was kindled against us. Blessed be the Lord, who hath not given us a prey to their teeth ! The chieftains amongst them were all cut off, either by sword or sickness, in the war time, excepting those in the eastern parts, whose ringleaders outlived their fellows ; but now God hath met with them. There were in special two of those Indians who shed much innocent blood, viz. Simon and Squando. As for bloody Simon, who was wont to boast of the mischiefs he had done, and how he had treacherously shot and killed such and such Englishmen, he died miserably the last winter. Another Indian discharging a gun, hapned to shoot Simon, so as to break his arm. After which he lived two years, but in extremity of pain, so as that the Indians when enquired of how Simon did, their usual answer was, " Worse than dead." He used all means that earth and hell (for he betook himself to *powaws*) could afford him for his recovery, but in vain. Thus was the wickedness of that murtherer at last returned upon his own head.

Concerning Squando, the Sachem of the Indians at Saco, the story of him is upon sundry accounts remarkable. Many years ago, he was sick and near unto death, after which he said, that one pretending to be the Englishmans God appeared to him in the form of an English minister, and discoursed with him, requiring him to leave off his drinking of rum, and religiously to observe the Sabbath-day, and to deal justly amongst men, withal promising him that if he did so, then at death his soul should go upwards to an happy place; but if he did not obey these commandments, at death his soul should go downwards, and to be for ever miserable. But this pretended God said nothing to him about Jesus Christ. However, this apparition so wrought upon Squando, as that he left his drunkenness, and became a strict observer of the Sabbath-day; yea, so that he alwayes kept it as a day of fast, and would hear the English ministers preach, and was very just in his dealing. But in the time of the late Indian war, he was the principal actor in the bloody tragedies in that part of the countrey. The last year the pretended Englishmans God appeared to him again, as afore, in the form of a minister, requiring him to kill himself, and promising him that if he did obey, he should live again the next day, and never die more. Squando acquainted his wife and some other Indians with this new apparition; they most earnestly advised him not to follow the murderous counsel which the spectre had given. Nevertheless, he since hath hanged himself, and so is gone to his own place. This was the end of the man that disturbed the peace of New-England.

CHAPTER XII.

AN ACCOUNT OF SOME REMARKABLES AT NORWICH IN NEW ENGLAND.

Special answers of prayer made in that place. That people marvelously preserved. The scandalous miscarriage of one so over-ruled by Providence, as to be an occasion of the conversion of several others. A further account of some personal deliverances in Norwich. Concerning sudden deaths which have hapned in New-England.

THERE is lately come to my hand an account of some remarkables which have hapned at Norwich in New-England, drawn up by Mr. Fitch, the judicious and eminently faithful pastor of the church in that place; which, that others may be incouraged to follow his example, in observing and recording the special works of Divine Providence, I shall here insert, as I received it, and so hasten to finish this essay. It is that which follows.

Remarkable Providences at Norwich.

1. "Many times the heavens have been shut up; but God hath answered our prayers in sending rain, and sometimes so speedily and so plentifully, after our seeking the Lord by fasting and prayer, that the heathen, now for more than twenty years upon occasion of want of rain, will speak to us to call upon the name of the Lord our God; one especial instance of this kind I have already given, and its

upon record in the history of the war with the Indians in New-England.

2. "Many among us have been in more than ordinary hazard by rattlesnakes; some have set their feet upon them; some have been bitten by them upon the skin; and one, as he was stooping down to drink at a spring of water spied a rattlesnake, within two foot of his head, rising up against him. Thus manifold wayes in danger by this venimous creature, and yet none of us have suffered any harm, but only one was bitten in the finger, and in a short time perfectly healed.

3. "In the time of the wars with the Indians we were not only preseved from the heathen in the midst of the heathen, but by the Lords making some of them to be a wall of defence unto us; and thus were saved by a destroying means.

'And at this time the providence of God was very remarkable in preserving many of our people in one of our garrisons, who were driven to garrison several houses; and the house of which now I speak did contain about sixty persons; and in this house one of the souldiers taking a gun loaden with bullets into his hand, as he stood in a lower room, the lock being half bent, and he holding the gun right upwards, the gun was discharged; though many people were in the chamber, yet none of them suffered any harm, because Providence did guid the shot into the summer—that piece of timber which is the support of the chamber.

"Also, one in the same house, looking with a candle under a bed for something he wanted, fired some flax, which filled the room with flame and smoke; and two small children lay sleeping in this peril, but were preserved from the fire or any harm by the throng of people in the room.   At length one of the children was taken up by one of the men, with a purpose of throwing it out of the chamber window; but at that very moment there was such an abatement of the flame, and hope that the worst of the danger was past, that he held the child in his arms; and yet presently after the fire brake out again in the uppermost room in the house, nigh to a barrel of gunpowder; but some were guided, strengthened, and succeeded in their endeavour to the extinguishing the fire; so that the lives and limbs and goods of all these was preserved by the good hand of God, who doth wonderfully when we know not what to do.

4. "One of the children of the church (grown up, though not in full communion) was left to fall into a most notorious abominable practice, which did occasion the church to meet and humble their souls by fasting and prayer; and at this time, in the sermon and prayer, it was declared, that the Lord had determined either to bring our children nearer to him, and not to suffer them to live out of full communion with his church, or else he would in his anger leave them to such abominations as shall cut them off from his church.   And since this time many young people have, by the grace of the Lord, been prepared for full communion, and have taken hold of the covenant, confessing that they have felt the impression of that Work upon that abashing occasion spoken.   And thus the fall of one hath been the rising of many. Where sin abounds the Lord can make grace to superabound."

" Concerning some Personal Deliverances.

"There was a young man endeavouring to subdue a

young horse; and a rope at one end of it was fastned about the horses neck, but the horse running with great speed, the other end of the rope caught the foot of this young man, as in a snare, and was so entangled therein, that he was drawn ten rods upon his back in a very rough and uneven place of land, he being unable to free himself, and none at hand that could help him; and thus it being come to this extremity, the horse of himself stood still so long, and no longer time, than that the young man did clear his foot out of the rope; and thus was delivered out of the danger, and suffered not a broken bone, nor any considerable bruise or harm.

"There was another young man, who sat upon a plough-beam, and suddenly his cattle moving, his plough turned, and one of his legs were entangled within the plough, and the plough irons pressing hard against some part of his body, but could not free himself; and the more he called to the cattle the more speedily they moved, and thus was in danger of being torn in pieces; but in this extremity it was not long before the cattle of themselves stood still.

"There was another young man, who did fall about ten foot from some part of the mill timber into deep waters, and a place of many rocks, a stream very violent, and he was carried about eleven rod down the stream, where there was a great piece of ice; and while he was in this confounded and amazed posture, his hand was guided to take hold of that ice, and there to hold, until one who saw him fall, did adventure upon that ice, and drew him out of the waters, and thus they were both delivered.

"There was a very aged man among us, who, riding in his cart over a river; and when the cattle were coming out of the river, he endeavoured to come out of the cart; but he did fall down so nigh to the wheel, that it began to press hard against his breast; and he only speaking to the cattle, they stood still, and ceased moving till he was removed out of the danger, otherwise, if they had moved a few inches more, he had been prest to death."

Thus far is Mr. Fitch's narrative. Had all others been as diligent in observing the works of God, as this worthy person has, the account of New-Englands Remarkables would have been more full and compleat. But other things must be left for another attempt of this kind. I shall only add at present, that there have been many sudden deaths in this countrey which should not pass without some remark; for when such strokes are multiplied there is undoubtedly a speaking voice of Providence therein; and so it hath been with us in New-England this last year, and most of all the last summer. To my observation in August last, within the space of three or four weeks, there were twelve sudden deaths (and it may be others have observed more than I did), some of them being in respect of sundry circumstances exceeding awful. Let me only add here that sudden death is not alwayes a judgment unto those who are taken out of an evil world: it may be a mercy to them, and a warning unto others, as the prophet Ezekiels wife was. Many of whom the world was not worthy, have been so removed out of it. Moses died suddenly, and so have some excellent persons in this countrey done. Governour Eaton at New-Haven, and Governour Haines at Hartford, died in their sleep without being sick. That excellent man of God, Mr. Norton, as he was walking in his house in this Boston, was taken with a syncope, fell down dead, and never spake more. The like has hapned to other servants of God in other parts of the world. Famous Mr. Vines, on a Lords Day, after he had preached and administered the sacrament, went to bed well, and went to heaven that night. Nor is there any rule or reason for Christians to pray absolutely against sudden death. Some holy men have, with submission to the will of the Most High, desired and prayed for such a death; so did Mr. Capel, and God gave him his desire; for on September 21, 1656, having preached twice that day, and performed religious duties with his family, went to bed, and died immediately. The like is reported by Dr. Fuller, in his *Church History,* concerning that angelical man, Mr. Brightman, who would often pray (if God saw fit) that he might die rather a sudden than a lingring death, and so it came to pass; for, as he was travelling in the coach with Sir John Osborne, and reading of a book (for he would lose no time), he was taken with a fainting fit, and, though instantly taken out in the arms of one there present, and all means possible used for his recovery, he there died, August 24, 1607. The learned and pious Wolfius (not the divine who has written commentaries on several parts of the Scriptures, but he that published *Lectionum Memorabilium et Reconditarum Centenarios*), on May 23, 1600, being in usual health, was, after he had dined, surprised with a sudden illness, whereof he died within a few hours. That holy man, Jacobus Faber, who did and suffered great things for the name of Christ, went suddenly into the silent grave. On a day when some friends came to visit him, after he had courteously entertained them, he laid himself down upon his bed to take some repose, and no sooner shut his eyes, but his heaven-born soul took its flight into the world of souls.

The man who being in Christ, shall alwayes be doing something for God, may bid death welcome whenever it shall come, be it never so soon, never so suddenly.

גדלים מעשי יהוה דרושים
לבל־הבציהם

Psalm iii, 2.

תם

FINIS.

AN ESSAY

FOR THE

RECORDING

OF

Illustrious Providences:

Wherein an Account is given of many Remarkable and very Memorable Events, which have hapned this last Age,

ESPECIALLY IN NEW-ENGLAND.

By *INCREASE MATHER*,
Teacher of a Church at *Boston* in *New-England.*

Psal. 107. 8. *Oh that men would praise the Lord for his goodness, and for his wonderful works to the Children of Men.*

Psal. 145. 4. *One Generation shall praise thy works to another, and shall declare thy mighty Acts.*

BOSTON IN NEW-ENGLAND,

Printed by *Samuel Green* for *Joseph Browning* and are to be sold at his Shop at the corner of the *Prison-Lane* next the *Town-House.* 1684.

Printed in the United States
1004300001B